IDEOLOGY
and
LEADERSHIP

IDEOLOGY and LEADERSHIP

Marvin J. Folkertsma, Jr.

Grove City College

PRENTICE HALL, Englewood Cliffs, New Jersey 07632

Library of Congress Cataloging-in-Publication Data

FOLKERTSMA, MARVIN J. [DATE]
  Ideology and leadership.

  Includes index.
  1. Political leadership—Case studies. 2. Political
science. 3. Ideology. I. Title.
JF1525.L4F64   1988   303.4′4   87-25751
ISBN 0-13-450198-5

Editorial/production supervision: *Edith Riker*
Cover design: *George Cornell*
Manufacturing buyer: *Margaret Rizzi*
Photo Research: *Kay Dellosa*
Photo credits: p. 1, *Donald Patterson/Stock Boston*; p. 15, 107, *New York Public Library*; p. 25, 53, *Library of Congress*; p. 83, *AFL-CIO News*; p. 115, 143, 197, *UPI/Bettmann Newsphotos*; p. 169, *Eugene Gordon.*

ISBN 0-13-450198-5

Prentice-Hall International (UK) Limited, *London*
Prentice-Hall of Australia Pty. Limited, *Sydney*
Prentice-Hall Canada Inc., *Toronto*
Prentice-Hall Hispanoamericana, S.A., *Mexico*
Prentice-Hall of India Private Limited, *New Delhi*
Prentice-Hall of Japan, Inc., *Tokyo*
Simon & Schuster Asia Pte. Ltd., *Singapore*
Editora Prentice-Hall do Brasil, Ltda., *Rio de Janeiro*

CONTENTS

PART TWO: MARXISM

PART THREE: FASCISM

PART FOUR: ISLAMIC FUNDAMENTALISM

to my wife
ANDREA

PREFACE

Surveys of modern political ideologies usually deal with individual contributions to a broader stream of thought, with references that must necessarily be very brief. The same is true for accounts that involve comparing different types of governments, or that provide an introductory overview of politics throughout the world, or, finally, that survey the main themes of international relations. Depth must be sacrificed in order to achieve breadth, and very often the *ideas* and *actions* of people under various circumstances, and the *differences* they have made, must be given less coverage. This is understandable, of course, because general treatments of politics must involve a broad sweep of historical, comparative, or institutional analysis, and can only stop to focus upon individual contributions on an occasional basis. But it is also regrettable, because the ideas and actions of people, en masse or on an individual basis, constitute the very stuff of politics. In fact, several very prominent leaders in this century, who have seriously acted upon their political convictions, have actually *created*, or at least very significantly changed, those institutions, organizations, and patterns of behavior that are studied in books that provide overviews of such topics. In short, leaders who are seriously committed to a set of political beliefs, and who possess the determination and means to act upon them, have made an enormous difference on the course of modern politics.

The purpose of this book is to study a select number of such individuals, certain *ideological leaders*. The goal here is to explain what they believed, how they acted upon their beliefs, and what difference it made to their countries and, where relevant, to the world about them. All of the leaders dealt with here are very familiar ones, and were selected on the basis of their historical importance—James Madison, Franklin D. Roosevelt, Martin Luther King, Jr., Joseph Stalin, Mao Zedong, Adolf Hitler, and Ruhollah Khomeini. With one exception they are all twentieth-century figures, and, with another exception, are all dead. The impact of their lives on twentieth-century politics, however, has remained enormous by any standard. And the terms that are employed here to describe their styles of ideological leadership—

founder, revisionist, practitioner, and missionary—are, I believe, readily suggested by the main themes that emerge from a study of their lives. Indeed, in some cases, the terms applied here were used by the leaders themselves to describe their own views and actions, and to define their own places in history.

I have tried to keep the length of the chapters that deal with the lives of the ideological leaders approximately equal in size. The main exception to this is the chapter that deals with Khomeini. There are several reasons for this chapter's expanded size. First, it deals with a topic with which many readers are not familiar, although there is much about it in the news of late—fundamentalist Islam. Secondly, it is my hope that many will find this book to be a highly useful supplement to other texts in political ideologies, comparative politics, or international relations. But many of these texts have little or no coverage of Islam, and therefore I thought it would be helpful to supplement more thoroughly what might be lacking in other treatments. Finally, Khomeini's Iran has traumatized not only the Middle East, but the United States as well, and it appears that the events surrounding that country will remain of abiding interest, regardless of what happens to him.

Naturally, in writing about topics such as political ideology and political leaders, it is difficult to submerge totally one's own biases toward the issues and people involved. I have tried to provide accounts that are well balanced, and to come to conclusions that are justified by the evidence rendered by experts in the various fields of study under consideration, regardless of my own personal views. Nonetheless, the reader will note an admiration on my part for the Americans chosen for this study, Madison, Roosevelt, and King—particularly King. Such are the perils of dealing with ideology and leadership.

I want to conclude by thanking all those who have helped me with this book, by reading excerpts, providing criticism, or enlightening me more thoroughly about some particular topics (especially Islam), in ways that I found extremely helpful—and, in some cases, indispensable. I especially want to thank those at Prentice Hall who worked with me on this project: Stan Wakefield, with whom I started the book; Karen Horton, who continued with patience, good advice, and encouragement; Edie Riker, who saw it through the production process; and Felice Swados, whose excellent task of copy editing saved me from innumerable errors. Although one wishes at all events to avoid making mistakes in presentation or in the many specifics of subjects under consideration, alas, there are always some that remain, and for these I take full responsibility.

LEADERSHIP AND MODERN POLITICS

1

INTRODUCTION

Political leaders are fascinating people, to their committed followers as well as to detached and uninvolved observers. In this century skillful practitioners of political leadership have succeeded in mobilizing masses of people to carry out tasks that they and others would have thought impossible otherwise. One of the most recent examples of this occurred in Iran. The government of the Shah was one of the most powerful, ruthless, and efficient police states in the world, respected by its allies and adversaries alike. Yet it was suddenly whisked away by hordes of frenzied, placard-waving religious zealots, led by a septuagenarian Muslim fundamentalist, the Ayatollah Ruhollah Khomeini—all before the eyes of incredulous foreign observers, who could scarcely understand what was going on, or why. Actually, however, this type of scene was not unique; it had been witnessed earlier in the century by millions of equally enthusiastic Germans, whose new leader proclaimed himself head of a state that would last a thousand years. Nor have Americans been immune from the allurements of political leaders with compelling messages and electrifying personalities. A scant generation ago saw the meteoric rise and tragic death of one of the most remarkable leaders ever to make his mark on the American political landscape—the Reverend Dr. Martin Luther King, Jr. Indeed, there is probably no nation that has not been deeply affected in some fashion, for good or ill, by a determined and flamboyant political leader.

Of course, not all leaders have been like Khomeini, Hitler, or King, three of the figures whom we shall be dealing with in this book. Joseph Stalin was short in stature, had a pock-marked face, and spoke with a weak voice, thick with a non-Russian accent. Although uninspiring in appearance and demeanor, he still succeeded in building the Soviet Union into a modern industrial state, but clearly by means of guile and brute power, and not by an inspiring personality. Still other important political leaders possessed neither overpowering personalities nor ruthless temperaments. For instance, James Madison was modest to a fault, unassuming, and physically frail, with a voice so soft that his colleagues had to strain to hear him speak, and often had to ask him politely to repeat what he had said. But Madison's towering and often domineering intellect resulted in the creation of an instrument of government, which, with suitable modifications, became the Constitution of the United States. Another famous American leader, Franklin Roosevelt, without question made up in charm and personality for what he lacked in intellect, and rivaled the very best orators of his day. And like them he could inspire people and move them to perform great tasks. But unlike them, he couldn't move himself in actual physical terms; he was confined to a wheelchair throughout his time in office. By vivid contrast, another leader whom we shall consider in this book, Mao Zedong, seemed to spend most of his adult life doing little else but moving around, and by every means available, too—donkey, horse, wheel-cart, armored car, airplane, as well as his own two feet—up and down the breadth and width of China. He kept himself in motion, and, with his leadership of that vast country, kept everyone else in motion as well. In short, modern political leaders have come in all forms, shapes, sizes, and abilities. Their sheer variety has also demonstrated that there are many ways to practice political leadership.

There are also many ways to evaluate and classify political leadership. Indeed, the literature on the subject is enormous, and it is beyond the scope of this inquiry to deal with it in any detail. Our present task is the more modest one of evaluating political leadership in terms of its relationship to some contemporary political ideologies. Before proceeding to that, however, we shall deal briefly with some treatments of leadership that have received the most attention in political science. This will allow us to put the present discussion against the background of previous efforts to come to grips with the prominent political leaders of the modern world.

CATEGORIES OF POLITICAL LEADERSHIP

Probably the most familiar method of classifying leadership was developed early in this century by the German sociologist Max Weber. His discussion of the evolution of societies led him to categorize leadership by reference to its source of authority. A second way to classify leadership is by personality type, a method that was first seriously developed by the American political scientist Harold Lasswell. A third way is illustrated by James MacGregor Burns, whose work has embodied much of the most recent scholarship on leadership, which emphasizes the relationship between the leaders and the led. Finally, we shall discuss the method applied in the present treatment, which explores the relationship between the leadership practices and the main themes of contemporary political ideologies.

Classifying Leaders by Source of Authority

In one of the most often-cited essays in social science, "Politics as a Vocation," Weber distinguished what he referred to as three "legitimations of domination." One of the most familiar of these derives from the "belief in the validity of legal statute . . . based on rationally created rules."[1] A public bureaucracy, of course, consists of a complex of offices created by legislative statutes, and exercises *"legal-rational"* authority. Naturally, there are private bureaucracies as well, and the positions in each type allow officials to exercise authority justified by the rules of the organization. Thus, the source of leadership in such cases is derived from the position that a person holds. One may or may not like the holder of the position or the orders that are given, but the position itself must be respected. It gives legitimacy to the exercise of leadership. Indeed, modern social and political organization is unthinkable without this kind of leadership.

A second source of leadership is also one that probably has fascinated social scientists more than any other kind—*charismatic* leadership. Weber defined charisma by reference to "a certain quality of an individual personality by virtue of which he is set apart from ordinary men and treated as if endowed with supernatural, superhuman, or at least specifically exceptional powers or qualities."[2] Thus, leaders are said to possess "charisma" precisely to the extent that they are able to inspire their followers with unshakable confidence in their ability to lead. The source of their authority lies in their own personalities. Weber also pointed out the category of "traditional domination," which is most often exemplified by the leadership exercised by a patriarch or tribal chief. One obeys such leaders because they have always been obeyed as long as anyone can remember. Weber discussed these legitimations of domination in terms of what he called "ideal types," which function as reference points more or less approximated by conditions in the real world, and provide for intelligent investigations into how real leaders and followers behave.

Weber's categories have been enormously influential, and social scientists have relied upon them heavily in continuing investigations of authority structures, leadership, and other social phenomena. Perhaps equally influential, however, have been attempts to develop political typologies of leaders and their followers on the basis of personality studies. That is, the development of political psychology has also contributed heavily to efforts that focus upon the needs, motivations, and patterns of behavior of individuals in a variety of settings. One of the trailblazers of this approach was Harold D. Lasswell.

Classifying Leaders by Personality Types

In a book published in 1930 with the slightly shocking title, *Psychopathology and Politics,* Harold Lasswell applied some methods of clinical psychology to the study of "political man." Influenced greatly by

Freudian psychoanalysis, he discussed a number of case studies that exemplified, in his view, the "displacement of private motives to public objects."[3] Much of his book reviews the life histories of representative political types, of which two stand out in his analysis. The first is the political agitator, a figure he describes in vivid terms as one who is interested principally in arousing the public to a fever pitch of political excitement for the pursuance of goals the agitator deems worthy. In Lasswell's own, highly descriptive language:

> Believing in direct, emotional responses from the public, the agitator trusts in mass appeals and general principles. Many of his kind live to shout and write. Their consciences trouble them unless they have periodic orgies of moral fervor. Relying upon the magic of rhetoric, they conjure away obstacles with the ritualistic repetition of principles. They become frustrated and confused in the tangled mass of technical detail upon which successful administration depends. Agitators of the "pure" type, when landed in responsible posts, long to desert the official swivel for the roving freedom of the platform and the press. They glorify men of outspoken zeal, men who harry the dragons and stir the public conscience by exhortation, reiteration, and vituperation.[4]

By contrast, political administrators are a somewhat more complex lot, and some of them actually share some characteristics with the agitators. A principle difference, however, rests upon an ability to take on tasks of a routine nature, and see them through to completion, without the fanfare, excitement, and inevitable sense of personal destiny that marks so much activity of the agitator. More important is the difference in temperament. One kind of administrator "often met in the public service is the conscientious, overscrupulous official, whose touchiness, fondness for detail, delight in routine, and passion for accuracy . . . preserve the integrity of the service."[5] Administrators as a group are more committed to the performance of specific tasks, are uncomfortable with abstractions, and tend generally to be less determined about shaping the events around them. He even suggests that the two types could actually be arranged on a continuum, with the agitator at one end and the administrator at the other. Successful administrators have moved from the agitator end of the scale in their personality development to the administrator end of the scale, "outgrowing," in effect, the characteristics of the previous stage.[6] This scheme is interesting, as it bears some similarity in individual terms to Weber's theory about the evolution of societies from the stage of charismatic rule to the "routinization of charisma" characterized by the development of legal-rational forms of authority.

At all events, interest in the relationship between personality and politics is as old as Plato, and tracing this development from the time of

Lasswell's work would lead us far afield from our present concerns.[7] The psychological approach illustrated by Lasswell has motivated many scholars to do detailed "psychohistories" of famous people, and no doubt has also inspired much of the present research into political cultures throughout the world and into the personality characteristics of citizens who live under different forms of government. Although Lasswell's work has in some respects been overtaken by more recent studies, it still retains its status as one of the classic approaches to the study and classification of political leadership—by reference to the personality types of the leaders in question.

Classifying Leaders by Relationship to Followers

One of the most important works on political leadership to appear in recent years has been James MacGregor Burns's *Leadership*. In this volume Burns reviews much of the literature on leadership that has derived from behavioral studies of power and influence, at the group and the societal level. His basic emphasis is that leadership cannot be understood without reference to the relationship between leader and follower. In his words, "I define leadership as leaders inducing followers to act for certain goals that represent the values and the motivations— the wants and needs, the aspirations and expectations—*of both leaders and followers*" (emphasis his).[8] Thus, unlike the two previous approaches, the characteristics of the followers and their circumstances are deemed as worthy an object of investigation as the characteristics of the leaders themselves. In fact, Burns's approach embraces aspects of Weber's and Lasswell's categories. For instance, the source of much leadership is found by reference to those needs in the followers that are satisfied by the actions of leader. Also, some leaders clearly possess various strengths of personality that make them stand apart from their followers. In short, both source and personality of leaders are dealt with by examining the leader-led relationship.

Burns defines two kinds of leadership, transactional and transformational. The first involves leaders reacting with followers in a way that approximates a commercial exchange—hence the appellation *transactional*. That is, the leader provides certain goods, values, or services in exchange for votes, money, or support of some sort on the part of the followers. Burns examines transactional leadership in the context of opinion leadership; group leadership in bureacracies, legislatures, and political parties; and executive leadership. He deals with all of these in separate chapters. Although important, transactional leadership is not particularly inspiring, as it is based only upon the objects of exchange that both parties in the equation find useful. Thus, the relationship between the leader and follower is functional in the sense that, like the purchase of a commodity in a store, each party has what the other one wants—hence a transaction is undertaken. But, as he points out, "a leadership act took place, but it was not one that binds leader and follower together in a mutual and continuing pursuit of a higher purpose."[9]

It is this higher purpose that distinguishes transformational leadership. Again, in his words, "transforming leadership ultimately becomes *moral* in that it raises the level of human conduct and ethical aspiration of both leader and led, and thus it has a transforming effect on both."[10] Burns provides cases of intellectual, reform, and revolutionary leadership in these terms, covering such figures as James Madison, Charles Grey of Great Britain, Alexander II of Russia, Gandhi, Lenin, and Mao Zedong. He also touches upon "heroic" leadership and ideological leadership, categories that overlap somewhat with Weber's charismatic authority as an ideal type, and Lasswell's notion of the political agitator. But the relational aspects of leadership remain the principle object of his focus, and Burns concludes his discussion with an overview of the purpose and impact of modern political leadership upon both leaders and followers, as well as on the course of world events generally.

Our discussion here will also involve these elements, as the political leaders discussed in this book—Hitler, Stalin, Mao, Khomeini, Madison, Franklin Roosevelt, and Martin Luther King, Jr.—influenced not only their immediate followers, but had a major impact upon world politics as well. And, like Burns's categories of leadership, the ones we shall discuss here overlap considerably with those of Weber and Lasswell, along with Burns's as well. That is because the criteria for classifying political leaders employed in our analysis involve a pervasive aspect of the modern politics—political ideology. Thus, the leaders we shall discuss were not only significant in terms of being agitators or administrators, charismatic authorities or bureaucratic officials, or transactional or transformational leaders, but were great *ideological* leaders as well. Before we can proceed to demonstrate this, however, we must deal with a few matters of definition. That is, before understanding what a great ideological leader is, we must understand what is meant by ideology and ideological leadership.

Classifying Leaders by Relationship to Political Ideology

Most textbook definitions of political ideology stress that the term refers to a network of beliefs and attitudes about the world of politics and one's place in it. Political ideologies may be understood by reference to the characteristics they all share, and by the functions that they perform for individuals and political systems. As we shall see, the characteristics of political ideologies are displayed rather prominently by the ideological leaders we shall describe in this book. They consist of famous persons (a hagiology), authoritative documents (sacred texts), and a theory of the meaning of political existence. Each of these characteristics is associated with a number of important functions. We shall review these as well, and devote special attention to those associated with the theory of the meaning of political existence.

Characteristics of Political Ideologies.

1. HAGIOLOGY.   This term refers literally to a "list of saints," and obviously derives from theological studies of persons regarded as especially inspired or chosen by God. In this context the meaning is similar, except that the figures identified as famous or particularly noteworthy in political ideologies, with the exception of Islam, are rarely called "saints." Indeed, very often they are called the opposite by their opponents. But at all events, the status accorded to many ideological giants is practically the same, in that the ideology in question simply cannot be understood without reference to them. In fact, the hagiology of some ideologies is so important that they are identified in terms of it.

Thus, devotees of Marxism-Leninism have special reverence, obviously, for Marx and Lenin—two figures who are often regarded as the Christ and St. Paul of that ideology. Indeed, anyone acquainted with the elaborate rituals associated with the visiting of Lenin's tomb in Moscow cannot fail to be impressed with the quasi-*religious* nature of his status in the Soviet Union. In Islam, of course, the list of saints is very much longer, and naturally the religious connotation remains. For *Shi'a Islam,* which we shall examine here, the hagiology includes, besides the Prophet Muhammad, the fourth caliph, Ali, his son Husayn, and a number of other figures known as the *Twelve Imams.* Democratic liberalism has an impressive hagiology too; who in the American tradition does not hold such figures as Thomas Jefferson, George Washington, and Abraham Lincoln in at least some esteem? In short, modern political ideologies are characterized, like the major religions of the world, by several prominent figures who function either as role models, ultimate sources of authority, special objects of veneration, or all of these things, for large numbers of people.

2. SACRED TEXTS.   Again, a religious term is applied here, but the emotional force lent by its use remains appropriate. All political ideologies have texts, famous writings, that are regarded as ultimate sources

of authority and as beyond reproach, or very nearly so. Indeed, it is often incumbent upon devotees to be very familiar with the sacred writings. This is especially the case with Islam, as the Qur'an is often cited as probably the most memorized book in the world. But it is also true with other ideologies that are less encompassing than Islam; that is, less concerned with all the intimate details of a person's existence. Thus, in the liberal tradition, John Locke's *Second Treatise of Government* retains its importance as a seminal treatment of liberal ideas. Americans are more familiar with the Declaration of Independence and the Bill of Rights, documents with enormously important status for liberalism in the United States. Marx and Engels's *Communist Manifesto* is required reading for communists and noncommunists alike, and Hitler's *Mein Kampf* remains probably the best summary of the Nazi ideology. In all cases, the function of the sacred texts is similar to that of the hagiology, which is to provide a source of authority for the interpretation and evaluation of political events.

3. THEORY OF THE MEANING OF POLITICAL EXISTENCE.   It is this characteristic of political ideologies that most writers focus upon as being the source of their many "functions" for individuals and political systems. In fundamental terms, political ideologies explain who a person is, where that person belongs or should belong in social and political terms, generally how the world works, what ideals should govern the actions of those committed to the ideology, and the meaning of political events. As all of these matters concern the most important functions of ideologies, we shall discuss each one separately.

A. A THEORY OF HISTORY.   Every modern political ideology is characterized by a particular understanding of history, which allows individuals to identify and place themselves and others in terms of a larger, temporal scheme. For instance, the Nazis regarded history, and, indeed, all existence, as the record of struggle between the strong and the weak, between the superior race and inferior races. Communists regard history as the record of class struggles; liberals following the enlightenment tradition generally see history as the record of people's progress toward rational self-governance. Muslims see history as the record of God's actions on this earth, and, correspondingly, their duties to Him in anticipation of the Last Judgment. All of these things may be understood in terms of the meaning of political existence provided by political ideologies, one of their most important characteristics.

B. POLITICAL IDENTIFICATION AND EXPLANATION.   Clearly, any theory of history allows individuals to identify themselves and others in terms of a larger conceptual framework. Also, political ideologies give individuals an outlook on the world that allows a person to identify politically relevant objects and to arrange political events into meaningful patterns. Thus, political figures are known as "liberals," "conservatives," "radicals," "communists," "racists," "fascists," or some other politically relevant label. Governments are "totalitarian," "authoritarian," or "democratic"; and some are fighting wars of "national liberation," or attempting to suppress "freedom fighters." Further, political events can have very different meanings to people who view them from different ideological positions. For example, the War in Vietnam may be looked upon as the result of indigenous nationalist forces who tried (successfully, as it turned out) to rid their country of imperialist aggressors, or it may be viewed as a prime example of international communism trying to extend its domain by subjugating an independent country fighting to maintain its freedom. The point is that no political figure and no political event in the world is ever value-neutral; how one interprets and evaluates either depends upon the complex of views known as one's political ideology.

C. JUSTIFICATION FOR ACTION. Ideologies provide justification for political action by political leaders and masses alike. Of all the functions of ideological systems, this one is probably the most important. If philosophy refers to the process whereby individuals are involved in a disinterested search for truth, then political ideologies may be understood as inspiring people to carry out political actions on the basis of truths already felt to have been discovered, or that, at all events, are firmly believed. *Action* is the key word in understanding modern political ideologies. No government that has failed to justify its actions on the basis of ideological beliefs widely shared by the populace is likely to stay in power for long. By the same token, competing ideologies within the same population is the usual pretext for civil war. Thus, in a fundamental sense, political ideologies provide legitimacy for government institutions and the actions taken on their behalf.

Indeed, the importance of ideology in justifying political institutions and their rulers can be seen by the dilemma faced by many communist governments today. For instance, most Western observers of the Soviet Union and China, as well as many critics within those countries, agree that both states face serious economic difficulties brought on by the structure of their politico-economic systems. With that in mind, Sovietologists and Sinologists are often asked whether or not the rulers of those two countries are still committed communists; that is, whether they still believe in the superiority of the Marxist-Leninist system, the scientific validity of Marxism-Leninism as a political ideology, the inevitable demise of the capitalist world predicted by Marxist thought, and so forth. The answers that are given vary, but on one point scholars of those communist states are practically unanimous: regardless of whether Soviet rulers, Chinese rulers, or Marxist-Leninist leaders anywhere remain in their hearts committed communists, they had better *pretend* to believe they are committed communists. The communist ideology is the only thing that grants legitimacy to their political systems and their high positions in them. As we shall see, the present rulers of these countries are coping with that difficulty in various ways.

And, of course, we shall see that there are various methods that political leaders may use to react to, act upon, or revise the basic tenets of the political ideologies they profess. The categories used here to classify ideological leaders are based upon those differences. Before proceeding to a treatment of these leaders, then, we must look briefly at the ways used to classify them in our analysis.

Categories of Ideological Leadership.   There are four categories of ideological leadership applied to the figures in our treatment: founder, revisionist, practitioner, and missionary. Following Weber here, we shall regard these terms as ideal types, recognizing that the leaders we shall consider approximate these categories to various degrees, but do not perfectly embody them. Although the terms are fairly self-explanatory, a brief explanation of each is in order.

FOUNDER.   This concept refers to those leaders who are most responsible for formulating and developing the ideology in question, in the following sense: an ideological founder is one who has provided an interpretation of an existing set of beliefs, and has acted upon them in a fashion that has resulted in a distinctive complex of political practices and institutions. Of the terms we shall employ here, the concept of the founder is perhaps the most problematic, because it seems to state too much. Who, after all, can truly be regarded as the sole founder of a political ideology in this century? But the key to understanding and applying the category rests less upon intellectual originality than it does upon the historical significance of the founder's particular views, along with his political actions, and the practical results flowing from them. In short, it is the *combination* of ideas, practices, and new institutions that distinguish certain ideological leaders of our day as founders. We might add that recognizing other contributors to a stream of thought that is most prominently associated with a single figure does not diminish the stature of that person as an ideological founder as we shall use the term here.

This consideration takes on added importance by virtue of the fact that, as we shall see, some founders actually were not terribly original thinkers. But they all were extremely adept at putting together various aspects of other people's ideas in ways that suggested something new. There is perhaps no better example of this than Adolf Hitler, one of the most devastating founders of the twentieth century. Hitler himself was not strikingly original. But he possessed a brilliant though erratic mind, and succeeded in melding together a number of prominent themes in the German historical and philosophical traditions to form something new. Indeed, Nazism and the Third Reich are practically inconceivable without Adolf Hitler. In fact, the Soviets' designation of the National Socialist experience in Germany is really more accurate than the terms commonly used in the West; they refer to it as "Hitlerism." Their term is not only more descriptive, but gives due "credit"—if that is the word— to the founder of the Nazi state.

Other founders also demonstrate the importance of individual renderings of existing ideological beliefs—Joseph Stalin, for instance. He was a Marxist, of course, but obviously he did not create that ideology. Stalin was simply one of the most important followers of Marxist thought—and Lenin's as well. But after a quarter century of his rule in Russia, there was no question that someting new had appeared in the ideological lexicon of world politics—"Stalinism." And it was Stalin who "founded" Stalinism, not Marx or Lenin. Indeed, his status as founder of the modern Soviet Union, in terms of institutions and practices associated with his name, is practically undisputed. All contemporary observers of the Soviet Union comment voluminously on the ramifications and implications of Stalinism, meaning by that a particular kind of regime, one characterized by a distinctive array of social, political, and economic institutions.

Two other individuals in our survey qualify as founders, James Madison and the Ayatollah Khomeini. Madison's case is particularly interesting because he is probably known more as one of the famous authors of the Federalist Papers than he is of the Virginia Plan at Constitutional Convention. The main reason for that had to do with his rather reserved personality; had Madison been as flamboyant as, for instance, Jefferson, he probably would have been better remembered. By contrast, one person who is unlikely ever to be forgotten is Khomeini. The Ayatolla possesses none of Madison's modesty, but was equally responsible for the creation of a new state, the Islamic Republic of Iran. Although his role in this regard was indispensable, for reasons that we shall discuss, he will be dealt with here mainly as a practitioner of Islamic fundamentalism.

REVISIONIST.   This type of ideological leader is identified in terms developing a major variant, or revision, of an existing political ideology.

The revision is recognized as significant enough to constitute a distinctive contribution, but still within the confines of a broader stream of thought. The term *revisionist* has been associated mostly with the development of Marxist socialism over the past one hundred years, and often has been used as a term of derision or condemnation by those supporting the Soviet point of view. In more recent years, probably the two most noteworthy revisionists have been Tito of Yugoslavia and Mao Zedong of China. Both have been thorns in the side of the Soviet leadership, especially Mao, who is the revisionist we shall consider here. Of course, we shall also see that Mao regarded the Soviet leaders as "revisionists," for reasons of his own. Thus, who belongs to this category depends upon who is applying the term, but we shall argue that the Soviet charge probably makes more sense.

PRACTITIONER.   The practitioner is a leader who may be regarded as an exemplar of the political ideology that holds his or her commitments. Without question there are more practitioners in the world than there are any other kind of political leader. But some of them stand out in rather significant ways, as we shall see with the practitioners chosen for study in our analysis, Franklin D. Roosevelt and the Ayatollah Khomeini. Roosevelt's presidency, which was so often bitterly criticized and confused by his opponents, was actually an embodiment of numerous very characteristic themes in American history. In a similar fashion, Khomeini seems to be virtually identified as a practitioner of Islamic fundamentalism, although we shall see that many of his ideas and practices are regarded as original by specialists. Also, he has inspired many people to actions consistent with our last category, the missionary.

THE MISSIONARY.   The leader as missionary is a person who, like his or her religious counterpart, attempts to extend ideological precepts to as many people as possible. In other words, the missionary literally has a mission in life—to spread his or her faith to others, and to gain converts to the ideology. Actually, the missionary we shall discuss here had a somewhat different sort of thing in mind, although it was equally important. Martin Luther King, Jr. gave his life for the purpose of reinstilling in Americans the ideals upon which the country was founded; that is, to *remind* them of what the United States was all about. Like an Old Testament prophet, King tried to turn the people to the ways of righteousness outlined in the principle summary of the American creed, the Declaration of Independence. In this sense King has not been the only missionary that the United States has produced, but he is the most recent, and generally regarded as the most significant. Indeed, of all the American missionaries, he is the only one to have his own birthday declared a national holiday.

Founder, revisionist, practitioner, missionary—these are the terms that we shall use in our survey of ideology and leadership in the world today. Before proceeding to a discussion of the ideological leaders, a final point should be made about how the categories were applied. Anyone familiar with the political careers of the figures treated in this book will recognize that much of what several did falls into more than one category. This, of course, is the difficulty of many concepts developed in political science to understand the complexity of the world of politics, to break it down into manageable portions and to arrange it in patterns that are instructive and meaningful. And the choices made here may not be agreed upon by all, at least in some details. Nonetheless, choices do have to be made. The ones made here reflect my views, based further upon my understanding of what many specialists have concluded about the principle contributions of the leaders in this book. Interestingly, several of the leaders under review here regarded *themselves* in terms of the categories used in our analysis. With that in mind, then, let us proceed to our treatment of ideology and leadership.

ENDNOTES

[1] Max Weber, "Politics as a Vocation," in H. H. Gerth and C. Wright Mills, trans. and eds., *From Max Weber: Essays in Sociology* (New York: Oxford University Press, 1958), pp. 77–128. Weber's extended comments on bureaucratic and charismatic authority are also contained in this volume. See "Bureaucracy," pp. 196–244; and "The Sociology of Charismatic Authority," pp. 245–52. See also Max Weber, *The Interpretation of Social Reality*, ed. J. E. T. Eldridge (New York: Schocken Books, 1980), pp. 229–37.

[2] Max Weber, *Interpretation of Social Reality*, p. 229.

[3] Harold D. Lasswell, *Psychopathology and Politics*, in *The Political Writings of Harold D. Lasswell* (Glencoe, Ill.: The Free Press, 1951), p. 75.

[4] Ibid., p. 79.

[5] Ibid., p. 142.

[6] Ibid., pp. 151–52.

[7] See the succinct overview provided by Robert Dahl, *Modern Political Analysis* (Englewood Cliffs, N.J.: Prentice-Hall, Inc., 1984), pp. 94–120. Dahl's discussion includes several references to the recent literature of personality and politics.

[8] James MacGregor Burns, *Leadership* (New York: Harper & Row, 1978), p. 19.

[9] Ibid., p. 20.

[10] Ibid.

THE ROOTS
OF AMERICAN
LIBERALISM

INTRODUCTION

Louis Hartz once commented that liberalism was "natural" to the United States, largely because of the absence of competing philosophical traditions.[1] That is, during the colonial fight for independence, as well as in the subsequent development of the country's political institutions, Americans did not also have to struggle against ideas defending such traditions as feudalism, the monarchy, or an aristocracy based on birth, because none of these things took root in the British colonies. The dominant tradition in the country had always been liberalism, and the American revolutionaries were in the position of addressing the British with a single voice. Ironically, this "natural liberalism" of Americans consisted of a set of ideas that was actually imported from Great Britain, inspired mostly by what Gordon Wood has referred to as the "Opposition view of English politics."[2] This referred to views developed by a distinguished group of British political thinkers and articulated in the United States by persons familiar to most Americans— James Otis, John Dickinson, Thomas Jefferson, James Madison, John Adams, and many others. By the time of the revolution, the main themes of American political thought were clearly stated by the prominent leaders of public opinion throughout British North America, widely accepted by most members of the population, and assumed to be universally applicable. Our first task is to outline briefly the major tenets of American liberalism as most thinkers understood them on the eve of the American Revolution.

Our second task will be to comment briefly upon the unique conditions in which the liberal tradition developed in America. There is no question that the circumstances in which liberalism took root in the United States contributed greatly to what Daniel Boorstin has called the "Genius of American Politics." This "genius" derived in large measure from settlers in the New World taking advantage of "the unprecedented opportunities of this continent," and "a peculiar and unrepeatable combination of historical circumstances."[3] Coping with these circumstances produced individuals with a distinctive set of attitudes and approaches to the world. These attitudes were as significant in the development of American political institutions as the more formally expressed elements of American liberalism, and we shall discuss them next. In short, liberalism in America was the product of a particular set of ideas imported from Europe and applied to the distinctive conditions of the North American continent.

MAJOR TENETS OF AMERICAN LIBERALISM[4]

By the time of the American Revolution, colonial political thinkers had arrived at the following conclusions about origins of government, and its purposes and functions.

Natural Law

The foundation of colonial beliefs was the conviction that underlying reality is a fundamental law that governs the workings of the universe as well as the moral and social relations among persons. It is an unwritten law, discoverable by human reason, confirmed by experience, proclaimed by God's commands, and thus accessible to anyone who wishes to inquire about it. Naturally, this idea has deep roots in the Greco-Roman tradition as well as the Judeo-Christian understanding of God's universal providence. The political treatments of fundamental law most directly relevant to colonial thinking were found in the works of British political theorists and jurists, such as John Locke (1632–1704) and Sir Edward Coke (1552–1634), who each talked about fundamental law as providing a standard to judge the actions of executives and legislators.[5] Most important, natural law guaranteed to all people their natural rights.

Natural Rights

Natural law was politically significant chiefly in its relationship to natural rights. The most important ones according to John Locke were life, liberty, and property. Jefferson, who authored the Declaration of Independence, changed the last item to the "pursuit of happiness"—a more expansive term that seems to include the previous two, as well as generally the right to live as one wishes without interference from others, provided one does not intrude upon their rights. The most significant characteristic of natural rights, however, was the fact that they are guaranteed by the law of nature, and not granted by the state. That is, they existed *prior to* the institution of governments; people possessed them whether or not there was any government in existence. Indeed, the whole point of establishing a government was better to safeguard individual rights.

During the disputes with Great Britain, the colonists had no trouble listing the number of rights that they felt were being threatened by parliamentary actions. These included freedom of speech, assembly, and association, and guarantees of periodic elections, and the right to impartial trials. But all these derived from their fundamental convictions that the "natural state" of all individuals was to live in freedom and equality. Freedom was interpreted largely in terms of not being subject to arbitrary and onerous acts of government, and being able to pursue individual interests as one saw fit. Equality was understood in moral and political terms; in Clinton Rossiter's words: "Men may be grossly unequal in appearance, talents, intelligence, virtue, and fortune, but to this extent at least they are absolutely equal: no man has any natural right of dominion over any other; every man is free in the sight of God and the plan of nature."[6] In short, freedom and equality were the primary values that enabled them to expand at length upon all the others. Clearly, few of their beliefs had more continuing relevance to the development of American politics than these.

Consent of the Governed

The solution to the problem of political obligation—why a citizen is obligated to obey commands of the government—lies in the principle of the consent of the governed. In short, individuals obey the government because they consented to obey. This consent is rendered in two ways. The first is associated with the original agreement, or contract, that establishes the structure of government, and outlines its functions and powers. Citizens agree to create a government and to give their allegiance to it in return for peace, security, and the continuing protection of individual rights. American colonists were very accustomed to this idea in practice, as they had been establishing governments at the local level almost literally from the day they arrived in the New World. The second form of consent centers upon representation, and concerns rendering continuing approval or disapproval of the acts of government. Obviously, the precise manner in which consent through representation is achieved is of crucial importance to the legitimacy of the government. Without question, one of the most lasting contributions of early American liberals was their conviction that a government that does not represent the people simply does not deserve to be obeyed. This idea has had wide application in American social as well as political history.

Duty of Resistance

When a government fails to carry out the functions assigned to it and becomes tyrannical, the people have a right to resist. More than that, they have a *duty* to resist. American colonists settled the age-old problem of how governments should deal with disobedient citizens essentially by turning the question around; that is, how should *citizens* deal with a disobedient *government,* one that has acted against the precepts of natural law, broken its trust with the people, failed to provide peace, order, and the protection of rights, and engaged instead in acts of tyranny? The answer that Jefferson gave in the Declaration of Independence represented the conclusion of many years of political reflection: dispense with the old government and create a new one. It is not only the right of the people, but a solemn duty as well. The colonists insisted that political authority is not something that should simply be taken for granted, but must be justified according to clearly defined standards.

As we shall see, statesmen have over the years applied these standards, the tenets of American liberalism, in various ways to fit the needs of the age. But their relevance to the continuing assessments of American politics has remained. In fact, American liberalism, although born in the dreams of European philosophers, theologians, and jurists, attained the status of a civil religion in the New World, summarized most succinctly in the Declaration of Independence, and widely accepted by all members of the population with little reflection or debate. Liberalism in America was and remains the American creed, a set of beliefs similar in force and application to religious dogma. Indeed, G. K. Chesterton (1874–1936), the noted British essayist, once described America as "a nation with the soul of a church," the only one in the world "that is founded on a creed."[7] It was a creed that James Madison struggled to apply in his proposals for the Constitution of the United States, and Franklin Roosevelt labored to preserve by his programs of the New Deal. Most recently, of course, it was powerfully reinvigorated by Martin Luther King, Jr. in the civil rights movement. Each was informed and guided by the basic tenets of American liberalism.

THE AMERICAN TEMPERAMENT

This rather old-fashioned term refers to the outlooks toward life, the habits of mind, produced by the reactions of successive generations of European immigrants to their experiences in the British North American colonies and, later, the United States. Admittedly, it is difficult to draw the line between what one observer would label distinctly as an aspect of American political theory—as developed by some political philosophers, for instance—and another simply as an element of American culture that has political significance. For example, Ralph Henry Gabriel, in his masterful book, *The Course of American Democratic Thought,* referred to the belief in fundamental law, the doctrine of the free and responsible individual, and the idea of America's mission in the world as the Doctrines of the American Democratic Faith.[8] Certainly all three have roots in systematic political and religious thought, and the first has already been discussed. We shall build upon Gabriel's analysis by discussing the other two as well, but in a fashion that differs from his treatment. The ideas of America's mission in the world, and the free and responsible individual, are also woven into the fabric of American culture, and constitute important elements of what we shall treat here as the American temperament. We shall discuss each in these terms.

The Mission of America

The conviction that America has a mission in the world derives chiefly from the Puritan experience in New England during the seventeenth century. At that time it was felt that God's almighty providence had singled out the Puritans to build a true Christian commonwealth, one that would constitute a shining example to a Europe wracked by religious conflicts and, in their view, corrupt, unreformed theology. John Winthrop, one of the principle founders of the Bay Colony in Massachusetts, expressed this idea succinctly in "A Model of Christian Charity," a sermon delivered to the passengers of the ship *Arbella,* on the way to the New World. "We must consider," Winthrop intoned, "that we shall be as a City upon a Hill, the eyes of all people are upon us."[9] In short, the Puritans judged their mission not only by their interpretations of God's special commands to them, but also against what Thomas Jefferson would later term "the opinions of mankind." These are demanding criteria, requiring the utmost effort and sternest diligence. Actually, the Puritans achieved many successes, but the feeling that their experiment never quite measured up to the standards they invoked continued to linger in American history. In fact, the conclusion that America had fallen short in carrying out its mission was without question a primary inspiration for the work of Martin Luther King, Jr., as we shall see.

By the end of the eighteenth century, the idea of America's mission had developed in directions that were more familiar to later generations of Americans. Its principle component rested upon the conviction that the United States of America was unique. It was the land of the free, the only place on earth where any person, regardless of previous national origins or social status, could begin life with a clean slate, and be whatever he wanted to be. It was the mission of America to set an example for all humanity, to show the world the boundless prosperity and benefits that accrue to individuals who live in a society based upon freedom, equality, and democratic institutions of governance. Although this idea took something of a drubbing from social criticism during the sixties, it has remained alive, and was recently rekindled during centennial celebrations of the Statue of Liberty. For instance, when President Reagan proclaimed, "We are the keepers of the flame of liberty," he expressed a sentiment that had deep roots in American political history. Clearly, the faith in America's mission to the world remains a salient aspect of the American temperament.

The Free and Responsible Individual

Closely related to the mission idea is the conviction that society consists of individuals who are free to develop as they please and are responsible for all actions they undertake. Again, individualism has a long history and has been developed in depth by Western political thinkers. But in America the notion of the free and responsible individual was more than just a theorist's concept or a popular aspiration; to the millions of Europeans who came to the United States for the purpose of starting their lives anew, it was a reality as well. This was confirmed by numerous foreign visitors, those sympathetic to the United States, at least, who made acute observations on American conditions over the years.[10] Many examples could be cited, but our review here will be confined to the comments of just two—one from the eighteenth century, and the other from the nineteenth: Michel de Crèvecoeur and Alexis de Tocqueville, respectively.

Michel de Crèvecoeur was a Frenchman who spent several decades living and working in the colonies around the time of their disputes with Great Britain. In his "Letters From an American Farmer," he ably described what it was like to be in America after growing up in Europe. "We have no princes for whom we toil, starve, and bleed," he said, "we are the most perfect society now existing in the world. Here man is free as he ought to be . . ."[11] "This fair country alone," he went on, "is settled by freeholders, the possessors of the soil they cultivate, members of the government they obey, and the framers of their own laws by means of their representatives."[12] Nearly everything de Crèvecoeur saw in America confirmed his view that it was a country unlike any other in the world.

Indeed, living in the new land had an invigorating effect upon people. The American was a "new man" who did things that he would not dream of doing anyplace else. De Crèvecoeur noticed that there was a sense of optimism and adventure among the common people that simply did not exist in Europe. "A European, when he first arrives, seems limited in his intentions as well as in his views; but he very suddenly alters his scale," he concluded. "He no sooner breathes our air than he forms schemes and embarks in designs he never would have thought of in his own country."[13] America was a place where people's fate was in their own hands, where dreams could come true and fortunes could be made (as well as unmade), and where nearly anything was possible. It was a land of adventure, where optimism reined supreme.

These sentiments were echoed by an even more famous visitor to the United States a half century after de Crèvecoeur, Alexis de Tocqueville. "America is a land of wonders," de Tocqueville observed, "in which everything is in constant motion, and every change seems an improvement."[14] In fact, the American preoccupation with novelty led many to change occupations quickly and with ease—something that rarely happened in Europe. The land of the free was also the land of the generalist, and "if the American be less perfect in each craft than the

European," de Tocqueville noted, "at least there is scarcely any trade with which he is utterly unacquainted."[15] And why not? "No natural boundary seems to be set to the efforts of man; and, in his eyes, what is not yet done is only what he has not yet attempted to do."[16] In short, freedom and responsibility, optimism, adventure, novelty—these were the characteristics that defined what we have termed here the American temperament.

It is important to keep in mind, however, at least two fundamental qualifications to these characteristics. First, the preceding assessments were made especially with Europe in mind, against the background of European conditions, patterns of thought, and behavior. And they were made by individuals who were frankly sympathetic to the new country. Although not relevant to our present survey, many foreign evaluations were filled with negative comments, especially about the state of American accomplishments in the arts and philosophy, for instance. Second, there was a darker side to American culture, represented principally by the treatment of Native Americans (Indians) and, of course, American blacks. Indeed, the most shameful characteristic of American culture centered upon the denial to black Americans the opportunities available to other immigrant groups. As we shall argue, America's mission could not, and cannot, be fulfilled without application of the American creed to all of the country's citizens.

In summary, liberalism and the American temperament consisted of a set of ideals, habits of thought, and ways of approaching the world that have had a distinctive influence upon American political development. Each of the Americans we will deal with here, James Madison, Franklin Roosevelt, and Martin Luther King, Jr., was inspired by various aspects of the tradition already described, in ways that made a difference in American history. Naturally, each one also exemplified different leadership styles in relationship to the liberal tradition and the American temperament—founder, practitioner, and missionary, respectively. Our next task is to discuss their contributions in these terms.

ENDNOTES

[1] Louis Hartz, *The Liberal Tradition in America* (New York: Harcourt, Brace & World, 1955), p. 5.

[2] Gordon Wood, *The Creation of the American Republic, 1776–1787* (W.W. Norton & Company, 1972), p. 14.

[3] Daniel Boorstin, *The Genius of American Politics* (Chicago: The University of Chicago Press, 1953), p. 1.

[4] The following discussion is drawn from a variety of sources. For good surveys of American political thought, see Lawrence J. R. Herson, *The Politics of Ideas: Political Theory and American Public Policy* (Homewood, Ill.: The Dorsey Press, 1984); Alpheus Thomas

Mason and Richard H. Leach, *In Quest of Freedom* (Englewood Cliffs, N.J.: Prentice-Hall, Inc., 1959); Ralph Henry Gabriel, *The Course of American Democratic Thought*, 2nd ed. (New York: The Ronald Press, 1959); Alan Pendleton Grimes, *American Political Thought*, rev. ed. (New York: Holt, Rinehart and Winston, 1960); and A. J. Beitzinger, *A History of American Political Thought* (New York: Dodd, Mead & Company, 1972). For studies of American political thought during the time of the Revolution, see, for instance, Clinton Rossiter, *The Political Thought of the American Revolution* (New York: Harcourt, Brace & World, Inc., 1963); Bernard Bailyn, *The Ideological Origins of the American Revolution* (Cambridge, Mass.: Harvard University Press, 1967); John P. Roche, ed., *Origins of American Political Thought* (New York: Harper & Row, 1967), in addition to Hartz, *Liberal Tradition*, and Wood, *American Republic*.

[5] An excellent treatment of this topic is found in Edward S. Corwin, *The "Higher Law" Background of American Constitutional Law* (Ithaca, N.Y.: Cornell University Press, 1929).

[6] Clinton Rossiter, "The Political Theory of the American Revolution," in Roche, *Origins*, p. 101.

[7] Quoted in Michael Novak, "The Nation with the Soul of a Church," in Richard J. Bishirijian, ed., *A Public Philosophy Reader* (New Rochelle, N.Y.: Arlington House Publishers, 1978), p. 94.

[8] Gabriel "The Doctrines of the American Democratic Faith," in *Democratic Thought*, pp. 12–25.

[9] John Winthrop, "A Model of Christian Charity," in Perry Miller and Thomas Johnson, eds., *The Puritans: A Sourcebook of Their Writings*, rev. ed. (New York: Harper & Row Publishers, 1963), p. 199. The spelling has been rendered into modern English.

[10] A useful collection of observations by foreign visitors to the United States is contained in Henry Steele Commager, ed., *America in Perspective: The United States Through Foreign Eyes* (New York: New American Library, 1947).

[11] Michel Guillaume Jean de Crèvecoeur, "What is an American?" in *The Annals of America*, Vol. 2, *1755–1783* (Chicago: Encyclopedia Britannica, Inc., 1968), p. 584.

[12] Ibid., p. 588.

[13] Ibid., p. 589.

[14] Alexis de Tocqueville, *Democracy in America*, ed. Andrew Hacker (New York: Washington Square Press, 1964), p. 118. The first edition of this book was originally published in French, in 1835–1840.

[15] Ibid.

[16] Ibid.

JAMES MADISON

Founder as Father of the Constitution

3

Every person seems to acknowledge his greatness. He blends together the profound politician with the scholar . . . and tho' he cannot be called an orator, he is a most agreeable, eloquent and convincing speaker . . . The affairs of the United States, he perhaps, has the most correct knowledge of, of any man in the Union. *William Pierce*[1]

The most eloquent man I ever heard. *John Marshall*[2]

I have known him from 1779, when he first came into the public councils, and, from three and thirty years trial, I can say conscientiously that I do not know in the world a man of purer integrity, more dispassionate, disinterested, and devoted to genuine Republicanism; nor could I in the whole scope of American Europe point out an abler head. *Thomas Jefferson*[3]

Give Mr. Madison the right side of a good cause, and no man could equal him in its vindication. *Charles Ingersoll*[4]

[With regard to my] estimate of Mr. Madison—his private virtues, his extraordinary talents, his comprehensive and statesmanlike views . . . in wisdom I have long been accustomed to place him before Jefferson. *Justice Story*[5]

The citizens of the United States are responsible for the greatest trust ever confided to a political society. If justice, good faith, honor, gratitude and all the other qualities which enoble the character of a nation & fulfill the ends of government, be the fruits of our establishments, the cause of liberty will acquire a dignity and lustre, which it has never yet enjoyed, and an example will be set, which cannot but have the most favourable influence on the rights of Mankind. *James Madison*[6]

INTRODUCTION

In a public address in 1827 Charles J. Ingersoll bestowed upon James Madison a title that he never accepted: Father of the Constitution. He later reacted by saying, "You give me a credit to which I have no claim . . . This [the Constitution] was not like the fabled goddess of wisdom the offspring of a single brain. It ought to be regarded as the work of many heads and many hands."[7] But this self-effacing judgment was not shared by his contemporaries, and for good reason. The major point of departure for the discussions during the Constitutional Convention was a proposal based upon the results of Madison's careful studies during the time preceding the opening of the debates. Moreover, he committed himself to the strenuous task of taking notes at the Convention, recording, in surprising detail, the events that took place. Indeed, scholars of the American founding acknowledge their tremendous indebtedness to his work. Clearly, in the minds of those who knew him personally and as an historical figure, Madison's contribution to the formation and governance of the Republic was indispensable.

Unfortunately for Madison admirers, however, there is little evidence on public display that gives testimony to his greatness as a founder. Americans are generally far more familiar with such figures as George Washington, Thomas Jefferson, Andrew Jackson, and Abraham Lincoln than they are with James Madison. Washington, of course, was Father of Our Country; Jefferson, the author of the Declaration of Independence; Jackson, the Great Democrat; and Lincoln, the Savior of the Union. And all of them have been commemorated in numerous public buildings and statues throughout the land. In fact, even some villains of American history, such as Aaron Burr and Benedict Arnold, are probably better known than Madison.[8] So where does this leave James Madison; just how should Americans refer to him as an historical figure? Madison the Wise, perhaps, or Madison the Astute? Possibly the title Madison the Obscure is the most descriptive. But it is also the most unfair. Ingersoll's suggestion is clearly the most appropriate: Madison the Father of the Constitution.

However, this designation is also incomplete, as the historical contributions of Madison went beyond even those associated with the founding of the republic. He was also the cofounder, with Thomas Jefferson, of the Republican (later called the Democratic) Party. Further, he was the cofounder, again with Jefferson, of arguments that contributed greatly to the near-destruction of the union of states that he had labored so hard to create and maintain. And these contributions were made before the most publicly visible aspects of his career in politics—his two terms as president—actually began. This constitutes a separate chapter in American history and will not be dealt with here. Our main emphasis will be placed upon Madison's role as founder and shaper of the momentous events of the 1780s and 1790s. We shall begin with a very brief account of his activities leading up to this crucial period.

THE MIND OF THE FOUNDER—
THE FORMATIVE PERIOD[9]

When the Constitutional Convention delegates met in Philadelphia in 1787, no one was better prepared for the coming debates than the thirty-six-year-old James Madison. In fact, he seemed to have been preparing for them his entire life. He had received a vigorous and exhausting education in the classics, which included completing a four-year course at the College of New Jersey (Princeton) in two years. He had extensive experience in the state government of Virginia, and had also become thoroughly acquainted with national affairs by serving in the Congress under the Articles of Confederation. In all of these endeavors, Madison was widely respected for his patient and scholarly disposition, two traits that proved to be indispensable for the trials that he and the country were to experience after the War for Independence. By 1787 he had come to a number of definite conclusions about the state of the union immediately prior to the opening of the Convention.[10] Before discussing these, however, a brief overview of his formative years is in order.

Madison and Virginia Politics

For three years after the Declaration of Independence, Madison served in Virginia state government, first as a member of the House of Delegates, and then as a member of the Governor's Council. He was elected to the Confederation Congress in 1779, served until 1783, and rejoined the House of Delegates in the spring of the following year. One of the most important aspects of his experience during these years was his collaboration with Thomas Jefferson, especially after Jefferson became governor of Virginia in 1779. Together they must have been an interesting pair: the tall, stately Jefferson and the diminutive Madison— "a withered little apple-john," cracked Washington Irving;[11] "no bigger than a half a piece of soap," another quipped.[12] But few friendships were more lasting or productive. Indeed, in his review of Madison's writings, Marvin Meyers concluded that "every major public project of their lives, from establishing the Virginia republic on liberal foundations in the 1770s to creating the University of Virginia in the 1820s, became a joint enterprise, drawing the two leaders closer."[13] Although they did not always agree, each benefited enormously from their joint endeavors.

One of the fruits of their early efforts together was also extremely significant for the development of Madison's political philosophy. It involved a measure that would disestablish the Episcopal Church from the state of Virginia—that is, withdraw from the church any financial support from the state. This was a volatile issue that inflamed the debates in the legislature for a decade, and Madison was usually in the middle of it. He defended disestablishment on the basis of his strong views about the value of religious freedom to the social order, which he insisted was promoted by separation of church and state. Moreover, he was convinced that denial of religious liberty had a stifling effect upon the imaginations and energies of the people: "Religious bondage shackles and debilitates the mind," Madison warned, "and unfits it for every noble enterprise, every expanded prospect."[14] Later he would draw the conclusion that tolerance extended to a multiplicity of religious sects actually guarantees freedom for them all, which was without doubt one of the most important insights into social relations he ever had. An extension of his argument into the realm of civil freedom would come in his famous Federalist Paper Number Ten. In short, Madison's grappling with the issue of religious freedom strongly influenced the views he expressed at the Constitutional Convention.

Madison in the Confederation Congress

Madison's political education continued when he was elected to the Confederation Congress in 1779. He was enormously active in that organization, serving on most of the important committees on both foreign and domestic affairs, frequently writing committee reports on various matters, and generally receiving an excellent overview of the operations of the national government during the war years. Unfortunately, everything he saw brought him to despair. He wrote agonizing letters to Jefferson, pointing out how the lack of adequate national authority undermined everything the government attempted to do, especially in supporting the war effort with appropriate funding. "The whole Confederacy," he lamented, "may be insulted and the most salutary measures frustrated by the most inconsiderable State in the Union."[15] Exasperated, he submitted a measure that would give the national government the authority to coerce a state to obey national laws. But since amendments to the Articles of Confederation required the assent of all the states, his proposal failed handily. He left the Congress in 1783, convinced that only a strong national government would be able to deal with the serious problems faced by the United States.

The Road to Philadelphia

By 1787 the United States was in a social, economic, and political mess. To Madison and many others, it seemed that the civic virtue, the willingness to sacrifice for the common good that was so often shown by people during the war years, had simply evaporated. Further, American citizens and their state governments were displaying all the vices and corruption that had been the doom of every republican government in the past. Selfishness and greed abounded in every city, village, and hamlet in the land; unconcern or outright contempt for the public good was widespread. Religious commitments seemed to decline, profanity fouled the air, litigation increased over trifling matters, and, worst of all, the Confederation government became an object of universal contempt, for both Americans and foreign governments. And no element of the population could be held blameless in contributing to the general demise of public morals—merchants, farmers, government officials at all levels, debtors and creditors alike—all were guilty. George Washington greatly understated matters by concluding that "we have probably had too good an opinion of human nature in forming our confederation."[16]

He was undoubtedly correct, but most Americans were realistic about the frailties of human nature. The vexing question centered upon what should be done about human failings—all those noisy and dangerous conflicts, divisions, and petty disputes that seemed to engulf public affairs at both the state and national levels. For instance, how could one reform what many regarded as those "vile state governments," who were ruled by legislative majorities that regularly passed legislation violating the rights of some group of its citizens—creditors, for instance; property owners generally; or those engaged in a specific industry, such as fishermen, cotton-growers, or shippers? Further, what could be done about conflicts *among* the states? What measures should be taken against states that passed tariffs against one another, thus restricting interstate commerce, or otherwise discriminated against one anothers' citizens? Finally, there was a serious problem about the United States's relations with foreign powers—principally Spain, Great Britain, and numerous Indian tribes—who threatened the borders of the country. All these questions converged upon the central consideration about the viability of the United States as a sovereign political entity.

It is instructive to point out that from the standpoint of American liberalism, these problems appeared unique, or at the very least, unanticipated. Certainly people continued to believe in liberal ideas about people and government—fundamental law, natural rights, freedom and equality, the consent of the governed, and the duty to overthrow tyrannical governments. But, as noted earlier, these ideals also constituted a summary statement of the *opposition* theory of British politics, applied to the colonial setting and directed against *British* rule. At this time the principle figure in American hagiology, at least from the standpoint of philosophical influence, was John Locke. And the main difficulty of his theory applied to current American conditions is that it reduced all the complexities of politics to a single problem of devastating simplicity: people versus government. The people were assumed to be good, and the government, at least a distant, unrepresentative one, was bad. So long as the enemy took the form of a monolithic tyranny located on faraway shores, matters remained uncomplicated.

But what if—in the words of the cartoon character Pogo—we have met our enemy and he is us? That is, what if the main problem of politics is no longer that of people versus government (us versus them) but rather that of the people versus people (us versus us)? Stated differently, how does one protect the rights of one part of the population—the lesser part, usually—against the demands of the majority? Moreover, there was another conflict of potentially more destructive consequences—governments versus governments. The state governments were not only pitted against one another in many cases, but were also defiant of national authority. Further, these conflicts did not occur in a context of "no taxation without representation"—the battle cry of the revolution—but rather under circumstances in which, as Madison astutely noted, there was unquestionably excellent popular representation in legislative councils![17] In short, between the end of the War for Independence and the Constitutional Convention, the problems of governance became much more complicated. Americans still wanted to maintain a system of ordered liberty, which is what they enjoyed under British rule for so long, but now the way to achieve that no longer seemed so clear.

But stunning events often function to clarify the thoughts of responsible people, and two significant ones took place within a year of the Convention. The first occurred in Massachusetts and had frightening implications for the maintenance of civil order. A group of farmers in the western part of the state attempted by force to close the civil courts, and thereby prevent any more foreclosures on their lands. This disturbance was known as Shays's Rebellion, because of the leadership role played by a certain Daniel Shays, a former army captain. It began in the late summer of 1786 and continued into the winter of the next year, when the last rebels finally submitted to the state militia. But the outburst had sobering effects upon property-holding classes everywhere, and provided a timely incentive for reform.

The second important event centered upon the efforts of Virginia and Maryland jointly to regulate commerce on the Potomac. The authority of the Confederation Congress was so feeble by this point that neither state even attempted to resolve their differences by appealing to that body. Instead, each passed a resolution asking the other states to meet at Annapolis in September 1786 to deal with common problems, and five states in all actually attended. The main accomplishment of the Annapolis Convention was to issue another call to the other states to review the problems arising from the existing constitutional arrangements, and "to devise such further provisions as shall appear to them necessary to render the Constitution of the Federal Government adequate to the exigencies of the Union."[18] The meeting was set for May 1787.

Thus, the stage was set for the Grand Convention. Nobody approached the meeting with more anticipation and greater study than James Madison. He spent the winter and spring prior to the Convention in Philadelphia, while Jefferson was in Paris, and the two exchanged notes and articles through the mail—books for Madison from Paris, and flora and fauna for Jefferson from the New World. While Jefferson dazzled his hosts with the assorted wonders of America, Madison went through an incredible amount of material in preparing himself for the convention. "The books arrived," says Catherine Drinker Bowen,

> not by the ones and twos but by the hundred: thirty-seven volumes of the new *Encyclopedie Methodique,* books on political theory and the law of nations, histories, works by Burlamaqui, Voltaire, Diderot, Mably, Necker, d'Albon. There were biographies and memoirs, histories in sets of eleven volumes on such timely productions as Mirabeau on The Order of the Cincinnati.[19]

Madison went through them all—some two hundred volumes—carefully taking notes and writing down his reactions as he went. By the time he was finished, he had some very definite ideas about how the new government should be formed.

The main object of his study focused upon the principles and operations of confederate systems of government, and whether or not their defects could be corrected. Nothing that Madison learned in his intense studies of the problem convinced him that confederations—including the American one—had any chance to survive. They all suffered from precisely those defects that were presently tearing apart the United States: localism and want of sufficient power in the center. Clearly, if the United States of America were to survive as a distinct political entity, it must be based upon a new design for popular, republican government, one strong enough to prevent anarchy, but not so powerful as to threaten the rights and liberties of its citizens.[20] In his notes written before the convention he said that he wanted to find a "middle-ground," which "may at once support a due supremacy of the national authority, and not exclude the local authorities wherever they can be subordinately useful."[21] In letters written to George Washington, Edmund Randolph, and Thomas Jefferson, he outlined a series of proposals that he thought would accomplish that purpose. These were introduced by Randolph at the convention in May, and were referred to as the Virginia Plan, or, sometimes, the Randolph Plan. But actually it was Madison's, and the discussion of his ideas at the convention began the most creative and important part of his life as Father of the Constitution and principal founder of the American democratic republic.

THE FRAMING OF THE CONSTITUTION

The Constitutional Convention

The original point of departure for the debates at the convention was the Virginia Plan formulated by Madison and submitted by Governor Randolph.[22] It called for the creation of a new national government with three branches, executive, judicial, and legislative. The executive was to be chosen by the legislature, which consisted of two houses. The lower house was to be popularly elected, and the upper house would comprise members elected by the lower from lists submitted by state legislatures. Most important to Madison, however, were the provisions that supported national supremacy. One of these would give the national government the power to "negative" any act of a state legislature, and another called for marshaling the "force of the Union against any member of the Union failing to fulfill its duty under the articles thereof."[23] Everything in Madison's experience and study convinced him of the necessity of a strong national government, and the Virginia Plan was a vivid result of his convictions.

On many matters he was able to get his way. Most importantly, the convention began with a proposal that called for the formation of a new government, and not just a revision of the old. This set the tone for the debates, putting those in favor of the old constitutional arrangement on the defensive. Secondly, he was convinced that the separation of powers into three distinct branches of government was an institutional arrangement most conducive to the maintenance of freedom, citing as his authority a figure familiar to most students of constitutionalism, the Frenchman Charles de Montesquieu. Finally, the new government had to be popularly based, but in a fashion that would moderate the "transient and indigested sentiments" of the people, so that it would avoid the instabilities and threats to individual rights often associated with the state governments. In short, by 1787, Madison and the other nationalists felt a system of ordered liberty required taming the "excesses of democracy" with stronger central authority.

Other matters had to be worked out, however, and not all of Madison's proposals were adopted, especially those pertaining to the mode of selecting public officials. The so-called "Great Compromise" resolved that issue with regard to the Congress by providing for proportional representation in the lower house, equal representation in the upper, and upper-house members chosen by state legislatures. Madison lost on the selection method for the chief executive as well, and in the end an unusual arrangement that relied upon an institution called the Electoral College was adopted. He was also opposed to the inclusion of a federal bill of rights, arguing that a limited government with carefully enumerated powers did not require such additional guarantees. Although the document approved in Philadelphia did not include them, supporters of the Constitution in the state ratifying conventions pledged to work for a federal bill of rights once the new government was approved. This bargain was kept, and Madison again showed his leadership role. Historian Edward Channing pointed out that as a member of the House of Representatives, "Madison seemed to be almost the only one who had any interest in the first batch of amendments," which became the Bill of Rights.[24] Clearly, his leadership role involved the willingness to compromise as well.

However, Madison remained adamant about asserting national supremacy over state authority, and tenaciously defended his proposal that would allow the national government to coerce a state. He gave up only after it was clear that he could not win. But he also changed his mind on this point, as did many others in favor of strong national government. As the debates proceeded, it became more clear that a truly national government that was approved by, received its authority from, and could act directly upon its citizens did not need such a power.[25] That is, the new national government rested upon *individuals,* and not the states. This point was underscored by the method of ratification chosen—approval by special conventions (not the state legislatures) chosen by the people of the states. A vote of nine states was considered sufficient for ratification. In short, the states were considered only as convenient means to convey popular desires.

Madison drew upon his very considerable talents to explain and justify the new government he had labored so hard to bring forth. His efforts, combined with those of John Jay and Alexander Hamilton, resulted in the most significant contribution to modern political science ever produced in the United States—the Federalist Papers. These were actually a series of numbered articles that appeared in some New York newspapers, written for the general public, and in support of the new government. They were all signed "Publius," but, thanks to the efforts of Douglas Adair, we now know that Madison wrote twenty-six to twenty-nine out of a total of eighty-five essays.[26] These include some of the most significant social and political analyses ever written. In order to understand Madison's importance as a founder, the arguments he presented in these papers must be dealt with. Before proceeding with this, however, we shall first review the problems of Constitution-writing that the delegates at the convention had to grapple with, which were later explained in such eloquent detail by the authors of the Federalist Papers.

Explaining the Constitution: Problems of Constitution Writing

Applying Declaration Principles.   There were two fundamental difficulties that Madison and the framers of the Constitution had to deal with at the convention. The first was the more general one of attempting to apply the basic tenets of liberalism—as formulated in the Declaration of Independence, for instance—to the practical tasks of constructing a government. Clearly, the Declaration proclaimed the right of the people to establish a government that protected their rights. But, as we have seen, the postwar experience showed convincingly that merely asserting the principles of self-government could not by itself resolve the thorny problems of governance. In short, the Declaration did not dictate the particular *form* that the government should take; it only asserted the "right of the people . . . to institute new government . . . as to them shall seem most likely to effect their safety and happiness." This seemed to leave the options open.

Indeed, Martin Diamond makes a point that is often lost on contemporary readers: "by any form of government the Declaration emphatically includes—as any literate eighteenth century reader would have understood—not only the democratic form of government but also aristocratic and monarchical government as well."[27] Thus, the American Constitution must be considered as the *particular* application of Declaration principles that was finally settled upon by the framers in Philadelphia, and approved by the people. Still, Diamond singles out Madison's contribution by adding that it was his "theoretic *wisdom* [italics are his]" and "sober clarity regarding democracy [that] gave the shape and thrust to our unique democratic form of government and way of life."[28]

The Problem of Republicanism.   The second difficulty of Constitution-writing involved trying to solve a problem that had never been solved in the history of mankind. Madison's analysis of the problem and his explanation of the solution represented by the Constitution are found in Federalist Ten. This is unquestionably his most famous essay, and we shall draw from it extensively in our treatment of his positions. The following references, unless otherwise noted, are taken from this paper.

Madison defined a republic as "a government in which the scheme of representation takes place," and understood it as a government in which the people are represented, wholly, or in part. The fundamental problem of republican, or "popular," governments, throughout history was their inability to control the "violence" of faction. He defined a faction as consisting of "a number of citizens . . . who are united and actuated by some common impulse of passion, or of interest, adverse to the rights of other citizens, or to the permanent and aggregated interests of the community." His exhaustive study of republican governments led him to conclude the "mischiefs of faction" explain why "popular governments have everywhere perished." Further, the "latent causes of faction are . . . sown in the nature of man," and cannot be eradicated; attempts to do so simply destroy the liberty that give diverse interests such free play. The solution, therefore, lies in controlling their effects. Madison asserted that "the regulation of . . . various and interfering interests forms the principal task of modern legislation, and involves the spirit of party and faction *in the necessary and ordinary operations of government* [italics added]."

This was an extraordinary conclusion, given the assumptions that guided political thinkers up to the drafting of the Constitution. Madison did not, for instance, insist that a republic could survive only if its people were virtuous—a common assumption in American political thought before and during the Revolutionary War.[29] Madison and his contemporaries had a bellyful of experience that proved without a doubt that Americans were no more (or less) virtuous than any other people in the world. He also rejected absolutism in any form, feeling that the solution was worse than the disease. Thus he dismissed the conclusions of Thomas Hobbes, the famous seventeenth-century British political theorist, whose horror of factious behavior led him to recommend nearly unquestioning obedience to an all-powerful sovereign. Plato's suggestion for a philosopher-king, charged with the task of forcing "these clashing interests" to be "subservient to the public good," he dismissed as well. Such people "will not always be at the helm," and in any event are always in short supply. In short, Madison rejected all the classical solutions to the problems of republicanism. A new political science was necessary, one that went beyond all the old theories that had been tried and failed.

Madison insisted that there was a *republican* solution "for the diseases most incident to republican government." What was it? He gave the answer in Federalist Ten, and spent the greater portion of his remaining essays explaining it: "In the extent and proper structure of the union," he said, can one find "the cure for which we are seeking." That is, size and structure both function to *filter the popular impulses in a fashion that redounds to the benefit of all,* or at least not to the detriment to the public good. Thus, the inelegant expression "filtration device" captures the purpose of the specific measures found in the Constitution to maintain a system of ordered liberty in the American republic. Each deserved separate treatment.

Explaining the Constitution: Madisonian Political Science

The Principle of Size. In her studies of the opposition to the Constitution, Cecelia Kenyon pointed out that "the fundamental issue over which the Federalists and Anti-Federalists split was the question whether republican government could be extended to embrace a nation, or whether it must be limited to the comparatively small political and geographical units which the separate American states then constituted."[30] Patrick Henry, one of the major foes of the Federalists, summarized the common view by concluding that "one government cannot reign over so extensive a country as this is, without absolute despotism."[31] Indeed, some very prominent figures, including John Adams and Alexander Hamilton, expressed the opinion that Americans eventually would have to adopt some form of monarchical government. Further, these pessimistic reactions were based upon the received wisdom of the day, drawing from centuries of practice, about the perils of maintaining an extensive republic.

Madison totally rejected this analysis by completely turning it around. He chided his opponents for confusing the differences between a "pure democracy," which he agreed "can admit of no cure from the mischiefs of faction," and a republic. Pure democracies are unstable and unjust precisely because of their small size. It is easier for a combination of factions to constitute a majority and "concert and execute their plans for oppression" in a small area than it is in a large one. In an extensive republic, however, the situation is entirely different. In Madison's words:

> Extend the sphere, and you take in a greater variety of parties and interests; you make it less probable that a majority of the whole will have a common motive to invade the rights of other citizens; or if such a common motive exists, it will be more difficult for all who feel it to discover their own strength, and to act in unison with each other.

In other words, the principle of large size serves as a filtration device for the whole republican system essentially by keeping local passions local. "The influence of factious leaders may kindle a flame within their particular states," Madison concluded, "but will be unable to spread a general conflagration through the other states."

Further, Madison suggested that a large republic would actually function to moderate extreme views. In Federalist Fifty-One he argued that the knowledge that one is operating in an extensive republic would generate the desire among all parties, weak and strong, for a just and impartial government. "A coalition of a majority of the whole society could seldom take place upon any other principles than those of justice and the general good," he concluded. Thus, instead of being inimical to the principles of a free society, a large republic actually promotes them! In summary, the principle of size acting as a filtration device for extreme views offers one of the republican remedies "for the diseases most incident to republican government."

Substituting Representation for Virtue.   The second republican remedy for the problems of republicanism is the principle of representation. It is hard to overemphasize the importance of representation in American government. In Federalist Sixty-Two Madison stated categorically that "the difference most relied on between the American and other republics consists in the principle of representation, *which is the pivot on which the former move*" [italics added]. He was not alone in this view. Edmund Randolph asserted that representation was "a thing not understood in its fullest extent till very lately."[32] James Wilson, one of the finest legal minds in America, concisely summarized the Constitution by saying that "all authority of every kind is derived by representation from the people and the democratic principle is carried into every part of government."[33] In short, the principle of popular representation throughout government, so commonly accepted today as the basis for public authority, was regarded as an innovation of monumental proportions by Madison and the other framers of the Constitution.

Why was that the case? The idea itself was certainly not new; representation in theory and practice had been around at least as long as the Greeks, and Madison gave credit to the discovery of the "great principle" of modern representation to current European practices. Nonetheless, "America," he asserted, "can claim the merit of making the discovery the basis of unmixed and extensive republics" [Federalist Fourteen]. The word *unmixed* is crucial here, and, Martin Diamond reminds us, "must be read in its full force."[34] The ancients had seen governments "wholly popular" in the sense that Madison referred to as a pure democracy. Modern European governments were partly representative of the people, but were "mixed" in the sense of being based also upon representation of other elements in society; namely, aristocratical, monarchical, or clerical. What made the American republic so different was that *popular* representation was the basis for *all* governmental authority, and on a scale that was unmatched in history. For instance, the American Senate did not represent an aristocracy; there was and could not be any aristocracy to be represented in a polity where only the people are sovereign. The Senate simply represented the people in a different way from the House of Representatives. In short, the United States was the world's first *democratic* republic, founded wholly on the basis of popular representation throughout every branch of government.

But how does representation act as a filtration device? Madison answered this in several places in the Federalist Papers, but probably his best explanation is found in his defense of the Senate in Federalist Sixty-Three. "There are particular moments in public affairs," he stated,

> when the people, stimulated by some irregular passion, or some illicit advantage, or misled by the artful misrepresentations of interested men, may call for measures which they themselves will afterwards be the most ready to lament and condemn. In these critical moments, how salutary will be the interference of some temperate and respectable body of citizens, in order to check the misguided career, *and to suspend the blow meditated by the people against themselves until reason, justice, and truth, can regain their authority over the public mind?* [Italics added]

The crucial point to understand here is that representation as a filtration device is the principle of government that the Constitution substituted for public virtue. The people had to be protected against themselves, not by the constant invocation of higher motives, but by a system of representation that filtered out the more destructive tendencies of popular impulses. Representation is the functional substitute for virtue in an extensive republic.

There are other substitutes as well that operate within the government, like the system of checks and balances. Indeed, some of Madison's most well-known assertions were made in defense of such things as the presidential veto power and senatorial advice and consent. In all cases, virtue is not expected; rather, the careful balancing of interests in a way that protected the people—represented in different ways throughout the government—against themselves. In Federalist Fifty-One Madison confessed that the multiplicity of these constitutional safeguards "may be a reflection on human nature"; but, he explained, "what is government itself, but the greatest of all reflections on human nature? If men were angels, no government would be necessary." However, men are not angels, and must govern themselves. In an extensive republic, "a dependence on the people is, no doubt, the primary control on the government; but experience has taught mankind the necessity of auxiliary precautions." The sum total of these "auxiliary precautions" was contained in the "proper structure" of government that he and the other framers hoped would endure through the ages.

In Federalist Thirty-Seven Madison expressed his pride as well as some amazement that the constitutional system devised in Philadelphia met with the approval of most of the framers. "It is impossible, for the man of pious reflection, not to perceive in it a finger of that Almighty Hand, which has been so frequently and signally extended to our relief in the critical stages of the revolution." He did not know, when he wrote this, that the "critical stages of the revolution" were not quite finished yet. Nor were his days as a founder over. After ratification, Madison, along with Jefferson, became involved in a series of heated controversies over the direction of public policy the new republic would take. Together they worked to found the first political party in the nation's history. Their activities also resulted in the development of constitutional arguments about the nature of the "more perfect union" created in Philadelphia, which were to haunt the Father of the Constitution for the rest of his days.

THE FOUNDING OF THE REPUBLICAN PARTY

Madison's role in the founding of the Republican party emerged from his opposition to Washington's administration's policies in domestic and foreign affairs. His activities provided him also with the opportunity to clarify his thoughts on the nature of republicanism and, with Thomas Jefferson, establish an institutional and ideological foundation for a "loyal opposition" to the existing officeholders.[35] This opposition focused upon two significant controversies of the 1790s: the economic proposals of Alexander Hamilton, the Secretary of Treasury, and the events surrounding the president's reaction to the French Revolution.

The Hamiltonian Program

Hamilton's proposals were directed toward winning the allegiance of the merchant, manufacturing, and landholding classes to the new government.[36] Accordingly, in 1790 and 1791 he submitted a series of reports on the public credit that called for full funding of the national debt through the sale of interest-bearing securities, assumption of debts incurred by the states and the confederacy, the establishment of a national bank, and a tariff to protect domestic manufacturers. It was supported by all the specific groups targeted by his program: merchants, traders and ship-builders, holders of the public debt, bankers, financiers, speculators, factory owners—all the "haves" of American society. Together they formed the nucleus of the emerging "Federalist" party—those in support of the federal, that is, national, government. He also generated media support in a newspaper called the *Gazette of the United States*, which became something of a Federalist mouthpiece. But the most important ally of the Federalists was undoubtedly George Washington, a figure who enjoyed enormous prestige in the country.

Madison, of course, had recently championed the cause of stronger national government, but he had no stomach for Hamilton's blatant catering to the better-off elements of society. The Treasury secretary's contempt for ordinary folk was well known, and his program smacked of "antirepublicanism," in Madison's view. Actually, it was Jefferson, always good with a turn of the phrase, who best summarized the republican reaction: "equal rights for all, special privileges for none." That indeed was the problem with the Federalists; Madison and Jefferson felt that the Hamiltonian program granted special privileges to the "rich and well-born," and was crassly insensitive to the interests of the common people. For instance, they were both outraged by Hamilton's proposal for the federal government to assume all state and confederacy debts at face value as many of these securities were originally held by veterans whose desperate straits forced them to sell their holdings to speculators. This total disregard for the nonprivileged sectors of society, the great mass of ordinary citizens, in their view endangered the foundations of democratic, republican government.

Madison wasted no time in reacting. As a member of the House of Representatives, "he took the floor . . . more frequently than any other member, and he was also busy behind the scenes, trying to persuade other members, carrying on a substantial political correspondence, and devising strategy."[37] Part of this strategy was to generate grass-roots opposition to the program. He answered Hamilton's publications with articles of his own, which appeared in a paper called the *National Gazette*, during the fall and spring of 1791–1792. In one of his articles he referred to the Republican party as the one that supported "Republican principles"—an obvious attempt to give it an identity distinct from that of the Federalists. In this he succeeded, but neither his efforts in the House nor Jefferson's objections as a member of the administration—he was Washington's secretary of state—were sufficient to block the passage of Hamilton's program.

The differences between the Federalists and the Republicans were clarified during the early debates on economic issues. But, as William Nisbet Chambers points out in his study of the origins of the party system, "the crystallizing elements—particularly for the Republicans—

were issues of world politics and broad ideology."[38] Jefferson's contribution in this regard became more visible after he resigned from the cabinet in 1793. This not only relieved him of the burden of being constantly at odds with the Treasury secretary, in situations in which "Hamilton and myself were daily pitted in the cabinet like two cocks," he acidly commented, but also allowed him to speak out more freely.[39] This was important, as his stately and confident demeanor gave the Republicans an important symbolic leader, one who could complement the efforts of the more reserved and considerably less flamboyant Madison. However, their joint leadership of the opposition to the Federalists led each to develop Republican principles in dangerous directions, as we shall see.

Foreign-Policy Debates

When the French Revolution began in 1789, Madison shared the optimism of many Americans whose sentiments were with their recent ally in the war for independence against Great Britain. But the situation in revolutionary France soon deteriorated, leading to declarations of war among the major European countries in the early 1790s. President Washington declared a policy of neutrality toward all the warring powers, and Madison and Jefferson immediately objected to it on constitutional and legal grounds. However, the specific reasons for their objections are less noteworthy than the activities they undertook that made the Republican party a permanent fixture on the American political scene. For instance, Madison continued his attempts to generate grass-roots opposition to the Federalists by circulating letters to local Virginia politicians, urging their support of Republican protests against administration policy. He also remained active in Congress by trying patiently to generate opposition to administration policies. In fact, as the decade wore on, Madison's efforts in the House succeeded in coalescing a body of members opposed to Federalist policies on ideological and partisan grounds.

This can best be seen by the reaction in Congress to the Jay Treaty, an agreement negotiated by John Jay with Great Britain to resolve some commercial disputes between the two countries. Republicans felt that its terms were outrageously inimical to American interests, and howls of protest were heard across the land. Indeed, the vehemence of opposition at the popular level was impressive. The following words were written in large letters on a Boston street wall: "Damn John Jay! Damn every one who won't damn John Jay! Damn every one who won't sit up all night damning John Jay!"[40] Although Madison shared these sentiments, at least somewhat, there was in fact little that he could do about "the Treaty," as it became known, since approval of such agreements was the constitutional responsibility of the Senate. But he did lead an active opposition in the House to the implementing legislation, and the results of the vote, which took place in 1796, show clearly how partisan loyalties had developed. With a few exceptions, the vote was strictly along partisan lines: forty-four Federalists and seven Republicans in favor, and forty-five Republicans and three Federalists (all from Virginia) opposed.[41] This remarkable split was not only a reflection of the issue's importance, but also of Madison's leadership efforts over the years in organizing and developing the Republican Party in the House.

The commercial disputes between Britain and the United States over the rights of neutral shipping were not resolved until Madison's own presidency, and then only by a second war between the two countries. In the meantime a far more dangerous matter arose, one that affected the nature of the Union of States bound by the Constitution. In response to intense partisan controversies over America's relationship with France, the administration of John Adams, which followed that of Washington, passed some measures known as the Alien and Sedition Acts. The furious opposition to these laws by Madison and Jefferson produced constitutional arguments that would be used by others to question the nature and utility of the "more perfect union" embodied in Mr. Madison's Constitution.

The Nullification Controversy

The Alien and Sedition Acts.   These measures were attempts by the Adams administration to stifle dissent that it felt bordered on treason. They were passed by a Federalist-controlled Congress in 1798, when there appeared to be a serious danger of war with France. There were three acts in all, two dealing with Federal authority to deport aliens deemed a threat to the security of the United States; and a third, the Sedition Act, made it a crime for any person to express criticism of the United States government. The third was unquestionably the worst, and a review of some of its language shows why the Republicans reacted with outrage and fear. The Sedition Act made it a crime to publish "any false, scandalous and malicious writing . . . against the government of the United States, or either house of Congress . . . or the President . . . with intent to defame . . . or to bring them, or either of them into contempt or disrepute; or to excite against them, or either or any of them, the hatred of the good people of the United States."[42] In short, the Act forbade not just actions, which are demonstrated by judicial means, to overthrow the government—a standard criterion for judging sedition—but mere *criticism* of government policies.

The extreme nature of the Sedition Act is perhaps best appreciated by looking at the unequivocal language of the First Amendment, which reads in part: "Congress shall make no law . . . abridging the freedom of speech or of the press; or the right of the people peaceably to assemble." With that in mind, Madison bristled with indignation, claiming that the new Act granted the federal government the power, "which, more than any other, ought to produce universal alarm, because it is levelled against that right of freely examining public characters and measures, and of free communication thereon, which has ever been justly deemed the only effectual guardian of every other right."[43] Clearly, he stated the view most consistent with liberal tenets about the sanctity of freedom, in beliefs, actions, and expressions of opinion, subject to the *reasonable* restraints of not violating the rights of others to do the same. In fact, as constitutional historians Kelly and Harbison point out, Madison asserted "virtually for the first time what was to become the classic 'extreme liberal' position on the [first] amendment."[44] This was especially ironic, considering that he had originally opposed the inclusion of a bill of rights in the Federal Constitution. And now he was the staunchest defender of what he (and others) regarded as the most important right of them all—freedom of expression.

If Madison had not taken his objections any further, he would have remained on solid liberal and constitutional grounds. Unfortunately, he and Jefferson desperately wanted to apply other means of redress against the obnoxious law. To this end they persuaded the state legislatures of Kentucky and Virginia to pass some resolutions—the Kentucky and Virginia Resolutions—that carried their arguments a step further. Each document contained language that spoke of the states' "interposing" their authority between the federal government and the people, thus by implication raising the very serious issue of the legal nature of the Union of the States. It was a step neither ever should have taken.

The language of Jefferson was generally more extreme than Madison's—it usually was—but Madison's own words were strong enough. Consider the following passage:

> This Assembly doth explicitly and peremptorily declare that it views the powers of the federal government as resulting from the compact to which the states are parties, as limited by the plain sense and intention of the instrument constituting that compact—as no further valid than they are authorized by the grants enumerated in that compact; and that, in the case of a deliberate, palpable, and dangerous exercise of other powers, not granted by the said compact, the states who are parties thereto have the right, and are duty bound, to interpose, for arresting the progress of the evil, and for maintaining, within their respective limits, the authorities, rights, and liberties appertaining to them.[45]

This is absolutely horrible language for the founder of a federal, constitutional government! In fact, it is not the language of federalism at all; it is the language of confederation, not federalism. Without question the Virginia Resolution is diametrically opposed to the whole tenor of Madisonian thought as expressed at the Constitutional Convention and in the Federalist Papers. Clearly, he lost sight of what constituted the foundation of both the state and federal governments, namely, the people. After all, the preamble to the Constitution does not read, "We the States," but rather, "We the People." The central government derived its powers not from the states, which had acted only as legal conveniences for the purpose of ratification, but from the people of the United States. In short, the line of thinking expressed in the Virginia Resolution was directly opposed to the political science of the American Constitution.

Two years after he wrote the words embodied in the Virginia Resolution, Madison returned to the fray with a document entitled the *Virginia Report.* Realizing that he might have gone too far, he tried to explain away some of the positions he had taken earlier, with a long and tedious examination of the previous document. Madison labored to explain that it was the states collectively, and not each individual state, that had the power to interpose. And it was the "people composing those political societies, in their highest sovereign capacity," to which he was actually referring, and not the states themselves.[46] Further, interposition did not mean to imply, after all, nullification—the act of a state declaring null and void a federal law within its boundaries. But if the Virginia Resolution did not mean that, then, pray tell, just what did it mean? It was an expression of opinion, Madison stated evenly, for the purpose of "exciting reflection." Thus, the people, who alone "possess absolute sovereignty" collectively through the instruments of the states, expressed their vigorous disapproval of the actions of the federal government. That was the Virginia Resolution.

This was too clever by half, and seemed to many to miss the point of his arguments in 1798. Later advocates of nullification and secession simply read into his document what they felt was the plain meaning of it. And the plain meaning of it seemed to be the following: the states, as sovereign entities, were parties to a contract that created and approved an instrument of governance called the United States Constitution. If at any time the government of that Constitution violated the interests of the parties that created it—by passing an obnoxious law, for instance—the parties had the option of "interposing" their authority and declaring such a law null and void within their legal jurisdictions. And if that failed to protect the interests of the aggrieved state, it could then exercise its ultimate right, as a sovereign "party to the contract": to secede from the union and go its separate way. This was precisely the argument of Southern statesmen who felt that far more was at stake in their political fortunes than the First Amendment to the Constitution. Thus, Madison's Virginia Resolution went considerably beyond "exciting reflection"; it excited sedition as well.

Nullification and the South.   The nullification doctrine did not become a salient national issue until the late 1820s. It briefly gained some notoriety in the War of 1812 when some spokesmen from Federalist New England, which had been especially hard hit by the conflict with Great Britain, threatened secession. An early end to the hostilities prevented any further development of the idea in that part of the country. Its relevance then shifted to the South, whose leaders found it a particularly useful vehicle for the expression of sectional grievances against what they felt was discriminatory national legislation. After the Missouri Compromise in 1820, the most famous exponent of nullification and secession was John C. Calhoun, a dashing South Carolinian, and one of the most articulate and eloquent speakers in the United States Congress. Calhoun actually began his career as an ardent nationalist during the administration of Madison, but he ended it as the most prominent spokesman for the Southern cause prior to the Civil War.

The reasons for Calhoun's dramatic transformation can be traced to the economic changes that had occurred in his home state since the early 1800s. Once a thriving agricultural center with a flourishing seaport, South Carolina had gradually been losing population and business to other Southern states, which had fresher soils and more slaves. But its most serious complaint centered upon what was called the "Tariff of Abominations," passed in 1828. This measure put the South in an economic vise. It set extraordinarily high duties on imported manufactured goods, forcing Southerners to buy from Northern factories at prices that were well above those they would have had to pay for goods shipped in from abroad. The tariff also had the effect of restricting the exports of cotton, especially to Great Britain, and thus reduced the competitiveness of Southern goods on world markets. Thus, Calhoun argued that the tariff fattened the pockets of Northern manufacturers by reducing the South to a condition of abject serfdom. A more vicious piece of economic legislation could hardly have been envisioned.

This potentially explosive economic issue generated intense constitutional arguments, the first of which was outlined in Calhoun's anonymously published, "The Exposition and Protest" in 1828. The sectional tensions reached a fever pitch in 1830, with a brilliant exchange on the floor of the Senate between Senator Hayne of South Carolina and

Senator Daniel Webster, who spoke on behalf of New England interests. The issue between them originally was sparked by a controversy over Western land policy, but it soon developed into a full-scale constitutional debate over the nature of the union. Hayne contemptuously made reference to New England's treasonable behavior during the late war with Great Britain, and then introduced a proposal that was equally treasonous—nullification. Webster was incensed, and responded with a torrid speech that lasted some four hours and covered every issue that divided the sections of the country, North, South, and West. He ended with a peroration that rang in the hearts of his countrymen for the next generation, and became required reading for generations of American schoolchildren long after that: "Liberty and Union, now and for ever, one and inseparable!"[47] For all their brilliance, Hayne and Calhoun had met their match.

So where did Madison fit into all this? Such perfervid prose could not go unanswered, of course, and the nullifiers needed more ammunition for their cause. Who better to ask than the Father of the Constitution, the author of the Virginia Resolution, the only Founding Father still alive, and, perhaps most importantly, a famous Virginian (and Southerner, naturally) as well? But Madison would have none of it. In the October 1830 issue of the *North American Review*, he gave his own answer to Hayne, and in 1833 he wrote directly to John C. Calhoun, the prime instigator of what Madison felt was constitutional nonsense. In each case he vigorously denied any paternity to doctrines of nullification and secession currently in fashion, and vehemently denounced them as "twin heresies" from sound constitutional doctrine. "Nullification," Madison snapped, "has the effect of putting powder under the Constitution and Union, and a match in the hand of every party, to blow them up at pleasure."[48] Although he did not convince his enemies, Madison's unambiguous denial of the South Carolinian position on its relationship to the Union helped greatly to prevent his home state of Virginia from joining its neighbor.[49] Most importantly, the nullifiers were denied the use of his services.

Madison did not live to see the final outcome of his interposition doctrine played out on the field of battle. He was already in his eighties when Calhoun led South Carolina in its first challenge to the Constitution. Although he succeeded in disassociating himself from the secessionist cause, he never did admit that the ideas that he and Jefferson had developed years before had anything to do with what Calhoun and others were claiming. Irving Brant suggested that "a lifelong unwillingness to admit error or inconsistency was one of the marked elements of James Madison's character."[50] Nowhere was this demonstrated more dramatically than in the debate over nullification and secession.

JAMES MADISON THE FOUNDER

Madison left government service in 1817, after serving as Jefferson's secretary of state beginning in 1801, and as President of the United States for two terms. His service to the republic continued into the last years of his life, until he quietly passed away in 1836. By that point all the institutions he had worked so diligently to build and uphold were firmly in place, and his status as the most important contributor to the framing of the Constitution was well established. Madison's most considerable contributions, however, were made before he entered the executive branch of government, and may be summarized as follows:

First, at the Constitutional Convention, Madison applied the tenets of American liberalism to the actual construction of a constitutional government. That is, he succeeded in the difficult task of creating workable, institutional embodiments of the ideals expressed in the Declaration of Independence. It is hard to overestimate the enormous significance of this accomplishment, especially in an age suffused with the pronouncements of lofty ideals. Indeed, revolutionaries today typically discover that proclaiming a set of noble goals in some ringing "manifesto" statement is really the easy part—practically anybody with a talent for bombastic expression can do that. The hard part comes when one attempts seriously to deliver on revolutionary promises. Jefferson, Madison, and the framers of the Constitution were revolutionaries also, and they, too, attempted to deliver on the promises and ideals of self-government expressed in the Declaration of Independence. The success they achieved in devising a government that has lasted for two centuries is due in large part to the role played by the man known as Father of the Constitution—James Madison. His role as a founder is undisputed.

Second, Madison succeeded, with Jefferson, in creating the Republican (later called Democratic) party of the United States. This accomplishment actually completed the work of the first, by providing a permanent "loyal opposition" to the rulers holding office under a Constitution accepted by all. Interestingly, this task of developing an opposition view to the government was carried out *within the context* of a political theory that in fact already constituted an opposition view of politics (British politics), as expressed in the Declaration of Independence. It is true they both worked with familiar materials, in that their expression of Republican principles borrowed heavily from Jefferson's statements in the Declaration. But the effect of Madison's contributions was to clarify partisan loyalties in a society already guided by liberal tenets. Democratic theorists generally agree that the existence of legitimate opposition parties, who enjoy the opportunity to win office by lawful means, constitutes the very definition of democratic government. In this sense, the achievement of Jefferson and Madison in creating the world's first democratic political party is as significant as the framing of the Constitution.

Finally, Madison must be credited with creating arguments that very nearly reversed everything else he tried to do in his public life. Clearly, the principle of "interposition" and its infamous constitutional progeny, nullification and secession, was the most dangerous product of Madison's reflections on government. Although not as lasting as his other contributions, the "states' rights" assertion of authority against federal law still lingered stubbornly into the twentieth century. Ironically, the guiding theme of the Virginia Resolution completed the analyses of constitutional principles that began with his criticism of the Articles of Confederation. In his life's work, Madison alternately stressed the importance of asserting national authority with constitutional safeguards against the "excesses of democracy," followed by the vigorous defenses of popular opposition to national policy that surrounded his partisan activities against the Federalists, and ending with his statements about interposing state sovereignty between the national government and the people. In short, Madison's genius as a founder led him to cover all the territory of American liberal thought about government and politics in the early days of the Republic—national authority, states' rights, and popular sovereignty.

However, it was the Union of the States that captured his early imagination and inspired his most enduring commitments. The talk about nullification and secession was heartrending to the founder of the republic, and he closed his years by offering the following comments to his countrymen: "The advice nearest to my heart and deepest in my convictions is that the Union of the States be cherished and perpetuated. Let the open enemy to it be regarded as a Pandora with her box opened; and the disguised one, as the Serpent creeping with his deadly wiles into Paradise."[51]

Unfortunately, Madison's cherished Union of States faced dangers in later years as serious as those that he and Jefferson had to cope with in their day. In this century, the nation governed by Mr. Madison's Constitution has had to cope with crises that have wracked the republic as much as disunity and nullification. The first one, the Great Depression, was dealt with by a leader who regarded himself as a faithful follower of the constitutional principles, and was also a vivacious practitioner of the American temperament—Franklin D. Roosevelt. And the second crisis, the blight of centuries of racial injustice, was attacked by a leader who followed the same principles of the American creed that guided Madison in his role as Father of the Constitution—Martin Luther

King, Jr. Together, as practitioner and missionary, Roosevelt and King showed the continued relevance of Madisonian and Jeffersonian principles in the continuing story known as the American experiment in self-government.

ENDNOTES

[1] Quoted in Max Farrand, *The Framing of the Constitution of the United States* (New Haven, Conn.: Yale University Press, 1913), p. 17. William Pierce provided a number of thumbnail sketches of the participants at the Constitutional Convention.

[2] Quoted in Neal Riemer, *James Madison* (New York: Twayne Publishers, Inc., 1968), p. 13.

[3] Quoted in Irving Brant, *The Fourth President: A Life of James Madison* (New York: Bobbs-Merrill, 1970), p. 44.

[4] Ibid., p. 644.

[5] Ibid.

[6] Quoted in Marvin Meyers, ed., *The Mind of the Founder* (Hanover, N.H.: The University Press of New England, 1981), p. 25.

[7] Quoted in Brant, *Fourth President*, p. 197.

[8] Riemer makes these points very effectively. See *James Madison*, p. 7.

[9] This section title is adopted from Marvin Meyers's book, *Mind of Founder*.

[10] Brant, *Fourth President*. The information about Madison's life is drawn from Brant's biography.

[11] Quoted in Richard Hofstadter, William Miller, and Daniel Aaron, *The American Republic to 1865* (Englewood Cliffs, N.J.: Prentice-Hall, Inc., 1959), p. 332.

[12] Quoted in Catherine Drinker Bowen, *Miracle at Philadelphia* (Boston: Little, Brown & Co., 1966), p. 13.

[13] Meyers, *Mind of Founder*, p. 155.

[14] Ibid., p. 5.

[15] Quoted in Brant, *Fourth President*, p. 64. Madison had Delaware in mind when he made this comment, but Rhode Island (sometimes referred to as "Rogues' Island") was also a problem.

[16] Quoted in Gordon Wood, *The Creation of the American Republic: 1776–1787* (New York: W. W. Norton, 1969), p. 472. This material is drawn from Wood's excellent treatment, pp. 257–469.

[17] Wood, *Creation of Republic*, p. 410.

[18] *Corwin and Peltason's Understanding the Constitution*, 6th ed., rev. by J. W. Peltason (Hinsdale, Ill.: The Dryden Press, 1973), p. 12.

[19] Bowen, *Miracles*, p. 14.

[20] See Madison's reflections in Meyers, *Mind of Founder*, pp. 47–57.

[21] Ibid., p. 66.

[22] There are several excellent summaries of the events of the Constitutional Convention. In addition to Bowen's *Miracle*, see Clinton Rossiter, *1787: The Grand Convention* (New York: Macmillan, 1966); and the accounts in Martin Diamond, Winston Mills Fisk, and Herbert Garfinkel, *The Democratic Republic* (Chicago: Rand McNally, 1970), pp. 15–159; and Alfred H. Kelly and Winfred A. Harbison, *The American Constitution: Its Origins and Development*, 4th ed. (New York: W. W. Norton, 1970), pp. 114–47.

[23] "The Virginia Plan of a Federal Constitution," in Irving Brant, *James Madison and American Nationalism* (Princeton, N.J.: D. Van Nostrand Co., 1968), p. 178.

[24] Quoted in Hofstadter et al., *American Republic*, p. 263.

[25] This point is well explained by Kelly and Harbison, *American Constitution*, pp. 122–24.

[26] Cited by Clinton Rossiter, ed., *The Federalist Papers* (New York: New American Library, 1961), p. xi. All references to the Federalist Papers are by number and are taken from this volume.

[27] Martin Diamond, "The Revolution of Sober Expectations," in Stephen J. Tonsor, ed., *America's Continuing Revolution* (Washington, D.C.: American Enterprise Institute, 1975), p. 31. Diamond is especially worth reading for insights into the formation of the Constitution. See also his essay, "The Federalist," in Leo Strauss and Joseph Cropsey, eds., *History of Political Philosophy*, 2nd ed. (Chicago: Rand McNally, 1972).

[28] Diamond, "Revolution of Sober Expectations," p. 39.

[29] For analyses of American political thinking before the revolution, see Wood, *Creation of Republic*, pp. 1–118; Clinton Rossiter, *The Political Thought of the American Revolution* (New York: Harcourt, Brace & World, Inc., 1963); and Bernard Bailyn, *The Ideological Origins of the American Revolution* (Cambridge, Mass.: Harvard University Press, 1967).

[30] Cecelia Kenyon, "Men of Little Faith: The Anti-Federalists on the Nature of Representative Government," in John P. Roche, ed., *Origins of American Political Thought* (New York: Harper & Row, 1967), p. 240.

[31] Quoted in Riemer, *Madison*, pp. 39–40.

[32] Quoted in Wood, *Creation of Republic*, p. 596.

[33] Ibid., pp. 603–64.

[34] "The Federalist," in Strauss and Cropsey, *Political Philosophy*, p. 639.

[35] Adrienne Koch's treatment of the relative contributions of Madison and Jefferson to the development of the Republican party is especially worth noting. See her *Power, Morals, and the Founding Fathers* (Ithaca, N.Y.: Cornell University Press, 1961).

[36] For an excellent overview of the origins of the party system in the United States, see William Nisbet Chambers, *Political Parties in a New Nation* (New York: Oxford University Press, 1963). Much of our discussion is based upon this fine account.

[37] Ibid., p. 54.

[38] Ibid., p. 76.

[39] Quoted in Chambers, *Political Parties*, p. 59.

[40] Quoted in Hoftstadter et al., *American Republic*, p. 279.

[41] Chambers, *Political Parties*, p. 87.

[42] "The Sedition Act," in Donald O. Dewey, ed., *Union and Liberty: A Documentary History of American Constitutionalism* (New York: McGraw-Hill Book Company, 1969), p. 71. See also the discussion in Kelly and Harbison, *American Constitution*, pp. 196–99.

[43] Quoted in Meyers, *Mind of Founder*, p. 244.

[44] Kelly and Harbison, *American Constitution*, p. 198.

[45] Quoted in Meyers, *Mind of Founder*, p. 232.

[46] Quoted in Brant, *Madison and American Nationalism*, p. 98.

[47] See the review in William W. Freehling, ed., *The Nullification Era* (New York: Harper & Row, 1967), pp. 62–91.

[48] Quoted in Brant, *Madison and American Nationalism*, p. 216.

[49] Ibid., pp. 209–17 for Madison's positions on these matters.

[50] Ibid., p. 96.

[51] Ibid., p. 217.

FRANKLIN D. ROOSEVELT

Master Practitioner

4

To describe Roosevelt you would have to describe three or four men for he had at least three or four different personalities. He could turn from one personality to another with such speed that you often never knew where you were or to which personality you were talking . . . . *William Phillips*, Roosevelt's Under-Secretary of State[1]

There is no basic stuff in the man. There are no deep-seated convictions. He is a tremendously agreeable and attractive person, but there is no bedrock in him. He is all clay and no granite. *Rabbi Stephen Wise* to Felix Frankfurter[2]

A second-class intellect—but a first-class temperament. *Oliver Wendell Holmes*[3]

No biographer of Roosevelt, I think, feels that he really understands the man, nor, evidently, does any member of his family. *James MacGregor Burns*[4]

Francis Perkins, FDR's Secretary of Labor, tells the story of a naive young reporter who attempted to pin the chief executive down on his political philosophy:

"Mr. President, are you a Communist?"

"No."

"Are you a capitalist?"

"No."

"Are you a Socialist?"

"No."

Frustrated over his inability to get the President to commit himself philosophically, the reporter finally asked:

"Well, what is your philosophy, then?"

"Philosophy?" the President replied, somewhat baffled by the question. "I am a Christian and a Democrat—that's all."[5]

INTRODUCTION

No chief executive has stimulated and intrigued professional observers of the presidency more than Franklin Delano Roosevelt. Richard Hofstadter referred to him as the "the Patrician as Opportunist."[6] James MacGregor Burns, who has written the most complete biography of Roosevelt, refers to him as "the Lion and the Fox."[7] Presidential scholar James David Barber classified him as an "active-positive" type of leader. The first term of this category of leadership refers to the level of energy devoted to the execution of his duties, and the second refers to his attitude about himself as well as his orientation toward life in general.[8] John G. Stoessinger comments about Roosevelt's conduct of American foreign policy by classifying him as both a "crusader" and a "pragmatist."[9] But regardless of the terms used to describe and label Franklin D. Roosevelt, most scholars agree that the modern presidency traces its origins to his first term in office.

Roosevelt also evoked very strong and varied reactions from his contemporaries. Some of his most vocal opponents dubbed him either a communist or fascist. Many of his supporters, on the other hand, saw him as the savior of American capitalism, of the United States, of Europe (during World War II), or of Western civilization in general. FDR was the kisser of babies, the shaker of hands, the soother of troubled minds, and the savior of homes, farms, and banks. He was the wrecker of the "old order" and the prophet of the new: he was compared to Hitler, Stalin, and Mussolini—to name a few prominent villains—along with Jefferson, Lincoln, Teddy Roosevelt, and Jesus Christ—to name a few prominent American heroes (with one exception). In the space of about twelve years, he managed to lift the spirits of a nation in utter despair, bring the national government closer to the American people than it ever had been, lead the mightiest military machine in world history against the most formidable challenge to Western civilization since the Islamic invasions, and create more government agencies than most observers have been able to keep track of. Indeed, both friends and foes of Franklin Roosevelt run out of words to use in describing their reactions to him. No president has engendered more intense feelings than FDR.

Above all, the man had class. As the Great Depression reached its lowest point—when women and children starved, while thousands of husbands and fathers threw themselves off of tall bridges or out of hotel-room windows ("Do you want this room for sleeping or jumping" was the common question), and the land teemed with homeless and helpless vagabonds, riding on trains going nowhere in particular, or sleeping in parks, wrecked cars, or improvised tent cities called "Hoovervilles"; when millions attempted to sell apples or pencils or their homes, bodies, souls, or sacred honor simply to stay alive, to survive—in short, when the United States of America stood on the verge of the most gargantuan social and economic collapse experienced by any civilization since the fall of the Roman empire, Franklin D. Roosevelt proclaimed boldly that "the only thing we have to fear is fear itself." Now that's class.

That's confidence, too—self-confidence, which Roosevelt rarely lacked. Indeed, even his most characteristic pose—his profile—inspired confidence: his chin prominently juts upward, and a long cigarette holder—like the jib boom of a magisterial ship of the line, brazenly proclaiming the direction—sticks in firmly clenched teeth, easily exposed by a broad, commanding smile. Roosevelt hardly ever doubted himself or wondered seriously if he could do the job. He certainly never questioned that the presidency was exactly where he belonged. With confidence to spare, he led a troubled and unsure nation out of a social and economic morass, at the same time that other modern nations were descending into the barbarisms of totalitarian rule. When he died in office, the United States was enormously better off than it was at the beginning of his first term.

Thus, it would seem that it is difficult to overstate the contributions of Franklin D. Roosevelt. In some respects, it would also seem that he should be treated as a founder. Without question Roosevelt contributed enormously to the development of liberalism in the United States, associating with that term an activist federal government committed to promoting the welfare of the great mass of ordinary Americans. And in terms of institutional practices, presidential scholars generally agree that the modern presidency traces its origins to his terms in office, as he made the executive branch the focal point of policy initiative in American national politics on a permanent basis. He was also the first to develop on a large scale the sort of media-oriented politics that is standard fare today. He put together a new Democratic party coalition consisting of blue-collar labor, less-well-off farmers, and numerous minority groups and "have-nots" in American society. In short, much of what was new in American politics and government is due to the efforts of Franklin Roosevelt.

For all that, however, he did not found a brand-new government or construct a completely novel constitutional arrangement; nor did he attempt to refashion every institution on the American social landscape. That is, he was not a founder in the sense of the others considered in our treatment, such as Hitler, for instance, or Stalin—both of whom consciously attempted completely to rebuild the societies they ruled over. Certainly Roosevelt tried to institute a number of important changes, but he quite correctly regarded his efforts as consistent with the main themes of the American political tradition. At all events, the argument that we shall pursue here is simply that one of the most *interesting* as well as noteworthy aspects of his leadership centers upon the manner in which he carried out his tasks—his style, if you will. And of course, although he was notoriously unreflective about what he was doing most of the time, he did have serious ideological commitments, and we shall examine them as well. Indeed, the substance of his beliefs and the manner in which he acted upon them is what made him such a distinctive leader. In short, our goal is to emphasize that, for all his reknowned contributions to the development of American political institutions, he was in fact an even grander exemplar of the American temperament, as well as a person who practiced a particular brand of American liberalism

We shall explore these matters by dealing briefly with his life up to the 1932 election, followed by a survey of his first two terms in office. Roosevelt's wartime experiences will then be covered. We shall conclude with some remarks about the ideology and style of Roosevelt, which made him one of the greatest practitioners of American liberalism as well as one of the most notable embodiments of the American temperament in our history.

PREPARATION FOR LEADERSHIP

Few chief executives in American history enjoyed an upbringing with as many advantages as Franklin Delano Roosevelt. Born in 1882, he was the only child of an established Hudson River family, and received lavish amounts of loving attention from both parents.[10] His education involved attendance at Groton, Harvard, and Columbia, with majors in history, government, and the law. He was generally mediocre as a student, but excelled in those extra-curricular activities that allowed him to display his natural charm and gregariousness. Although considered an intellectual lightweight, Franklin had been instilled from his days at Groton with values emphasizing commitment to God, country, and one's fellow men, and women, which he carried with him throughout his entire life. He entered politics in 1910, after winning a spirited election to the New York State Senate. His brief stay there earned him the reputation for being a supporter of progressive causes, along with the enmity of the Democratic establishment. Roosevelt was untroubled by this, as he had charted out for himself a career in national politics that in fact bore remarkable resemblance to the path actually taken by his famous distant cousin, Theodore. And when Woodrow Wilson was elected president in 1912, the resemblance assumed an uncanny identity. Shortly after the inauguration, Franklin resigned his elected position to begin duties as assistant secretary of the Navy.

This was a job Roosevelt absolutely relished. As a boy he had read extensively about naval matters, and had mastered the art of boating on his father's schooner. Now he had a whole government department to play around with, and he quickly gained the reputation for being one of the greatest movers and shakers the Navy had ever seen. Indeed, anyone who studies his torrid pace as an administrator in the Navy can see visions of the New Deal to come. He flitted from one thing to another, tried anything that looked promising, and dropped anything that fizzled out. For example, against tradition, established common sense, and naval officialdom of all persuasions and ranks, Roosevelt fought for a separate air arm for the Navy, lobbied hard for the construction of a new vessel called a subchaser, and even proposed laying a gargantuan string of mines across the North Sea to protect Allied shipping through this vital area. In pushing for these and other projects, he scissored through an enormous amount of red tape, showed no respect at all for established ways of doing things, bruised egos left and right, and instigated enough adminstrative exasperation to generate a tremendous sigh of relief when he left office. Nathan Miller points out that after the war FDR chuckled about having broken enough rules to put him in jail for about a thousand years.[11] But the job got done, and that is all Roosevelt ever really asked for in his long career in politics and administration.

By the war's end Roosevelt had attracted enough attention to become a national political figure. In May 1919 he gave a speech before the Democratic National Committee; in the following year he ran as the vice-presidential candidate on the Democratic ticket, waged a vigorous campaign, and lost. But this did not discourage him—nothing ever seemed to—as he was a rising political star whose future in the Democratic Party and in national politics looked very promising.

Then tragedy struck. In 1921 Roosevelt contracted polio, a disease that crippled him for the rest of his life. Up to this point, the only adversity he had ever suffered occurred in the context of waging various political battles, running for office, or knocking heads in assorted bureaucratic melees. But this was a blow that seemed, to many, at least, sufficient to end his political career permanently. But Roosevelt was made of stern stuff, and would have none of that. Instead of succumbing to the disease, he made every attempt to overcome it, including trying out things that the experts insisted would not work. In fact, Roosevelt became an expert himself on his disease. He developed a treatment center in Warm Springs, Georgia, and nagged medical specialists until they finally came around to recognizing the utility of his methods. More than that, he did what no expert would ever do about a matter as grave as polio: he joked about it. "I have renewed my youth in a rather unpleasant manner," he once said, "by contracting . . . infantile paralysis." At the end of conversations, he would close by saying, "Good-bye, I've got to run."[12] In short, Roosevelt succeeded in turning what could have been a fatal blow to his political aspirations into a definite political asset.

So it was back to politics as usual. In 1924 Roosevelt chaired Alfred Smith's campaign for the Democratic nomination for the presidency, and in the process occasioned one of the most touching and dramatic events in his lifetime as well as in American political history. Franklin was supposed to give the nominating speech for Smith at the national convention, a task made more difficult, of course, by his paralysis. But with the help of his son, James, he struggled up the platform, steadied himself behind the rostrum, and, in a gesture that was to become vintage FDR, flung his head back and broke into a wide, confident smile before the tumultuous cheers of the audience. Throughout that year, he worked hard to establish himself as the "consensus Democrat," the one man whose personal courage and political integrity towered over the petty factional disputes that had so divided the party over the years. The *New York Evening World* pointed out that he was "the one leader commanding the respect and admiration of delegations from all sections of the land."[13] Roosevelt turned personal adversity into a political asset, and defied the predictions of those who insisted that a cripple could not have a political career.

He also defied the political trends of the day. In 1928, a Republican landslide year that brought Herbert Hoover to the White House, Roosevelt ran for the office of the governor of New York, and won a narrow victory. He quickly established himself as a formidable political presence, particularly after the onset of the Great Depression in the following year. There was perhaps no better testing ground for nationally relevant policies than the state of New York, and FDR made the most of it. He fought for public-works projects, business regulation, labor legislation involving maximum hours and minimum wages, and unemployment relief, and established executive independence in budgetary matters and legislative initiative—all against the background of a hostile Republican Assembly. His reelection in 1930 added to his political experience, in that it gave him an opportunity to try at the state level the sort of campaign techniques he would later apply at the national level. Clearly, Roosevelt's tenure as governor of the nation's most populous state gave him the sort of national exposure and political experience that was instrumental in securing his presidential nomination in 1932.

His campaign for that position succeeded with his nomination on the fourth ballot at the Democratic National Convention that summer.

Roosevelt waged what was in many ways an incredible campaign. While the country was in absolutely horrible shape, he did his best to stress the positive—even in the choice of the theme song for his candidacy: "Happy Days are Here Again." He said that most Americans wanted work and security—as if anyone needed to be told those things—but also proclaimed that these should be regarded as spiritual values and thus pursued with all the fervor of a religious crusade. However, the most remembered statement he ever made came near the end of his acceptance speech for the nomination, as it contained the phrase that would be one of his lasting contributions to the American political lexicon:

> I pledge you, I pledge myself, to a new deal for the American people. Let us all here assembled constitute ourselves prophets of a new order of competence and of courage. This is more than a political campaign; it is a call to arms. Give me your help, not to win votes alone, but to win in this crusade to restore America to its own people.[14]

A new era in American political history had begun.

ROOSEVELT IN OFFICE: THE FIRST EIGHT YEARS

The New Deal

An American president had not entered office under such dire political conditions since Abraham Lincoln began his first term in 1861. The condition of the United States at this time was simply awful. One-quarter to one-third of the work force was unemployed; many millions more were either underemployed or living in constant fear of losing their jobs. The agricultural sector had nearly ceased to function, and farm prices were down even from their already depressed 1929 figures. The values of shares on the New York Stock Exchange had fallen to about one-fifth of their 1929 figures. Around ten thousand banks had failed, destroying the savings of millions of small investors.[15] Every index of economic activity revealed a commercial and industrial complex nearing a state of total collapse. No foreign enemy could have ever inflicted as much damage on the United States as did the Great Depression.

But these figures, gruesome as they were, concealed a reality of such abject misery as to defy one's imagination. Many fathers and husbands committed suicide; others, some two million of them, roamed the countryside for work. Staying with one's family often meant shivering together in tents during the coldest period of winter, or improvising shelters out of old barrels or wrecked cars, and cooking over wood fires—assuming, of course, that one had something to cook. Millions didn't: men fought over cans of garbage; children were kept out of school because there was no food; those who did go often fainted in class from hunger—as did their teachers, many of whom no longer were paid, but kept on teaching anyway.[16] This in fact was the standard nearly all of America struggled with: to keep on going in life anyway, regardless of how hopeless it seemed.

To this misery must be added a note on the staggering irrationality of it all. While people starved, the *New Republic* reported in 1932 that there were "fields of unpicked cotton" in an area stretching from the Carolinas into New Mexico, because no one could afford to pick it, to sell it, or to buy it. Further, there were "vineyards with grapes still unpicked, orchards of olive trees hanging full of rotting fruits and oranges being sold at less than the cost of production."[17] Starvation in the midst of plenty; production in the midst of want. Someone pointed out to Roosevelt that if he succeeded in dealing with this extraordinary crisis he would go down as the greatest president in American history; if he failed, he would be remembered as the worst one. "If I fail," Franklin replied somberly, "I shall be the last one."[18]

He wasted no time in taking action. The first thing he did was to declare a national banking "holiday," the effect of which was to close all the banks for four days. His purpose, of course, was to prevent further collapse of the nation's financial system, but its symbolic effect was at least as important. "This is the happiest day in three years," quipped Will Rogers, the good-natured humorist. "We have no jobs, we have no money, we have no banks; and if Roosevelt had burned down the Capitol, we would have said, 'Thank God, he started a fire under something!' "[19] Indeed he did, but under the authority of the Trading with the Enemy Act, a law that Hoover felt, probably correctly, could not possibly be construed to allow such an action. Therefore it had to be explained. So the president proceeded to explain it, by a method that was soon to become vintage FDR—the Fireside Chat. In a national radio address given on March 12, Sunday evening, at ten o'clock, Roosevelt calmly outlined the current crisis, the measures he was taking to deal with it, and his reasons for acting the way he did—all in langague that was clear, straightforward, and without a hint of condescension. In short, he explained the banking situation so well, Will Rogers again observed, that even the bankers understood.

And so did everybody else. "In one week," wrote Walter Lippmann, "the nation, which had lost confidence in everything and everybody, has regained confidence in the government and in itself."[20] But this was just the beginning. For the next three months Roosevelt generated so much legislative activity that this period of his presidency has simply been labeled "the One Hundred Days." The country demanded bold, persistent experimentation, he had said, and that is exactly what the country got.

The list of Roosevelt legislation passed during this period is impressive.[21] March 16 saw the passage of the Agricultural Adjustment Act, a measure designed to raise farm income. Farmers' needs were also addressed by the Farm Credit Administration (FCA), an agency created by a law enacted on the following day. On the twenty-first the Civilian Conservation Corps was created. The CCC emerged from FDR's life-long fascination with conservation and reforestation projects, and of all the New Deal enterprises, it was probably the one closest to his heart. It was designed to put unemployed young men to work in forests and national parks, planting trees, clearing roads, protecting wildlife, and doing flood-control work. Another unemployment measure was passed on the same day, the Federal Emergency Relief Act (FERA). This set up an agency designed to help the states directly with the hordes of unemployed that had overwhelmed their relief capacities. It was run by Harry Hopkins, a brusque, no-nonsense type ("Hunger is not debatable," he once snapped), who had run a similar agency in the state of New York. He took about 50 percent cut in salary to take the position, and wasted no time in dispensing relief—some $5 million in his first two hours on the job.[22]

Most New Deal legislation, like FERA and FCA, was designed to deal with specific problems affecting clearly defined and usually rather large groups. The Home Owners' Loan Act, which was inspired by the appalling number of mortgage foreclosures and evictions, falls in this category as well. Passed on April 13, its purpose was to provide immediate assistance to beleaguered homeowners by providing low-interest money to keep up payments on mortgages. Eventually, one in every five mortgaged dwellings was refinanced by the Home Owners Loan Corporation (HOLC), the agency created by the act. Another public corporation, the Federal Deposit Insurance Corporation (FDIC), was created by the Glass-Steagall Act. This was not really part of the president's program, but has been included among the noted New Deal efforts, probably because its purpose—to insure savings deposits—was so consistent with other FDR legislation.

Some New Deal legislation created agencies whose initials became very well known among the general population. And some of them were permanent. The Tennessee Valley Authority (TVA) was one of these. It was the first, the most ambitious, and the most successful effort at regional power development in American history. It set up a public corporation with authority to develop and manage the water resources of an area comprising over six hundred thousand square miles, and covering several states. It remains one of the most impressive legacies of the New Deal.

Equally well known (at the time, at least), but not nearly as successful, was the National Recovery Administration (NRA), an agency created by the National Industrial Recovery Act (NIRA). It also had a symbol, the blue eagle, with an inscription underneath saying, "We Do Our Part." The NIRA was the result of Roosevelt's determination to do something about what he and many of his advisers felt was the ruinous effect of "cutthroat" competition in American industry. It was the first and only serious attempt on the part of the federal government to engage in national economic planning. It allowed trade and industrial groups to set the terms of economic relationships in their own industries, by granting powers to set wages, prices, working conditions, and marketing and production quotas—the so-called "codes of fair competition." Although introduced with a great deal of fanfare and initially greeted by many affected groups with much enthusiasm, the NRA opened a Pandora's Box of troubles for the administration. The large corporations, many of which were at first slow to sign up, eventually dominated the price- and wage-fixing mechanisms, generating complaints from labor, small businessmen, and consumers. The Act was an attempt to please everybody, but it ended up satisfying no one. It died an ignominious death in May 1935, when the Supreme Court, appalled by its shoddy legislative standards, declared the NRA unconstitutional.

Other New Deal efforts met with greater degrees of success. For example, the Civil Works Administration (CWA) employed over four million persons, including artists and writers ("They have to eat too," FDR stated), and some fifty thousand teachers, by the opening of 1934. Together they built or improved one-half million miles of roads, forty thousand schools, thirty-five hundred playgrounds and athletic fields, and a thousand airports. Under the auspices of FERA, 5000 buildings and 7000 bridges were constructed; one and a half million adults were taught to read and write, while over one hundred thousand students were given help to attend college.[23] Students were also assisted by the National Youth Administration, which was created in 1935, and gave over two million highschool and college youths part-time work. The Civilian Conservation Corps also performed impressively, giving employment to over two and a half million men, whose efforts were responsible for more than half of the forest planting in the history of the nation.[24] All of these programs reflected Roosevelt's determination to commit the federal government to serving the needs of the great mass of citizens.

These and other New Deal projects reflected Roosevelt's particular influence in other ways as well. For example, many of these organizations had overlapping jurisdictions, and it required no small amount of administrative sophistication to tell the differences among them. This sort of thing never bothered Roosevelt. After Congress created a relief agency, and he noticed that there were still millions of people out of work or with nothing to eat, his response typically was to create an additional agency to do the same or similar things as the existing one. Thus, in addition to the Public Works Administration, for instance, there was another agency that had a very similar-sounding name: The Works Progress Administration (WPA)—an enormously productive organization created by the Emergency Relief Appropriation Act of 1935. Also, FDR was not daunted when some part of his program ran into trouble, for whatever reason. For instance, when the AAA was declared unconstitutional in 1936, he pressed for the passage of the Soil Conservation and Domestic Allotment Act, which revived at least a portion of the previous measure by encouraging farmers to restore land and productivity. During his first term in office, Roosevelt's persistence usually paid off.

Thus he did not respond, as Hoover perhaps would have, to Supreme Court opposition to the New Deal by quietly acceding to the wishes of the justices. On the contrary, FDR took advantage of the Democrat's increased numbers in the Congress—the Republicans actually *lost* seats in the off-year election in 1934—to generate a flurry of legislative activity that has since been dubbed "the Second Hundred Days." In a fairly rapid order, the tired and harried Congress responded to Roosevelt's initiatives by passing some of the most significant legislation in American history. This included, for instance, the Wagner Act, which set up the National Labor Relations Board, thereby giving unions considerably more muscle in their dealings with employers than they had ever enjoyed in the past. The agricultural sector was brought more into the mainstream of American life by the Rural Electrification Administration, an agency that eventually carried electricity to the nine-tenths of American farms that had none. Congress also passed the Banking Act, the Public Utilities Holding Company Act, an astonishing piece of legislation called the Wealth Tax Act, and one of the most significant laws in American history, the Social Security Act. Exhausted, Congress adjourned in late August 1935, and the president contemplated the electoral situation for the next year.

It hardly seemed necessary to do so. From the standpoint of his reelection chances, Roosevelt's position was virtually unassailable. Every index of industrial activity was significantly higher than four years before: national income was 50 percent higher, six million more jobs had been created; industrial output had nearly doubled, corporate profits were high, electrical output was at an all-time high, and Detroit was producing more autos than any time before, except in 1929.[25] The Republican candidate, Alf Landon, quickly gave up the election as lost as soon as he became aware of the latest business indices. Jim Farley, a close aide to the president, predicted that FDR would take every state except Maine and Vermont; he was exactly right.

Buoyed by his overwhelming victory at the polls, Roosevelt entered his second term with optimism. Of course, there was some unfinished business to attend to, some additional legislation to pass, a few old scores to settle—particularly with the Supreme Court—and some old-fashioned partisan politicking to cement the coalition that had formed around the presidency. Actually, however, Roosevelt's agenda for his second term differed in numerous respects from the New Deal. He wanted to cut back on some of the more obvious efforts on the part of the federal government to maintain relief—this had always bothered him—and let business return more or less to its proper role as the stimulant of the American economy. He also wanted to streamline the government's administrative operations, and work to bring the remainder of impoverished Americans into the mainstream of the country's economic life. He was not to get his way on any of these matters.

The Second Term

Roosevelt's second term was in many ways a disappointment. It began with his poorly conceived attempt to influence the Supreme Court, and ended with the president engaged in largely futile efforts to educate the American public about the dangers of fascism in Europe. Between these points were all sorts of frustrations. These included an economic downturn, a feisty and generally uncooperative Congress, strike-ravaged industries pleading for help, renewed attacks from all parts of the political spectrum accusing him of being a fascist, communist, or socialist, and the continuing depression that simply refused to go away. Throughout all this FDR managed to remain reasonably level-headed, but clearly the exhilarations of his first term were not to be repeated, at least not in domestic affairs.

It cannot be said that he always used the best judgment. Nowhere was this better demonstrated than by his attempt to "pack" the Supreme Court. During his first term the Court was unsympathetic to the New Deal, and viewed it with equal parts of horror and astonishment. Accordingly, by the summer of 1935 it had declared the NIRA unconstitutional, along with about a dozen other pieces of New Deal legislation.[26] FDR's exasperation led him after the 1936 election to propose a bill that would increase the size of the court from nine to fifteen members. This, of course, would give him the opportunity to appoint people whose political philosophy was more in line with his own. But it was a ploy that fooled absolutely no one. Worse than that, it was seen by many as an attack upon an old and venerable institution, and added further evidence to those arguments that painted Roosevelt as a dictator. Foolishly and uncharacteristically, FDR stuck to a position that was politically hopeless. He even tried to justify his proposal by pointing out how the tremendous work load of the Court was putting a strain on its (rather elderly) members—which was of course about the last thing on his mind. But Congress was not impressed by his pious pronouncements of concern about the judges' health, and quietly tabled the bill in mid-July 1937.

Although the Court's opinions changed rather dramatically after this incident, Roosevelt's prestige suffered in the process. And the second half of 1937 dealt further blows to his image as a producer of political and economic wonders. Probably the most politically damaging thing centered upon the activities of the newly emboldened labor unions. Encouraged by the generally prounion orientation of the NLRB, two of the nation's largest unions led a series of sit-down strikes against the auto and steel manufacturers, which severely cut down the production in both industries. The strikes were accompanied by an economic downturn complicated greatly by the cutoff of federal funds to the WPA and PWA. This made little economic sense at the time, but followed consistently from FDR's conviction about the role of the federal government in the American economy. He decided simply that it was time to see if the economy could now "stand on its own two feet" without constant infusions of federal support.[27] Obviously, it could not; when the crutches were removed, the patient collapsed. And so did FDR's prestige.

When the spring of 1938 showed no improvement, Roosevelt went into high gear. The first thing he did was to return to the big-spending policies that had worked well in his first term. All the various "alphabet agencies" received enormous influxes of new funds. Second, he recommended to Congress that it investigate the workings of concentrated economic power in the United States, and this resulted in a three-year investigation by a congressional committee. Much of this effort smacked of presidential scapegoating, but there is no question that Roosevelt genuinely felt big business had let the country down. And so had the Congress, aside from granting the administration a few legislative victories inspired mainly by presidential prodding. For example, its treatment of an executive reorganization bill, a very carefully crafted measure by experts outside the government, was met with utter disdain. "A dictator bill," someone cried; it thrusts a "dagger into the very heart of democracy," screamed another, as the bill was defeated in April.[28] Thoroughly disgusted, Roosevelt campaigned extensively during the 1938 congressional elections in an effort to "purge" the party of some antiadministration members. This ended up as a colossal failure that backfired as well. The Republicans gained eighty-one seats in the House and the Senate, becoming again, after a lapse of six years, a political force to be reckoned with.[29]

They were not the only ones. In addition to a stubborn Congress, a rejuvenated Republican Party, and a nation now grown a bit skeptical about Roosevelt's initiatives, the president also had to contend with adversaries from abroad. The rise of fascism in Europe had brought to power a flamboyant German dictator hungry for territory and revenge, and a posturing Italian despot eager to renew Italy's honor and establish its place in the sun. Further, Japan was carrying out an aggressive war against China, while contemplating further conquests in the Pacific. The last real victories of the New Deal, the Fair Labor Standards Act and a renewed AAA, were passed in 1938, the same year that the Western European powers committed an historic act of appeasement at Munich. Thereafter, FDR's attentions would be increasingly absorbed by foreign affairs.

Before dealing with his activities as commander in chief, however, it may be useful to summarize the principle aspects of his leadership role as a practitioner of American liberalism. There are several reasons for interrupting our survey of Roosevelt's career to do this. First, by the time his attention was diverted to foreign affairs, near the end of the thirties, the main patterns of his presidency were rather well established and the New Deal had become a fact of American life. Also, most of his domestic initiatives were behind him by the time war broke out in Europe, and his principle accomplishments after that point were to articulate further the beliefs that had guided him over his years as president. Finally, his activities as commander in chief can scarcely be understood without reference to the beliefs and practices for which he had become famous in domestic politics. In fact, we shall argue that FDR's approach to foreign policy was in many respects an extension of his manner of dealing with domestic problems.

ROOSEVELT THE PRACTITIONER

FDR and the Liberal Tradition

Although he was often surrounded by advisers who tended to be ideologically sensitive to the implications of New Deal policies, Roosevelt himself was usually unreflective about his political philosophy, as we have seen: "I am a Christian and a Democrat—that's all," he once asserted flatly. But actually he was more than that, and on numerous occasions he stated his beliefs quite clearly. Of the tenets of American liberalism most directly relevant to Roosevelt's views and actions as chief executive, the concept of individuals' rights and the purpose of constitutional government were probably the most important. But he was also mindful that governments rest upon the consent of the governed, and cannot indefinitely ignore popular needs without risking a loss of legitimacy that could lead to revolt. Certainly this seemed the lesson of the European experience during his life. But at the foundation of everything he tried to do in domestic as well as foreign affairs was a commitment to the common good, along with a particularly American way to achieve it.

We shall discuss these matters in four sections. The main components of Roosevelt's liberalism included, first, a combination of the ideals of Thomas Jefferson with the methods of Alexander Hamilton that redefined liberalism, giving it a modern application, and investing it with the meaning that it has today. This entailed, second, an emphasis upon preserving America's historical commitment to individualism by stressing the social responsibilities individuals have to one another, which can be realized through public means. Third, Roosevelt expanded upon the concept of individual rights that was emphasized so much during the formative years of the republic, by giving it an economic as well as a political content. Finally, we shall note that Roosevelt was a practitioner of modern liberalism in a fashion that was strikingly consistent with the American temperament, as understood by de Crèvecoeur, de Tocqueville, and more current observers of the American scene.

Hamilton Jeffersonianism.   One of the most systematic outlines of Roosevelt's political philosophy was presented in a speech before the Commonwealth Club in San Francisco in September 1932. He focused on a review of the contributions to American political thinking and practice of Alexander Hamilton and Thomas Jefferson. He explained that they represented opposing political views, but each had played an important role in the development of American political institutions. Most importantly, the task of modern American government was to draw upon the best that each tradition—Hamiltonian and Jeffersonian—had to offer for the solution of contemporary problems.[30]

The first portion of his address consisted of clarifying the differences between Hamilton and Jefferson. Hamilton, he explained, was the "most brilliant, honest, and able exponent" of a view that had little regard for the abilities of most people, and that assumed the business of government was best carried out by "a great and strong group of central institutions, guided by a small group of able and public spirited citizens . . ." In short, good government must be grounded on property, and must receive its primary support from the better-off elements of society, the property-holding classes. To this he opposed the ideals of Jefferson, which placed great emphasis upon the rights of "personal competency"—freedom of thought and actions, freedom of "personal living each man according to his own lights"—and property rights. Jefferson realized that the exercise of property rights by some could interfere with the enjoyment of personal competency rights by others—an analysis that neatly fitted Roosevelt's own concerns. He also emphasized Jefferson's feeling that it was the duty of government to intervene, should this situation ever come about again, "not to destroy individualism, but to protect it."

Most of the time throughout American history this was not necessary. That is, the lot of common people was never so absolutely wretched that Jefferson's condition for government intervention was satisfied. But all this had changed in the twentieth century, and it was now time for the central government to act vigorously. Jefferson had always feared that the encroachment of governmental power would be destructive of people's liberties, particularly as such oppression probably would come about as a result of political power in the hands of the rich and well-born. But this was not the situation today. It was not a highly centralized, Hamiltonian government that was oppressing the people, said Roosevelt, but rather a highly centralized, irresponsible economic elite that had lost its sense of social responsibility and any regard for the common people of the land. Jefferson strongly believed that government rested upon the great mass of ordinary citizens, and was not the special province of the gifted few. Clearly the circumstances today required the central government to act on behalf of the vast majority of Americans, as its instrument, to curb the oppressors and work for the common good. In short, it was necessary to use Hamiltonian means to achieve Jeffersonian ends.

This was "Hamiltonian Jeffersonianism." Roosevelt believed, with Hamilton, that the central government had an active role to play in bettering conditions in society. And he also believed, with Jefferson, that the power of the government should be used to promote the common good; that is, to help the ordinary folk and not just the privileged few, those who had, in Hamilton's terms, a "stake in society." To FDR everyone had a stake in society. And how he achieved Jeffersonian goals with Hamiltonian means was a matter of indifference to him: Roosevelt would try anything that worked. Thus, critics who ascribed all sorts of foreign-sounding adjectives to the New Deal were actually "trying to make very complex and theoretical something that is really very simple and very practical," he pointed out in a Fireside Chat in 1934.[31] There was nothing foreign about Hamiltonian Jeffersonianism—that is, modern American liberalism as understood and practiced by Roosevelt. It was "Americanism" at its best. Indeed, it was as American as hot dogs and apple pie.

The Common Good. The Jeffersonian side of Roosevelt's liberalism was more important to him, and he often articulated his views about the common good in radio addresses and other public speeches. For example, in a speech given in August 1934, he stated that the goal of the New Deal was to "cement our society, rich and poor, manual worker and brain worker, into a voluntary brotherhood of freemen, standing together, striving together, for the common good of all."[32] This required on everyone's part the realization of "our interdependence on each other," and that "if we are to go forward, we must move as a trained and loyal army willing to sacrifice for the good of a common discipline."[33] His vision involved all people recognizing their duties to one another in a common national enterprise where each citizen is committed to the welfare of all. "I always hate the frame of mind which talks about 'your group' and 'my group,'" he once asserted.[34] He was confident of his ability to bridge the widest gaps among contending groups, if he were given the opportunity to appeal to their higher interests. Indeed, he felt that if every group based its actions on common-good premises, they would all agree on policy matters.

The hard thing, of course, was to get every group to think that way. In fact, Roosevelt's vision may have been laudable, but it was clearly naïve, seen against the assumptions that guided the framing of the American constitutional system and the century and a half of experience since its founding. James Madison, of course, felt that the structure of the federal government was conducive to the achievement of the common good, because it made it so very difficult for any combination of groups (factions, in his terms) to impose its own partial interests upon the rest of society. The government itself was considered an arena for the interplay of group conflicts. Its policy outputs represented the outcome of the ongoing struggles among various interests in American society. Strictly speaking, however, the governmental apparatus itself was supposed to be a neutral mechanism.

Roosevelt completely changed this around. Instead of being a neutral arbiter for all, "the state under FDR," Richard Hofstadter pointed out, "could be called neutral only in the sense that it offered favors to everyone."[35] In fact, nothing else better explains the something-for-everyone approach of the New Deal: jobs for the unemployed, relief for the needy, price supports for the farmers, collective-bargaining guarantees for the worker, protection from competition for business, pensions for the elderly, low-interest mortgages for home buyers—in short, guaranteed help of some form for whomever needed it. There was little notion of sacrifice in any of this, of course, but at least the idea that everybody should try to help one another in some fashion was clearly in evidence. And the national government was the means of doing so. Indeed, FDR was convinced that national relief programs were the only way left to restore the freedoms of economic security and opportunity for individual citizens that had been so ravaged by the depression. Thus, under the auspices of federal governmental initiatives, as Ralph Henry Gabriel put it, "the maintenance of individual freedom was made a national community project—collective action supporting individual liberty."[36]

To Roosevelt this made eminently good sense, especially since the doctrine of the free and responsible individual seemed to be so painfully irrelevant in an economy ruled by vast conglomerates of private power. During the depression millions of people were out of work, out of food, and often out of their homes for reasons completely beyond their control. That is, one-third to one-half of the American population was in miserable straits not because of *personal* irresponsibility, but because of the workings of an economic system that, in Roosevelt's view, was in the hands of an insensitive and uncaring elite. He did not, however, engage in a wholesale condemnation of American capitalism; quite the contrary, Roosevelt remained convinced that its proper role was to be the main stimulant of and provider of jobs in the American economy. But he had bitter complaints against some segments of big business that frequently put their own interests against those of the community. For instance, the charter of the American Liberty League, a group formed by some wealthy industrialists in 1934 to organize opposition to the New Deal, read like a conservative economic catechism. Roosevelt didn't object to those portions of the charter that preached about the necessity of government to safeguard individual initiative, or even about the right to acquire property. But "there is no mention . . . " he snorted, "about the concern of the community," or about the government's duty to do other things, such as "the protection of the life and liberty of the individual against elements in the community which seek to enrich or advance themselves at the expense of their fellow citizens."[37] As we have seen, in his first term, businessmen got the NIRA; in his second, they were investigated.

Roosevelt's commitment to the common good involved more than initiating programs for afflicted groups, or trying to play the role of a broker to arbitrate differences among them. It was manifested by the personal interest he took in the many programs passed by the New Deal. He was ever the empiricist; government programs had a flesh-and-blood meaning to him that constantly invigorated the common-good ideals that inspired their creation. When the First Lady traveled around the country, Franklin gave her advice always to be aware of the conditions she saw: "Watch people's faces," he intoned. "Look at the condition of their clothes on the wash line. You can tell a lot from that. Notice their cars."[38] He wanted to know what people were eating and how much, how they lived, what their education was like, what they seemed to need, what their concerns were—in short, did they seem happy and well-off? For many of the more ideologically inclined advisers around him, New Deal programs had value as embodiments of new principles of government and society. But for Roosevelt, always impatient with abstractions, they meant that the people of America were indeed better off in the ways that counted—in the immediate details of their everyday lives.

In fact, his commitment to the improvement of national living standards led him to formulate in concrete terms what he felt was the responsibility of the national government to provide for the common good of the country. Near the end of his tenure, Roosevelt outlined a program that required the federal government to secure an "Economic Bill of Rights" for all Americans.

The Economic Bill of Rights

In his eleventh annual message, given in January 1944, Roosevelt presented the agenda that he intended to follow after the conclusion of the war. As before, his analysis neatly drew from the tradition of early American liberalism, in this case as expressed in the Declaration of Independence and the first ten amendments to the Constitution. "This Republic," he asserted, "grew to its present strength, under the protection of certain inalienable rights," which were essentially political in nature—freedom of expression, worship, trial by jury, and so forth. However, in the twentieth century "these political rights proved inadequate to assure us equality in the pursuit of happiness." Then he concluded: "We have come to a clear realization of the fact that true individual freedom cannot exist without economic security and independence. 'Necessitous men are not free men.' People who are hungry and out of a job are the stuff of which dictatorships are made."[39]

Essentially Roosevelt suggested that the preservation of traditional American liberalism required changes consistent with contemporary needs. Thus, the old Bill of Rights was not discarded as irrelevant or no longer important; it had to be supplemented, not discarded. Individual freedom in a political sense clearly remains important, but it "cannot exist without economic security and independence." Further, he was acutely sensitive to the fact that rebellions occur for reasons other than to secure the protection of certain political rights, as in the case of the American Revolution. In an age of fascist and communist totalitarianism, FDR was convinced that economic deprivations generate revolutions just as surely as political oppresssions; indeed, they "are the stuff of which dictatorships are made." In short, a government that rests upon the consent of the governed needs to do more than protect political rights.

The "second Bill of Rights" that Roosevelt had in mind reads like a shopping list of individual and group needs, which had at least in part been addressed by New Deal programs, but still required additional action on the part of the federal government. These included the right to a job, to adequate food, clothing, and shelter, to education, and to adequate medical care and old-age assistance—in short, security. All elements of the population were cited by him as well—farmers, housewives, factory and office workers, and business people large and small. Everyone was equally deserving to be assured of this economic bill of rights, except, of course, those "selfish pressure groups" that had sought over the years to look after their own interests to the exclusion of the public good.

Naturally, this program represented a significant departure from the traditional understanding of rights, and of course it required an activist role on the part of the federal government. This obviously was the Hamiltonian side of FDR's liberalism. However, government intervention clearly had some precedent in American history, both in theory and practice. The Populists, who were rural reformers during the last third of the nineteenth century, vigorously sought for government regulation of railroads and banks—usually at the state level, and with mixed success. The Progressives, their urban counterparts, whose influence was felt mainly during the first two decades of this century, leveled their attacks against corrupt political "bossism" in the cities, and further advocated national legislation to protect the living and working conditions of Americans. Some American presidents were comfortable with interventionist government too, especially Woodrow Wilson during the First World War. He had also sought for more regulation of American business, particularly securities. And Theodore Roosevelt campaigned on the platform of "New Nationalism," and gained a reputation as a great trust-buster. In short, government intervention was far from a novelty when Roosevelt took office.

But what made the New Deal so distinctive was that it went beyond all these things, on the basis of a permanent commitment on the part of the national government, and on a scale never before practiced in American history. It is true that there were elements of Populism, Progressivism, and national planning in New Deal Programs. But Roosevelt regarded himself and his programs as "liberal," and succeeded in identifying the Democratic Party as the party of liberalism, an association that has remained today.[40] This was a significant achievement, of course, but it was also the result of his "first-rate temperament" as much as it was from a systematic application of certain political ideas. Indeed, Roosevelt was anything but systematic, which is perhaps why he has held such fascination for observers of the presidency. In fact, many feel that the most interesting aspect of Roosevelt's leadership was his style of operation, and not his political philosophy. There were few things more fun to observe than the Roosevelt style, to watch Roosevelt in action. Indeed, his temperament and style were as thoroughly grounded in the American liberal tradition as his political ideas.

Roosevelt and the American Temperament

As noted at the outset, one of the most striking aspects of liberalism in America was the context in which it took root and developed over the years. That is, American conditions were conducive not only to the development of liberal ideas, but also to the formation of habitual practices and modes of thought that so deeply impressed such observers as de Crèvecoeur and de Tocqueville. As we have seen, they felt that America was a unique land, a place defined by such values as novelty, optimism, generalized competence in a variety of occupations, and, above all, a spirit of adventure. There is probably no president in American history who exemplifies all of these traits more than Franklin Roosevelt. Of course, commentators like de Crèvecoeur and de Tocqueville made their observations during the eighteenth and nineteenth centuries, respectively, and FDR is a twentieth-century figure. But more recent analyses confirm these early judgments, indicating that Roosevelt truly represented the values we have cited as graphically as any of the characters ever examined by past reviewers of the American scene.

In one of the best recent treatments of the American temperament, the historian Daniel Boorstin has provided intriguing accounts of the types of people who settled and developed the country. One of these types he refers to as the "Go-Getters," individuals who "went in search of what others had never imagined was there to get."[41] They were the entrepreneurs, the explorers, the experimenters, the frontiersmen, the movers and shakers, the dashing adventurers of American history—in short, those imaginative and daring souls who blazed new trails for others to follow and opened up new vistas for the world to marvel at. The Go-Getters embodied what was most exciting in the American spirit—that willingness to challenge life with boldness and vision, to push for as much as one could get. The Go-Getters made America.

And so did Franklin Delano Roosevelt. Indeed, nothing better captures the life and political style of FDR than the designation "Go-

Getter"; he went in search of what others could not imagine was possible or did not dare to try. His whole life consisted of trying one thing after another, never losing faith if something failed, and, above all, never giving up, even in the face of enormous personal adversity. Like a true American Go-Getter, he had always been an experimenter: he experimented with curing his polio; he drove the bureaucracy in the Navy to hair-pulling distraction with one scheme after another; during the twenties he engaged in all sorts of business schemes, none of them terribly successful or even very much related to one another; and, of course, he experimented wildly in the hectic days of the New Deal. "This country needs," he stated at a commencement address in 1932, "and unless I mistake its temper, the country demands bold, persistent experimentation. It is common sense to take a method and try it. If it fails, admit it frankly and try another. But above all, try something."[42] No statement better illustrates the Go-Getter attitude toward life than this one.

Thus, he approached life in general and politics in particular in the same way: with a playful, experimental, let's-try-it-and-see-what-happens attitude. In fact, his very lack of seriousness in dealing with serious matters was frequently a cause for exasperation among his associates. Raymond Moley, one of FDR's earliest and most-influential "Brain Trust" members, recounted a very revealing and rather funny story—although it was not funny to him at the time—that illustrates this point beautifully. At one point during the campaign in 1932 he presented Roosevelt with two drafts of speeches on the tariff issue. The positions outlined were diametrically opposed, and Roosevelt was asked which one should be used, which one best represented his views. Moley, a conscientious academic type, always careful to make his distinctions clear and his statements unambiguous, was absolutely staggered by Franklin's reply: "Weave the two together," he answered effortlessly. One can only imagine the havoc wreaked by this casual response on Moley's sensitive academic intellect.[43]

So just how does one weave together the unweavable? If there were a way to do it, Roosevelt would find it. This was especially true in administrative relations, an area in which FDR seemed to take pride in exasperating people. He had the annoying habit of assigning two people to the same task, while he sat back to watch them fight it out. Assistant secretaries who were known to hate their superiors were appointed, apparently for the purpose of making life difficult for those around them. Authority in single departments was often divided; several agencies were sometimes given the same tasks with overlapping jurisdictions and, as we have seen, often with very similar-sounding names! And all manner and variety of aides, assistants, advisers, and officials had a direct line to the presidency, without consulting some chain of command. FDR once justified this "administration by competition" to Frances Perkins, his Secretary of Labor, by saying that "a little rivalry is stimulating, you know. It keeps everybody going to prove he is a better fellow than the next man. It keeps them honest too."[44] It also had the effect of assuring that only one person ever really knew what was going on—the president

Actually, these bizarre administrative habits reflected a great deal of political ability, along with considerable skills in human relations. Most of all, however, Roosevelt's leadership qualities illustrated the Jack-of-all-trades approach to occupational specialities at which de Crèvecoeur and de Tocqueville so marveled. That is, Roosevelt did not have the specialized skills of his advisers, and was not interested in acquiring them. What FDR had was not skill but what Boorstin calls "Know-How"—a generalized competence that enabled him to understand the tasks at hand and to know what was necessary to get them done.[45] And he practiced his Know-How with an enormously engaging personality that served him better than sheer intellect ever could have. Roosevelt was very "people-oriented" in every way. He loved to talk a lot, joke with his friends, persuade them, manipulate them, and more than occasionally play tricks on them. But the kindest remark ever made about his intellect came from Oliver Wendell Holmes, who called it "second-rate." Of course, he went on to say that Roosevelt had a first-rate temperament. Without question, his Know-How and first-rate temperament proved to be of far more importance than an overpowering intellect.

These considerations also indicate the foolishness of the many charges made against him while he was in office. Many of his critics were traumatized by the events in Europe, and tended to equate the New Deal with all sorts of foreign and sinister machinations. Herbert Hoover, for instance, icily accused Roosevelt of adhering to the "same philosophy of government which has poisoned all Europe . . . the fumes of the witch's caldron which boiled in Russia."[46] Like many, the former president was so enthralled by the horrible things going on in Germany, Italy, and the Soviet Union that he could not recognize how totally American Roosevelt was. Or, to put it another way, there was nothing at all "un-American" about FDR. He was not a practitioner of communism, fascism, socialism, or any alien-sounding *Ism*. Quite the contrary; everything he had ever done in and out of politics indicated that he was a traditional American Go-Getter—a Go-Getter with Know-How.

Unfortunately, both of these things were far more palatable to Americans than they were to citizens from other lands. To a very large extent, the same was true with Roosevelt's political ideas, which he tried to apply valiantly, but with little success, to the conduct of international affairs. But, as with his domestic endeavors, FDR must be given great credit for trying, especially since he often had to deal with an audience far tougher than anything even the Liberty League could come up with.

THE PRACTITIONER AND FOREIGN AFFAIRS

Roosevelt brought to the international scene the value system that had inspired the New Deal; namely, his commitment to the common good, his faith in "Hamiltonian Jeffersonianism," and, of course, his belief in the effectiveness of honest, good-natured arbitration among various interests. In short, he attempted to be a Go-Getter in applying "Americanism" to the world. This often required more Know-How than even he, the master practitioner, had at his disposal.

But he still did his best, and his best was very good indeed. It had to be, given the constraints of domestic politics and the numbing military catastrophes inflicted by fascist armies in the early years of World War II. On the home front FDR had to contend with a series of Neutrality Acts, the first of which was passed in 1935, by a Congress acutely conscious of American entanglements prior to World War I. Generally, they forbade American vessels from carrying munitions to any belligerent nations, prohibited Americans to sail on belligerent ships, and authorized the president to prevent the shipment of specified goods to foreign nations. However, a warring nation could get around these restrictions if it used its own ships to carry away needed goods and paid for such on the spot—"cash and carry," it was called. In this fashion the United States could wrap its oceans around itself and let the "rotten old nations" of Europe fight it out among themselves. Americans would remain aloof and try to cope with the more immediate demands of domestic politics.[47]

It didn't work—not for very long, that is. World War II began when Germany invaded Poland and exchanged declarations of war with Great Britain and France. After the Polish campaign, the conflict took on the character of what one observer called a "phony war"—a long period of military inactivity by any of the belligerents. This was broken with savage swiftness when Nazi armies descended upon Scandinavia and Western Europe. Of course, no one had expected Poland to last long, but when France, widely regarded as a first-class military power, disintegrated under the force of the German onslaught in less than six weeks, the Third Reich of Adolf Hitler looked invincible. The German Fuhrer followed up his victories on the ground with a massive attack upon Great Britain from the air. And as British cities were slowly being reduced to smoke and rubble, German submarines were sinking more ships than His Majesty's Government was able to build. Instead of England's using its navy to starve Germany, as it had in the First World War, quite the opposite was happening: England was being strangled to death by the fleet of Nazi U-boats. The British were not short of courage, but they were running out of practically everything else—money, weapons, food—resources of all kinds. They desperately needed help.

And Roosevelt was determined to give it to them. But the question was, how? In his traditional Go-Getter fashion, he used his Know-How to devise ways to help the British without violating the Neutrality Acts or somehow flagrantly putting the country at war. To this end he employed all manner of stratagems and explanations, and when these didn't work, he simply resorted to deception. For instance, American and British military staffs were involved in joint planning for several months in 1941, a fact conveniently hidden from the public until after the war. And when Congress became a problem, Roosevelt simply bypassed it. In September he agreed to provide the British with fifty "overage" destroyers for convoy protection in exchange for some bases in the Western hemisphere—a handy deal that was concluded by Executive agreement. In fact, "you can't attack a deal like that," moaned one isolationist Congressman. "Roosevelt outsmarted all of us . . . "[48]

But his efforts to outsmart people had limits. In September 1941, FDR in effect declared naval war against Germany after a German submarine shot a torpedo at an American destroyer. He denounced the act as "piracy," and pledged not to wait until the "rattlesnakes of the Atlantic" shot first; from now on, Americans would proceed with orders to "shoot on sight." Of course, this tough talk made it sound as though German submarine commanders had been deliberately seeking out American vessels, a policy they dearly wanted to follow, but that Hitler had steadfastly refused to authorize—so far. Actually, the opposite was true: American ships were put directly in the same routes used by British convoys, essentially inviting attack from Nazi subs. Indeed, the U.S.S. *Greer*, the first victim of the German attack, had been trailing the submarine with some help from a British aircraft, and finally drew its fire when the exasperated U-boat commander ran out of patience and options. Roosevelt knew all this, of course, but chose instead to make the matter appear like an unprovoked attack. And Congress was properly indignant, but would not declare war even after an American ship, the *Reuben James*, had actually been sunk. In fact, war was not declared until the United States lost a whole fleet of ships on the other side of the world, at Pearl Harbor. In short, no matter how hard the grand practitioner worked as a master manipulator of the facts, Congress and most of the public stood fast.

But FDR was able to win some victories before the Japanese attack removed all pretense from American war actions. Probably the most significant one occurred early in the spring of 1941, largely as the result of what one of his advisers called a "brilliant flash." It was brilliant, all right; in fact, it was so downright ingenious that Roosevelt had to use all of his Know-How to concoct a term to describe it. "Suppose," the master explainer-practitioner proceeded:

> my neighbor's home catches on fire, and I have a length of garden hose four or five hundred feet away. If he can take my garden hose and connect it up with his hydrant, I may help him put out the fire. Now what do I do? I don't say to him before that operation, 'Neighbor, my garden hose cost me fifteen dollars; you have to pay me fifteen dollars for it.' No! What is the transaction that goes on? I don't want fifteen dollars—I want my garden hose after the fire is over.[49]

And that deal was called Lend-lease. The bill embodying its provisions even had a patriotic number to it—1776. It was signed into law in March 1941, and was instrumental in transforming the United States into the "arsenal for democracy" in the fight against the fascist powers.

Unfortunately, the effectiveness of Rooseveltian Know-How, like American partisanship, seemed to stop at the water's edge. Although friends and foes alike responded well to FDR in personal terms—nearly everybody did—they were under no obligation to let his Go-Getter mentality interfere with their own designs. Thus, when Roosevelt tried his hardest to engineer a lasting agreement on Allied unity with two enormously egotistical Frenchmen, Charles de Gaulle and Henri Giraud, it broke down almost as soon as the two stopped shaking hands. Similarly, in a classic "weave-the-two-together" maneuver, Franklin asked for Churchill's forbearance at the Tehran Conference in 1943, while he tried to charm his way into Joseph Stalin's heart. Certainly the Soviet dictator seemed sufficiently amused—he was laughing and smiling by the time FDR ended his treatment—but still he refused to offer more than just vague assurances about instituting democracy in Eastern Europe. Indeed, Stalin was something of a Go-Getter with Know-How himself—Russian style. And that meant that the security interests of the Soviet state must always come before some airy proclamations about democracy and international goodwill among the major powers. To FDR's dismay, he was only president of the United States, not of the world.

Roosevelt's policy recommendations ran into as many problems as his style. It was his fervent hope that the old principles of international relations, based upon spheres of influence, power politics, and military strength, could be surpassed, and a new international order built upon a foundation of justice, mutual recognition of individual rights, and self-determination put in its place. These goals actually represented nothing less than the internationalization of New Deal ideas, most especially those of the NIRA. Thus, when he declared the whole world was one neighborhood, the New Deal took on global dimensions.

Probably nowhere is this better expressed than in his famous "Four Freedoms" speech, given in January 1941. "We look forward to a world," he proclaimed, "founded upon four essential human freedoms." These included freedom of speech and worship, and freedom from want and fear—"everywhere in the world." Further, this was "no vision of a distant millenium," but rather "a definite basis for a kind of world attainable in our own time and generation."(!) He concluded by saying that "the world order which we seek is the cooperation of free countries, working together in a friendly, civilized society."[50] Although he later modified his views about the attainability of this scheme during his lifetime, he did not alter his belief about the importance of working toward the goals outlined in this 1941 address.

The value orientation behind the Four Freedoms speech also informed his attempts in the later stages of the war to apply his "Four Policemen" notion to the building of the United Nations. He felt that if the most powerful nations on earth—represented by Great Britain, the United States, China, and the Soviet Union—would stick together and police the entire globe under the auspices of a new international organization, no one would dare to start an aggressive war. The possibility that one of these four might be an aggressor did not occur to him until later—too late, as it turned out. In his study of Roosevelt's thinking about world order, Willard Range commented that

> Roosevelt seemed to think that if national officials could develop the kind of personal relations neighbors have, who drop in for a drink, borrow each other's garden tools, and have conferences about community problems on each other's front porches, half the world's problems would disappear automatically and the other half would be readily soluble.[51]

The difficulty, of course, is that not everybody in the world wants to be a friendly neighbor.

But Roosevelt usually assumed otherwise. "You cannot hate a man that you know well," he once said.[52] On this matter FDR was as American as Will Rogers, who, incidentally, once said much the same thing—that he'd never met a man he didn't like. Of course, unlike FDR, he had never had to deal with the likes of de Gaulle or Stalin. And it may be that neither ever really entertained the possibility that an intimate knowledge of someone might actually cause one further to dislike—even hate—that person, and for perfectly good reasons. Familiarity does not necessarily breed friendliness; it may breed hatred and contempt. This is especially the case in world politics, where the enormous diversity of cultures, races, and belief systems have often bred centuries-old antagonisms, based not on ignorance or misunderstanding, but rather upon fairly accurate knowledge. In fact, most of Roosevelt's attempts to generalize from the American experience, to apply notions derived from his understanding of the common good, social interdependence, mutual understanding, and so forth, failed on practical grounds. However much the world might have benefited from the globalization of the New Deal, Roosevelt the great practitioner could not extend it beyond American borders.

But this does not diminish his many other accomplishments in the conduct of American foreign relations during the war. Roosevelt had succeeded in rallying the nation behind his policies to defeat the greatest foe the United States had ever faced. In doing so, he exercised the same skills, showed the same benevolence and the same genuine goodwill that had marked his efforts in domestic politics. And when he died in April 1945, it was the world, and not just the United States, that experienced a profound sense of loss. By that time, Franklin Delano Roosevelt, the Go-Getter with Know-How, the prophet of common good at home and universal brotherhood abroad, the Hamiltonian-Jeffersonian who embodied the best traditions in the American political experience—in short, the grandest practitioner of "Americanism" in the history of the United States—had become a legendary figure in the national and international political scene.

ENDNOTES

[1] Quoted in William E. Leuchtenburg, *Franklin Roosevelt and the New Deal* (Harper & Row, 1963), p. 167.

[2] Quoted in Nathan Miller, *FDR: An Intimate History* (Garden City, N.Y.: Doubleday & Company, Inc., 1983), p. 286.

[3] Ibid., p. 313.

[4] Quoted in Leuchtenburg, *New Deal*, p. 168, footnote 4.

[5] This story is related by Alpheus Thomas Mason, ed., *Free Government in the Making*, 3rd ed. (New York: Oxford University Press, 1965), p. 764.

[6] Richard Hofstadter, *The American Political Tradition* (New York: Vintage Books, 1955).

[7] James MacGregor Burns, *Roosevelt: The Lion and the Fox* (New York: Harcourt Brace Jovanovich, 1956).

[8] James David Barber, *The Presidential Character: Predicting Performance in the White House* (Englewood Cliffs, N.J.: Prentice-Hall, Inc. 1977).

[9] John G. Stoessinger, *Crusaders and Pragmatists: Movers of Modern American Foreign Policy* (New York: W. W. Norton & Company, 1979).

[10] This information about Roosevelt's youth and early political career is drawn from Miller, *FDR*, pp. 1–265. Miller is an especially valuable source for an overview of

Roosevelt's life and career before he became president. See also, Burns, *Roosevelt*, pp. 1–157. Burns devotes more attention to Roosevelt's presidency.

[11]Miller, *FDR*, p. 134.

[12]Quoted in ibid., pp. 190–91.

[13]Ibid., p. 206.

[14]In B. D. Zevin, ed., *Nothing to Fear: The Selected Addresses of Franklin Delano Roosevelt, 1932–45* (N.P.: Houghton Mifflin Company, 1946), p. 12.

[15]For information and economic statistics on the Great Depression, see Ross M. Robertson, *History of the American Economy*, 3rd ed. (New York: Harcourt Brace Jovanovich, 1973), pp. 696–703.

[16]See Leuchtenburg's succinct summary of Depression conditions in *New Deal*, pp. 1–4. Also consult the excellent portrayal of this era in William Manchester, *The Glory and the Dream* (New York: Bantam Books, 1975), pp. 3–263.

[17]Cited in Leuchtenburg, *New Deal*, p. 23.

[18]Quoted in Manchester, *Glory and Dream*, p. 83.

[19]Quoted in Miller, *FDR*, p. 309.

[20]Quoted in Manchester, *Glory and Dream*, p. 83.

[21]For discussions of the New Deal legislation passed during the One Hundred Days, see Miller, *FDR*, pp. 314–319; Leuchtenburg, *New Deal*, pp. 41–62; and Burns, *Roosevelt*, pp. 161–71.

[22]Miller, *FDR*, p. 315.

[23]Leuchtenburg, *New Deal*, pp. 121–23.

[24]Ibid., p. 174.

[25]Ibid., p. 194.

[26]For a discussion of Roosevelt's court-packing scheme and its consequences, see Alfred H. Kelly and Winfred A. Harbison, *The American Constitution: Its Origins and Development* (New York: W. W. Norton & Company, Inc., 1970), pp. 761–800. For relevant cases, see Martin Shapiro and Rocco J. Tresolini, *American Constitutional Law* (New York: Macmillan Publishing Company, Inc., 1975), pp. 285–99; and Donald O. Dewey, *Union and Liberty. A Documentary History of American Constitutionalism* (New York: McGraw-Hill Book Company, 1969), pp. 228–52.

[27]Leuchtenburg, *New Deal*, p. 245.

[28]Quoted in Burns, *Roosevelt*, p. 344.

[29]Leuchtenburg, *New Deal*, p. 271.

[30]Albert Fried, ed., *The Jeffersonian and Hamiltonian Traditions in American Politics* (Garden City, N.Y.: Anchor Books, 1968), pp. 414–44. Subsequent references to this speech are from this source. See also Miller, *FDR*, pp. 342–63, who develops this view as well.

[31]Quoted in Fried, *Traditions*, p. 428.

[32]Quoted in Burns, *Roosevelt*, p. 183.

[33]Ibid., p. 164

[34]Quoted by Leuchtenburg, *New Deal*, p. 164. Roosevelt's comment here was directed against liberals.

[35]Hofstadter, *The Age of Reform* (New York: Vintage Books, 1955), p. 307.

[36]Ralph Henry Gabriel, *The Course of American Democratic Thought*, 2nd ed. (New York: The Ronald Press Company, 1956), p. 433–34.

[37]Quoted in Burns, *Roosevelt*, pp. 206–208.

[38]Ibid., p. 173.

[39]Fried, *Traditions*, p. 483.

[40]A perceptive essay on this point is provided by Samuel Beer, "In Search of a New Public Philosophy," in Anthony King, ed., *The New American Political System* (Washington, D.C.: American Enterprise Institute, 1978), pp. 5–45.

[41]Daniel Boorstin, *The Americans: The Democratic Experience* (New York: Random House, 1973), p. 3.

[42]Quoted in Miller *FDR*, p. 263.

[43]Ibid., p. 285.

[44]Quoted in James MacGregor Burns, *Roosevelt: The Soldier of Freedom* (New York: Harcourt Brace Jovanovich, 1970), pp. 342–43.

[45]Daniel Boorstin, *The Americans: The National Experience* (New York: Vintage Books, 1965), p. 32.

[46]Quoted in Arthur M. Schlesinger, Jr., *The Crisis of the Old Order* (Boston: Houghton Mifflin Company, 1957), p. 437.

[47]For accounts of Roosevelt's wartime leadership, see William Range, *Franklin D. Roosevelt's World Order* (Athens, Ga.: University of Georgia Press, 1959); Robert A. Divine, *Roosevelt and World War II* (Baltimore: Johns Hopkins University Press, 1969), and Burns, *Roosevelt: The Soldier of Freedom.*

[48]Quoted in Manchester, *Glory and Dream*, p. 222.

[49]Quoted in Miller *FDR*, p. 460.

[50]Fried, *Traditions*, pp. 480–81.

[51]Range, *Roosevelt's World Order*, p. 60.

[52]Quoted in ibid., p. 63.

MARTIN LUTHER KING, JR.

An American Missionary

5

I never met a man in my life who has been so completely unaffected by the attention that has come to him in the world. He's always just Martin around anybody . . . . There isn't any swagger to his psyche at all. *Wyatt Walker*[1]

. . . the most notorious liar in the country. *J. Edgar Hoover*, Director of the Federal Bureau of Investigation[2]

I have a dream . . .

I have a dream that one day on the red hills of Georgia the sons of former slaves and the sons of former slaveowners will be able to sit down together at the table of brotherhood . . .

. . . when we let freedom ring, when we let it ring from every village and every hamlet, from every state and every city, we will be able to speed up that day when all of God's children, black men and white men, Jews and Gentiles, Protestants and Catholics, will be able to join hands and sing in the words of the old Negro spiritual, "Free at Last! Free at last! Thank God Almighty, we are free at last!" *Martin Luther King, Jr.*[3]

INTRODUCTION

In one of the most important books of the twentieth century Ralph Ellison, a prominent black writer, described himself as the "invisible man."[4] "No," Ellison explained, "I am not a spook like those who haunted Edgar Allan Poe; nor am I one of your Hollywood-movie ectoplasms. I am a man of substance, of flesh and bone, fiber and liquids—and I might even be said to possess a mind. I am invisible, understand, simply because people refuse to see me."[5] With this statement, the opening lines to a brilliant book, Ellison summarized the tragedy of the black experience in the United States. Blacks were invisible precisely because the white world around them refused to recognize their existence, which was made easier by the physical separation of the races throughout the country. For most Americans there was no race problem so long as blacks stayed "in their place." Indeed, that was the best way to keep them out of the way, out of mind, beyond anyone's concern—in short, "invisible." And what can be a better definition of invisible than something that people simply do not see?

Martin Luther King, Jr., made it his life's mission to change all that, to make blacks in America visible. It was his life's burning passion to stir the conscience of the country, to reinstill a national commitment to the ideals and fundamental purposes of the United States of America. Above all, King wanted to remind Americans, in terms that were familiar to them, of what the country was, of what the existence of the United States means. To do that he had to become a missionary in his own land—not to spread an alien faith, but to rekindle the allegiance of Americans to their existing faith, to the "faith of their fathers." In short, he worked to recommit Americans to the gospel of the American civil religion, especially as expressed in Jefferson's Declaration of Independence and in the utterances of the Great Emancipator, Abraham Lincoln. Indeed, if Thomas Jefferson could be considered one of the founders of the American civil religion, and Abraham Lincoln as one of its great expounders, then Martin Luther King, Jr., certainly was one of its greatest missionaries, perhaps the only truly great one.

For all that, he was not the first black leader to work on behalf of civil rights, nor was the organization that he founded, the Southern Christian Leadership Conference (SCLC) the most successful. The National Association for the Advancement of Colored People (NAACP) and the Congress of Racial Equality (CORE), to mention just two, were much older. And their leaders, although not as well known as the SCLC leader was to become in his career, had accomplished a great deal before Martin Luther King, Jr., really got started. But it does no disservice to other leaders and organizations to suggest that it was the work of King that electrified the Civil Rights movement in the United States. It was King who made the waves, who got the big headlines, who stirred things up, who excited the imaginations of nearly all blacks and the bitter hatred of many whites. It was King who became a figure whom all Americans—and not just black Americans—recognized as the leader of the Civil Rights movement. It was King who became known not as just another black leader, but who, more than anyone else, made blacks visible.

King's role as a missionary of the American civil religion will be explained by focusing upon three matters. We shall first deal with the social and economic conditions of American blacks—the Jim Crow system of segregation in the United States. In other words, to appreciate fully what King was reacting to in his missionary role, one must gain some understanding of what it meant (and, unfortunately for many, still means) to be black in America. No one described this better than King himself. Second, we shall briefly survey King's life, especially from 1955 to his death, in 1968. Finally, we shall analyze the meaning of his work in the context of understanding Martin Luther King, Jr., as perhaps the greatest missionary of the American creed in the twentieth century.

SEGREGATION IN AMERICA: THE JIM CROW SYSTEM

The Jim Crow system of legal discrimination against blacks and separation of the races had its origins in legislation passed by the Southern states in the generation following the Civil War.[6] These laws mandated racial segregation in churches, schools, housing, jobs, restaurants, hospitals, and public facilities of all sorts, including transportation systems, asylums, cemeteries, prisons, rest rooms, and ticket booths to public gatherings. Some of these measures took ridiculous extremes. Tools at working places were separated, as were entrances and exits, drinking fountains, nursing homes and poorhouses; there were even separate Jim Crow Bibles! And to exclude blacks from political participation, several state constitutions required them to pass literacy tests, pay poll taxes, or to meet the so-called "Grandfather Clause." This last measure required any voter to read and write any section of the state constitution at the request of the authorities. The requirement was waived in those cases where a person could prove that his forebears possessed the right to vote before January 1, 1866![7] And all these stipulations were reinforced by unneeded reminders in the form of "Whites Only" signs posted wherever it seemed relevant.

This system of exclusion was supported further by racist literature used in public schools, and in some cases by sheer terror. Schoolbooks, for instance, contained references to pseudo-scientific "findings" about the nature of the "inferior race," which of course justified the extreme racial discrimination practices by southern whites. The effect also was to minimize the significance of perpetrating terror against blacks. Indeed, the noted Swedish sociologist, Gunnar Myrdal commented in 1944 that "any white man can strike or beat a Negro, steal or destroy his property, cheat him in a transaction and even take his life, without much fear of legal reprisal."[8] Without *any* fear of legal reprisal would be more accurate; officers of the law were often involved themselves, either directly, or indirectly by prudently ignoring what everyone knew was going on. In short, even by the mid-twentieth century, no one in the South, black or white, needed to be told by anyone that blacks should be "kept in their place." After years of practice, reinforced by legal sanctions and buttressed by racist education and terrorist practices, you just *knew* it.

The cumulative effects of American racism had been well documented by the fifties, and the evidence was available to anyone who wished to look at it. To many Americans, especially the baby-boom generation that attended college in the sixties, reading accounts such as Kenneth B. Clark's *Dark Ghetto*, Charles E. Silberman's *Crisis in Black and White*, and the *Report of the National Advisory Committee on Civil Disorders* (the Kerner Commission Report) was a rude awakening to an ugly side of America. These accounts and many others all converged on a single point, most pointedly expressed by Kenneth Clark in his description of urban life for blacks: "The dark ghetto is institutionalized pathology; it is chronic, self-perpetuating pathology."[9] All of the indices of human misery—juvenile delinquency, drugs, prostitution, illegitimate births, high unemployment, mental illness, broken homes, street gangs, organized as well as unorganized crime of all sorts—made the ghetto hideous to live in and hideous to behold. But perhaps the most shocking aspect of the black experience was the fact that, one hundred years after the Emancipation Proclamation, the position of blacks in American society had not appreciably changed.

Without question, the most destructive aspect of American racism was its psychological effect upon blacks. In fact, it is almost impossible to exaggerate the consequences of race consciousness on the development of black Americans' identity and concept of self-worth throughout most of American history. Skin color literally made all the difference in the world, and said to every black man, woman, and child that for most of them there was no place to go in white society. Thus, for many, a vicious cycle developed: the early destruction of one's concept of self-worth led further to lack of motivation on the job, and less performance and productivity—because, after all, you were a Negro, you weren't supposed to excel, and if by chance you did, that would have constituted a threat not only to the white world, with its miserable stereotypes, but also to the black world, with its lowered expectations and consequent demand that people conform. In short, one couldn't be white, and being black didn't get you anywhere. James Baldwin summarized volumes of social and psychological analyses of the subject by commenting that "to be a Negro in this country and to be relatively conscious is to be in a rage almost all of the time."[10]

Although the racial factor prevented the vast majority of blacks from rising in American society, it did not prevent the federal government from asking them to defend that society and, if necessary, to die for it. America's participation in the two world wars was of crucial importance in at least two ways. First, it accelerated the migration of blacks from the rural South to the urban North, where they began to form a "critical mass" in political terms. Second, and more important, it raised the question about service in the armed forces that made whites uneasy and blacks increasingly indignant: why should American blacks fight for freedom and democracy abroad, when they were denied those very things at home? As the Second World War was fought against one of the most viciously racist regimes ever to exist, increasingly large numbers of blacks were asking that question: why indeed?

While these questions were being asked, however, the prospects for significant change were getting better. Although Franklin Roosevelt was in office for twelve years and had his hands full in fighting the Great Depression and World War II, he still managed, by executive order, to create an agency called the Fair Employment Practices Committee. Its task was to monitor defense contracts and employment conditions in defense-related industries, which employed large numbers of blacks. President Truman made further advances by issuing executive orders that ended discrimination in federal-government employment practices and in the armed forces. As a result, during the Korean War blacks and whites fought together in large numbers for the first time. Finally, the struggle against Jim Crow in the legal system, which had been carried out relentlessly by the National Association for the Advancement of Colored People, bore its most significant fruit in 1954. In *Brown* v. *Board of Education* the United States Supreme Court explicitly denied the separate-but-equal doctrine of *Plessy* v. *Ferguson*, an 1896 case that had the effect of allowing states to practice racial discrimination.[11] The walls of legal segregation in America were crumbling.

The stage was set for something dramatic, something electrifying, something that would inspire all Americans, black and white, to a recommitment to their national ideals. That is, the stage was set for the work of Martin Luther King, Jr.

THE LIFE OF DR. MARTIN LUTHER KING, JR.

The Road to Montgomery

Martin Luther King Jr., was born on January 15, 1929 into a family that belonged to the well-educated, black middle class of Atlanta, Georgia.[12] The senior King was an important man in his own right. A sturdy, no-nonsense type well known in his community, the Reverend King was the widely respected senior pastor of the Ebenezer Baptist Church in Atlanta, and an active member of the local NAACP. Next to him the most important influences upon young Martin's life were the figures he studied in the course of his academic training, which included attendance at Morehouse College, Crozer Seminary in Chester, Pennsylvania, and Boston College. The first of these influences was Walter Rauschenbusch, a noted advocate of the social-gospel teachings of the early twentieth century. Rauschenbusch emphasized the social duties of Christians to one another in this world, and called for the establishment of a new social order based upon the virtues of love, brotherhood, and fraternity among all peoples. The second important influence was provided by the life and teachings of an Indian, Mahatma Gandhi. From him King learned that nonviolent resistance to social evils was morally uplifting, for both the oppressed and the oppressors, and also could be fully as effective as more provocative measures. All three were instrumental in providing him with the character and values that guided him throughout his life.

King took his first church position in Montgomery, Alabama, in the spring of 1954, a landmark time in the history of the American Civil Rights movement. The Supreme Court had handed down its historic decision in the *Brown* v. *Board of Education* case, which had an electrifying effect upon blacks throughout the country. Even the black community in Montgomery, which had been demoralized and apathetic in the past, was stirred to action. Thus, in December of the following year, when a young black woman refused to yield her seat to a white patron on a city bus, the resulting incident generated a boycott of the entire bus system by blacks. The response rate among blacks was phenomenal—nearly 100 percent—an astounding reaction, given their nearly total dependence on public transportation. King became involved by being elected to a local organization, the Montgomery Improvement Association (MIA), that was formed to coordinate the local boycott efforts. His initial reluctance to take a leading role at such a young age was soon overcome by an observation made by one of his supporters: "You ain't got much time to think, 'cause you in the chair from now on."[13] Finding it impossible to refute that airtight argument, he smilingly agreed to do his best.

King's best was nothing short of phenomenal, and as the Montgomery story made national headlines, Martin Luther King was catapulted into national prominence. He was an extremely gifted orator, and the situation gave him many chances to keep in practice. In his own account of the events in Montgomery, *Stride Toward Freedom*, King observed that he "came to see for the first time what the older preachers meant when they said, 'Open your mouth and God will speak for you.' "[14] Certainly God never spoke more eloquently than when he delivered his message through the mouth of a certain Martin Luther King, Jr. Were they wrong in what they were doing? came the question. "If we are wrong, the Constitution of the United States is wrong. If we are wrong, God Almighty is wrong. If we are wrong, Jesus of Nazareth was merely a Utopian dreamer who never came down to earth. If we are wrong, justice is a lie."[15] Events were to prove that Martin Luther King, Jr., was not wrong.

But that did not mean that social justice in Montgomery would be attained without a struggle. King and the leaders of the MIA were insulted, sworn at, and vilified in all manner and variety of ways. King himself was labeled as a communist, radical, subversive, demagogue, anarchist, and agitator, and was accused of misusing MIA funds and taking advantage of the gullibility of poor blacks, who, it was said, would follow anyone with a good speaking voice. And while the city council snubbed him and the other MIA leaders, important white clergymen encouraged them all to give up this boycott foolishness, recognize their own shortcomings, avoid social action, and bend their souls toward their ultimate destinations in the Kingdom of God. But most blacks felt, with justice, that Heaven could wait; they were more interested in working for the Kingdom of God in America, on this real earth, here and now. In fact, of all the treatment he received from white leaders, King remembered with some sadness and disappointment that he was particularly disgusted with the white clergymen. They of all people, he felt, should have recognized the blatant injustice of a Jim Crow society and spoken out against it. Eventually, however, even this would come about.

In the meantime he had to go through some harrowing experiences. The worst one undoubtedly occurred one evening when he was at church, and his duties were interrupted by a breathless, agonized report that his house had been bombed. King asked if his wife and child were all right. The answer was that no one was sure yet, but that they had better all go there to investigate. To his immense relief, everyone was fine, but the house had been reduced to a shambles. There was also an angry crowd about, and many people were armed and ready for swift retaliatory action. King spoke to them in these words:

> If you have weapons, take them home; if you do not have them, please do not seek to get them. We cannot solve this problem through retaliatory violence. We must meet violence with nonviolence. Remember the words of Jesus: 'he who lives by the sword will perish by the sword . . . ' We must love our white brothers no matter what they do to us. We must make them know that we love them.[16]

Meet hate with love, he admonished—this from the man whose house was just bombed, and whose wife and child had nearly been killed. Meet hate with love.

Fortunately, their love had some help from outside sources. It came in the form of a Supreme Court decision in November 1956, which affirmed a local court ruling that declared Alabama's state and local segregation laws unconstitutional. Blacks in Montgomery and elsewhere were ecstatic, but the decision prompted a Ku Klux Klan terror ride through a black section of the town. Worse than that, outbursts of violence took a particularly ugly form in January 1957, when four churches and two parsonages were bombed; fortunately, without any loss of life. The outraged reaction to this included strident calls for vengeance, but King cautioned people to hold their tempers and remain committed to the doctrine of nonviolence. He ended his own account of the events in Montgomery with the suggestion that "the Negro may be God's appeal to this age," an appeal that overcomes the violence of racist hatred with the power of brotherly love.[17] His allegiance to the redemptive qualities of nonviolence was unshakable.

By 1957 Martin Luther King had "arrived" as a major figure in the Civil Rights movement in the United States. In August of that year he and one hundred other black leaders formed the Southern Christian Leadership Conference (SCLC), the main purpose of which was to extend to the rest of the South the lessons and methods of the "Montgomery Way," and to help communities to work for peaceful compliance with the Supreme Court's various desegregation decisions. King's efforts and his enormously effective symbolic appeal quickly made the SCLC the most visible civil-rights organization in the country. And King himself became the inspirational leader for all the civil-rights groups, a fact vividly illustrated by the dramatic public sermon on American ideals he gave in the nation's capital in 1963—the speech entitled, "I Have a Dream." Also, while serving a sentence in jail in the same year, he provided one of the most eloquent appeals to the American conscience ever written—the "Letter from a Birmingham Jail." Interestingly, both of these events were essentially impromptu responses on his part to the situations at hand, but were quickly recognized for their symbolic value, and have retained their importance as statements of the American creed.

Birmingham, Washington, and the Civil Rights Act

The years between Montgomery and the passage of the Civil Rights Act were very active ones for King, filled with both triumphs and disappointments. Among the latter was a particularly frustrating attempt to apply the Montgomery Way to the task of ending segregation in Albany, Georgia. King did all the things that had worked so well before—spending several months delivering speeches, leading marches, inspiring demonstrations, violating one city ordinance after another, and getting arrested and thrown in jail. But it didn't work in Albany, largely because of the cleverness of town officials. The police there carefully arrested all those who violated the law, kindly directed them to the paddy wagons, scrupulously drove them to the courts, where they were charged and sentenced, and very professionally locked them up in jail when met with refusals to pay the fines involved. For people who wanted to create an incident to dramatize the evils of segregation, this "kill them with kindness" approach was exasperating. Countering the Montgomery Way with the "Albany Way" seemed to defuse the drive for equal rights, and could have constituted a danger if applied consistently in other cities.

Although discouraged by his failure in Albany, King was determined to continue the struggle. A decision was made to continue the civil-rights offensive by targeting Birmingham, Alabama as the focus of activities. Naturally, the SCLC wanted to achieve another significant victory for the Civil Rights movement, but more than that, King wanted to marshal the resources of the federal government on the movement's behalf. He was convinced that more than just favorable court decisions was necessary to keep the movement alive. Civil-rights workers needed the power of the other two branches of government, spurred to action by injustices so flagrant that they could not be ignored.

Few cities met these requirements better than Birmingham, Alabama. It was located in the Deep South, the least reconstructed part of the Old Confederacy, and was a virtual lion's den of segregation, often compared to infamous counterparts in South Africa. Politicians there won elections by "outniggering" one another. Everything was segregated, including books on white rabbits and black rabbits. Even "Negro music" was prohibited, as it was considered as one of the worst things on earth. The other prohibitions included communism, socialism, journalism, and "integrationism"—this last term was given an honorary suffix because of its particularly odious nature. And to combat this particularly odious thing was a particularly committed sheriff, who embodied all of the virtues and defects of the southern good ol' boy complex, a man most appropriately named Bull Connor. Few people were less likely than

Bull Connor to try the kill-'em-with-kindness approach, or anything that even hinted of grace, tact, or cleverness toward King and the SCLC. A more made-to-order situation for testing the methods of nonviolence could scarcely be conceived.

The campaign was kicked off in April 1963 with a declaration called the Birmingham Manifesto. With its proclamation that the goal was the complete integration of all facilities in the city, the Battle of Birmingham had begun. Much of what occurred thereafter went more or less according to script, largely because the Birmingham officials reacted in ways that played into the hands of the SCLC. Bull Connor's unimaginative but predictable "jail 'em all" approach was particularly conducive to generating the sort of widespread publicity needed to focus attention on the suffering of the city's blacks. And suffer they did. At one point Connor unleashed police dogs and fire hoses into marching legions of youngsters, causing widespread havoc and many injuries, all in front of the incredulous eyes of television cameramen. King felt that if this sight did not arouse widespread indignation around the country, nothing would. He was right; nearly everyone, from the President of the United States to the viewer of the evening news, reacted in the same way: it made them sick.

King himself had his own difficulties. Naturally, he was imprisoned—that was no surprise—but he had to endure some episodes of sheer terror, through which he survived only by faith and determination. For example, there were no funds left in the SCLC's treasury to release him or any others on bail, should they get thrown in jail, and King knew that before he got arrested. At one point he was put in solitary confinement in a dungeonlike atmosphere sufficient to chill the heartiest soul. Of course, he was made of stern stuff, feeling that somehow the Lord would deliver him. And so the Lord did, this time through the persons of Harry Belafonte and John F. Kennedy, who both personally intervened on his behalf, the one with money, the other with the prestige of his office. Before he was released, however, King wrote the famous "Letter from a Birmingham Jail."

King's letter was just one of the dramatic events that occurred during these harrowing days. There were many others, as well, which he covered with great feeling in his book-length treatment of the Birmingham campaign, *Why We Can't Wait*.[18] Although the most gripping episodes deal with the confrontations between police and demonstrators, King's account also summarizes, with more effectiveness than scores of solemn sociological treatments of the subject, what it meant to be black in America. Consider the following words:

> . . . when you have seen vicious mobs lynch your mothers and fathers at will and drown your sisters and brothers at whim; when you have seen

hate-filled policemen curse, kick and even kill your black brothers and sisters; when you see the vast majority of your twenty million Negro brothers smothering in an airtight cage of poverty in the midst of an affluent society; when you suddenly find your tongue twisted and your speech stammering as you seek to explain to your six-year-old daughter why she can't go to the public amusement park that has just been advertised on television . . . when you are harried by day and haunted by night by the fact that you are a Negro . . . when you are forever fighting a degenerating sense of "nobodyness"—then you will understand why we find it difficult to wait. There comes a time when the cup of endurance runs over, and men are no longer willing to be plunged into the abyss of despair.[19]

And that was why black America couldn't wait.

The efforts of the SCLC were rewarded when agreements were reached in May 1963 with city authorities on ways to desegregate public facilities and open up job opportunities for blacks. However, probably more important was the symbolic importance of the Birmingham campaign. It served to dramatize the existence of racial injustice in the country, in all its ugliness, and also instilled an enormous amount of confidence in local groups, who had been battling the establishment for years. In addition, it gave the Civil Rights movement as a whole a boost of assurance needed for continuing the struggle. In short, Birmingham imparted courage and hope for the future.

For all that, however, it was not the high point of the movement. Most observers point to an event that took place a few months later, in Washington, D.C. It was the nation's capital that provided the setting for the most important and probably the most quoted message that Martin Luther King ever gave—his speech called, "I Have a Dream." The symbolism of the surroundings was not lost on anyone. In front of a crowd of a quarter of a million people, with the Lincoln Memorial behind him, King spoke to his audience—and to the conscience of America. Interestingly, his speech was supposed to last fewer than ten minutes—about the time it took for a good southern preacher just to get warmed up(!)—and he wondered if he could say anything important in so little time. But if he took more time, wouldn't the crowd get impatient? Wouldn't the other speakers—there were several—be resentful? he asked. "Look, Martin," he was advised, ". . . you go and do what the Spirit say do."[20] In the end this is exactly what King did—what the Spirit say do—and the result was the most electrifying speech in a career that included a great many electrifying speeches.

The rest of the year did not go well, however—for the Civil Rights movement and for the nation as a whole. J. Edgar Hoover received permission to eavesdrop electronically on prominent civil-rights leaders, especially Martin Luther King, and Hoover continued to harass him until King was murdered, in 1968. Worse than that, 1963 was remembered by many as a year of death. In September a bomb exploded in a Baptist church, killing four young black girls. Other blacks were killed, as violence and mayhem swept through much of the South during the summer and early fall. The worst blow came when President Kennedy was gunned down in November. This was a setback for the entire country, but especially for the Civil Rights movement, as the young president was becoming increasingly convinced of the need for strong legislative action at the federal level. However, it is fair to say that Kennedy did not die in vain. The president's death contributed to circumstances that resulted, in the middle of the following year, in the passage of a bill that King and other civil-rights leaders had long sought.

The year 1964 was one of tremendous ups and downs for King. It certainly began well enough; he was named as *Time's* Man of the Year, confirming his status as the country's most noted civil-rights leader. And it ended splendidly, as he received one of the greatest honors of all, the Nobel Peace Prize. Almost exactly between these glorious awards was his presence at the signing of the first serious Civil Rights Act in over a century. A book of his sermons was published, along with his account of the events in Birmingham, *Why We Can't Wait*. But interspersed among these enormous accomplishments, which had such national as well as personal significance, were some experiences that brought him to utter despair. Probably the worst one was the SCLC's failure to desegregate the town of Augustine, Florida, one of the most viciously racist communities in America. Also, civil-rights workers attempting to register blacks in Mississippi were regularly beaten up, and during the summer the country's cities exploded in race riots. Thus, in spite of his tremendous personal accomplishments, King and many civil-rights leaders saw much to give them sorrow in 1964.

But 1965 was a new year, and King was determined to make the most of it. He and the SCLC staff thought that it was especially important to test the new civil-rights law, especially as President Johnson did not seem interested in pressing the matter any further. King also wanted to push for federal voting-rights legislation, particularly given the sordid and often tragic experiences of those who tried to register blacks in Mississippi. Beyond that, the SCLC, NAACP, and other groups envisioned a domestic Marshall Plan, one modeled after the spectacularly successful foreign-aid package after World War II that had rehabilitated the Western European economies. Certainly the economic conditions of black Americans were as pitiful as those of their European counterparts, they argued; furthermore, they were *Americans*. Couldn't the American government do at least as much for its own citizens as it did for those in foreign countries? In short, King and his associates looked to the coming year with a crowded agenda. The first item on the list was Selma, Alabama.

Selma, Memphis, and the Death of Martin Luther King, Jr.

The voting-rights march covered the sixty-mile distance from Selma to Montgomery, Alabama, during the last week of March 1965. It took place in the context of some of the worst racial violence the South had ever seen. Earlier in the year in Selma, reporters for the national media were treated to gripping spectacles of police abuse, involving the use of billy clubs, bullwhips, police dogs, tear gas, and fire hoses emitting streams powerful enough to shear the bark off trees—all against singing and marching demonstrators. The decision to march to the state capital was made by King largely in response to this, in efforts to draw wider attention to the need for a stronger voting-rights law. Accordingly, he called upon religious leaders across the nation to join the local marchers. And when one of them, a white clergyman, was bludgeoned to death by a band of local toughs, President Johnson was sufficiently stirred to act again on behalf of the Civil Rights movement. He put the Alabama National Guard under federal authority, ordered it to protect the passage along the way, and appeared before Congress to announce that he would call for a stronger voting-rights bill. The stage was finally set for the dramatic march, which actually began on Sunday, March 21. It would quickly assume legendary status in the history of the Civil Rights movement in America.

The march took three days, amidst numerous catcalls, tauntings, and name-calling along the way, including a brief buzzing by an aircraft representing the "confederate air force." It ended most impressively with a procession of some 25,000 people advancing upon the capitol building to present a list of grievances to the absent Governor Wallace. The event culminated with another dramatic speech by King, and moved many people to feel that this was indeed the finest hour of their lives, as well as one of the most significant times in the country's history. It also contributed greatly to the dramatic victory in August 1965 with the signing of the Voting Rights Act, which guaranteed strong federal support for the right to vote in those portions of the country where voting registration was meager. More than anything else, the Selma-to-Montgomery campaign worked to unleash the political power of American blacks in the southern states, and elsewhere in the nation as well.

But it was also a tough act to follow, and King knew it. In fact, the Voting Rights Act of 1965 was the last significant victory of the Civil Rights movement while Martin Luther King was alive. The last three years of his life were very frustrating ones for him, and for the movement as a whole. In 1966 he nearly worked himself to death in managing two desegregation campaigns that had meager results—one in the North, in Chicago, and the other in Mississippi. He also found himself opposed by many blacks who openly rejected his philosophy of nonviolence; some, like the Black Muslims, scorned not only his methods but also his goals, and called for the separation of blacks from American life. King no longer commanded the unquestioning respect that he had as the leader of the Civil Rights movement, and was often derisively referred to as "de Lawd" by numerous dissidents in the movement. Further, these professional disappointments were aggravated by bouts of severe depression, which afflicted him with increasing intensity after the death of President Kennedy. His natural good cheer often was a put-on; frequently King was extremely disconsolate, causing his closest aides and friends to worry about him. And to make all these matters very much worse, there was a war going on.

Although he was not the kind to brood over his disappointments, the combined effect of domestic and international events during the last years of King's life caused him to change some of his views. For years, he said, he had "labored with the idea of reforming the existing institutions of the society, a little change here, a little change there. Now I feel quite differently. I think you've got to have a reconstruction of the entire society, a revolution of values."[21] He felt that the "barest minimum" of reconstruction involved a guaranteed national income, the nationalization of some key industries, and a concerted attack on problems of poverty and injustice in America. This broadened outlook was clearly in evidence by January 1966, when he declared war against all the forces that maintained slums in America. This was a rather large and complicated goal, much more difficult than that of simply registering more voters in some particular locality, and considerably more provocative as well. Further, King had decided to declare war on more than just social and racial injustice in domestic affairs; after 1966 he increasingly focused his attention upon what he felt was America's imposition of injustice abroad as well: the war in Vietnam.

After taking off the first few months of 1967 to write his last major book, *Where Do We Go From Here?*, King devoted his energies to the burgeoning antiwar movement in the United States. In February he made a major speech on American involvement in Vietnam, and took positions that were fast becoming standard arguments against the war. It was unjust, he declared; it was an "American tragedy" brought on by fanatical anticommunism that was blind to the fervent desires of the Third World "colored" peoples to throw off the yoke of Western imperialism. In the following months he made his views even more clear, linking up the domestic Civil Rights movement with what he saw as the struggles in the vast arena of the Third World against the last vestiges of Western colonialism. He felt that the United States could never begin to tackle its serious domestic problems if national energies were constantly being wasted in a senseless and unjust war abroad. King concluded that American national priorities were tragically deranged, and that it was time to force government leaders to set them straight before a social and economic catastrophe of gargantuan proportions afflicted the United States.

To this end, in August 1967 he began serious planning for a national poor-people's march to take place in Washington during April of the following year. His aim was to instigate a massive campaign of civil disobedience in the nation's capital to protest American foreign and domestic policies, and to focus attention on the plight of the nation's poor. Nearly everybody advised against such an undertaking. King's friends and enemies—liberal, conservative, and radical alike—all denounced his initiatives, fearing the consequences they would bring; President Johnson even appealed to him personally to call the whole thing off. The FBI eagerly stepped up its surveillance, and assorted hate groups intensified their threats to kill him, his children, his wife, his parents, or anyone who had anything to do with him; some even put a "price" on his head as a "wanted" figure—"dead or alive," but preferably dead! Clearly, he was stepping into a political minefield, one filled with portentous social ramifications as well as personal dangers.

The pressures of working under such circumstances took their toll on him. He continued to be afflicted with spells of depression and anxiety, confessed that he thought about death frequently, and found it increasingly difficult to relax. He also seemed to his colleagues to be constantly on his guard whenever he spoke in public, always gazing over the audience with fitful, nervous glances. He would wonder: the lunatic with the gun, the assassin, the demented creature who wants with all his heart to blow my brains out—where is he? Will I make it through this speech without being shot? Will someone bound onto the stage and plunge a knife into my chest? (This had actually happened once.) Or will there be a bunch of them, a band of thugs, who will quickly assault me when I happen to turn in this or that direction to address the crowd? Will a rock smash into my skull? Will I feel a billy club against the back of my head? Or will it be something else? But what? And by whom? Where? And, God help me, when?

His concerns were allayed briefly by an interruption that appeared to be the perfect break from his arduous schedule of planning for the national campaign. King became intrigued by a situation in Memphis,

Tennessee, that developed out of a strike by a black union, and he decided to contribute his talents to local efforts against city authorities. The location, of course, was ideal, and the circumstances seemed to call for the sort of tactics that had been so successful in the earlier days of the movement. An added advantage was that Memphis could provide a useful training ground for the national campaign, something that was badly needed. So a brief stopover in Memphis looked like the right move to make.

As it turned out, of course, it was the wrong move, one that started out badly and ended tragically with King's death. A demonstration at the end of March 1968 quickly degenerated into one of the worst urban riots in the South. This event took its toll not only in property damage and injuries, but also inflicted further damage to the already tarnished image of King and the SCLC. Moreover, he was enjoined by a court order not to lead any more marches. Not all the news was bad, however. King was heartened by Lyndon Johnson's opting out of the presidential race, and this gave him hope that the peace forces and Civil Rights movement could elect a president more to their liking—Robert Kennedy, for instance, for whom King had great admiration. Also, his spirits were buoyed by the thunderous applause that greeted a speech he made shortly before the second march was supposed to occur. Finally, on April 4, he heard the good news that a judicial change of mind had lifted the injunction, allowing him now to march with official permission. Thus, his up-and-down fortunes in Memphis were on the rise as he prepared for his second march.

He never made it. In the early evening of that day, while waiting for his friends to ready themselves for a dinner engagement, King strolled out to the balcony of his motel room. As he gazed out from the balcony perch, James Earl Ray, an escaped convict, loaded his high-powered .30–06 rifle and sighted it on his target. Moments later those inside the motel room heard the violent charge of the rifle. Ralph Abernathy, King's longtime associate and closest friend, rushed out to see him lying flat on the balcony. The force of the bullet had hurled him violently backward, and he was clutching at his throat, his head and face limp in a pool of blood. He was rushed to the hospital amidst the tears and agonized screams of despair of those around him. There was never really any hope. At about seven o'clock Martin Luther King, Jr. was declared dead. And on April 9 in Atlanta, Georgia, the leader of the Civil Rights movement, the apostle of nonviolence, the conscience of the United States of America, and one of the most influential figures in American history, was laid to rest. The man who had preached love, peace, and brotherhood of all peoples had now reached his final destination, in eternal peace and fellowship with his God.

KING AS A MISSIONARY

The American Civil Religion

King's relationship to American liberalism is best seen in terms of his commitment to the ideals expressed in the Declaration of Independence, which itself was a concise summary of American political beliefs at the time of the Revolution. In fact, in his leadership role as a missionary, King's link to Declaration principles was probably clearer than either Madison's or Roosevelt's, because his consistent and direct appeal to that document was unambiguous and required no clever interpretations or complicated explanations. As we have seen, Madison's relationship to the tenets of liberalism was essentially that of a founder, in that he devised constitutional principles designed to embody Declaration ideals within a workable governmental frame. Franklin Roosevelt carried Madison's work further by drawing upon the two main streams of Constitutional interpretation that developed after the new government was in place, the Hamiltonian and Jeffersonian. Also, he exemplified characteristic elements of the American temperament in the political arena. But King's ideological leadership as a missionary was related directly to specific assertions in the Declaration, which he continued to restate with devastating clarity. His task was to point them out and exhort Americans to act upon beliefs they already held.

In doing so, he was following a tradition that began immediately after Jefferson's famous document was signed and submitted to the British Crown. That is, since 1776, American statesmen, poets, authors, and writers of all sorts have appealed to Declaration principles as the best summary of the American civil religion ever expressed. Just what is a civil religion? In brief, American civil religion consists of a set of values that, in the words of Sidney Mead, "stand in constant judgment over the passing shenanigans of the people, reminding them of the standards by which their current practices and those of their nation are ever being judged and found wanting."[22] Robert Bellah, another authority on the subject, refers to civil religion as "an understanding of the American experience in the light of ultimate and universal reality."[23] Will Herberg points to another aspect of civil religion by referring to it as "the American way of life."[24] These perspectives converge upon this important point: above the actions of the people stands the civil religion of the republic, and it is in fact this, and not the American Constitution, that stands as the real "higher law" in the American political system.

King, of course, was not the only one to understand this; and the Declaration, for all its eloquence, is certainly not the only statement of the American creed. American presidents, especially, have appealed to higher values, which stand above the political system, and to the special mission of the United States to abide by them. Consider, for instance, the words of George Washington in his first inaugural address: "The propitious smiles of Heaven can never be expected on a nation that disregards the eternal rules of order and right which Heaven itself has ordained . . . "[25] A more recent example is provided by John F. Kennedy, whose inaugural comments called for Americans to "go forth to lead the land we love, asking His Blessing and His help, but knowing that here on earth God's work must truly be our own."[26] About midpoint between these two men was a figure whom many regard as the greatest civil theologian in American history, Abraham Lincoln. "I shall be most happy indeed," he once said, "if I shall be a humble instrument in the hands of the Almighty, and of this, his almost chosen people."[27] All of these men were very aware of their role as chief spokesman for the ideals of the American republic.

The place of Abraham Lincoln is especially instructive in this regard because he did not belong to an established church. Actually, he had grave doubts about the specificity and exclusiveness of the established religions in the United States, often wondering if they did more harm than good. But no one expressed the sort of generalized conclusions derived from American Christianity about the political behavior of the American people better than he did. Indeed, Reinhold Niebuhr, the noted American theologian, once concluded that "Lincoln's religious convictions were superior in depth and purity to those, not only of the political leaders of his day, but of the religious leaders of the era."[28] Clearly, Lincoln's most famous utterances are fairly bursting with references to God, country, and the Almighty's purposes for the American nation, along with frequently sober judgments about the United States from the perspective of the American civil religion. Consider, for instance, the following statement, drawn from his first inaugural address, on the eve of the Civil War: "Intelligence, patriotism, Christianity, and a firm reliance on Him who has never yet forsaken this favored land are still competent to adjust in the best way all our present difficulty."[29] The fact that these words just as easily could have been spoken by Martin Luther King, Jr., illustrates powerfully the extraordinary continuity of the American political tradition. In fact, King expressed great admiration for all the great expounders of the American faith—Jefferson and Washington, for instance, and, of course, Abraham Lincoln.

More than that, King was determined to reawaken the American conscience to come face-to-face with its own ideals, with the fundamental purposes of the existence of the United States of America. In this task, too, he was squarely within the American tradition. Two hundred years earlier, it was Thomas Jefferson who addressed the British as though they were brothers—wayward ones, to be sure—but still operating in the same moral and conceptual universe as the colonists, and able to understand what they were saying, even if they vigorously disagreed. In like manner, Martin Luther King, Jr., assumed that he was dealing with people who understood his language in their hearts, who shared essentially the same view of America that he did, but who refused to acknowledge the just claims of blacks as brothers and sisters and rightful partners in the pursuit of the American dream. For this purpose he had to struggle to his death in performing the role of the missionary—a voice from God espousing the American creed for His "almost chosen people."

Missionary of the American Faith

Although the missionary role played by King was a familiar one in American history, it was not the only one he could have assumed. Martin Marty has pointed out that there are actually two. He describes them with a neatly turned phrase, saying that one of them "comforts the afflicted," while "the other afflicts the comfortable."[30] The first he refers to as the priestly mode, and the second as the prophetic. Each has had its prominent spokesmen throughout American history.

The priestly mode of civil religion is probably the most familiar one, and certainly the most popular. It embodies the concept of the United States as a "nation under God." In this formulation, God is viewed as a sort of "generic" Supreme Being, acceptable to all or most of the particular religions in the country, and giving "identity, meaning, and purpose to the nation and its citizens."[31] He has chosen America as His new Israel, His missionary people, whom He has endowed to carry out His special purposes. Or, to use expression more familiar to Puritan ears, He has selected the nation to be a City on a Hill, to shine like a beacon across the land, to show to the world the blessings that are bestowed upon a free and independent people who follow divine will. The chief priest of the civil religion conceived of in these terms is very often the president of the United States. It has been a role that most presidents have relished, probably because of its largely ceremonial and self-congratulatory nature, and also because being a "chief priest" usually involves few commitments that require hard decisions to be made.

This is not the only role available for American chief executives, or even necessarily the most important one. Martin Luther King used to criticize President Eisenhower bitterly for failing to live up to the creed to which he was publicly committed; after all, this was the president who added the phrase "under God" to the Pledge of Allegiance. Just what sort of president could possibly conceive of his country to be under God, when its government regularly deprived one-tenth of its citizens of the full "blessings of liberty"? Although this criticism was probably true enough, it also was a little hard on Eisenhower, as he simply was not that kind of civil theologian. He was more of a priest, and, like many presidents, attempted to comfort the afflicted. Moreover, it is certainly true, as Marty points out, that "presidents could not be presidents if their main function was to call God down in judgment on his nation's policies."[32] Indeed, it is likely that few could keep their jobs if they constantly made their constituents feel uncomfortable.

That role has been left to others, the prophets, whose main task is to remind us that the God of the nation is also a God of judgment. Of all the American presidents who fulfilled this role, Abraham Lincoln probably did it the best. He reminded his fellow citizens, both North and South, that although each side prayed to the same God, only one side would win, and, most importantly, it would be that side whose actions were in line with God's purposes. This is also precisely what Martin Luther King did: he pointed an accusing finger at his fellow Americans and warned them, in terms that were embarrassingly familiar, that they were not living up to demands of justice for the "Kingdom of God in America," to use H. Richard Niebuhr's phrase. He accused America of straying from the paths of justice, from the "solidly structured" home, whose "pillars were soundly grounded in the insights of our Judeo-Christian heritage."

What were these pillars? "All men are made in the image of God; all men are brothers; all men are created equal; every man is heir to a legacy of dignity and worth; every man has rights that are neither conferred by nor derived from the state, they are God-given. What a marvelous foundation for any home! What a glorious place to inhabit! But America strayed away . . . "[33] King exhorted America to come home, away from the "far country of racism," to form an "empire of justice" for all people. In short, like Lincoln a hundred years before him, King wanted America to recommit itself to God's purposes, as he saw them expressed in the American civil religion. And to this end he noted that, like the apostle Paul, "who carried the gospel of Jesus Christ to the far corners of the Greco-Roman world, so am I compelled to carry the gospel of freedom" to the far corners of America.[34] He was a prophet in his own land.

Indeed, his best addresses consist of phrases that have resounded with prophetic fervor throughout American history. Consider his speech, "I have a Dream," variants of which he used throughout his career, with tremendous effectiveness. He began it in beautifully Lincolnesque terms, with the statement: "Five score years ago, a great American, in whose symbolic shadow we stand, signed the Emancipation Proclamation . . . " and continued by outlining the failure of the nation to live up to the promise of the proclamation, as well as to the ideals of the Declaration of Independence. Lincoln and Jefferson—two of the very best—in the same speech. Perhaps the most impressive part came near the end, when he continued with renditions of "I have a Dream . . . " and asserted that his dream was "deeply rooted in the American dream. I have a dream that one day this nation will rise up and live out the true meaning of its creed: 'We hold these truths to be self-evident; that all men are created equal.' "[35] What American could disagree with that? Equality of all people who are free to pursue their own dreams—wasn't that what America had always been all about? Clearly, King's role as a prophet of the American creed had few, if any, peers in the American national experience.

The pillars of Martin Luther King's faith—the laws of God as he saw them embodied in the American civil religion—also led him vehemently to denounce the violent alternatives to his positions—particularly those espoused by black-power advocates. In his last full-length book, *Where Do We Go From Here?*, King combined some hardheaded political analysis with some rather idealistic speculation about the course of the Civil Rights movement in the United States. Some of his most convincing remarks dealt with black power, which had become rather attractive to younger blacks especially. Many blacks were inspired by the inflammatory treatment of oppressed minorities presented in Frantz Fanon's *Wretched of the Earth*, which combined a searing denunciation of Western colonialism with justification and praise for the "liberating" effects of violence. But King had no use for this type of analysis, and rejected it as a "nihilistic philosophy, one born out of the conviction that the Negro can't win." More than that, it was based upon the view that "American society is so hopelessly corrupt and enmeshed in evil that there is no possibility of salvation from within."[36] In short, black power, with its glorification of violence, its call for separation and emphasis upon black identity, was diametrically opposed to everything that Martin Luther King, Jr., had ever stood for. Although he occasionally became discouraged about the slow progress of the Civil Rights movement, King never wavered from his commitment to the principles of American civil religion. He resisted, to the end of his life, succumbing to the destructive impulses of black power, with its messages of hate and violence.

Indeed, the conclusion about the odyssey of Martin Luther King, Jr., in his native land must be that he truly was a great person, an extraordinary figure, unquestionably a courageous man, and undeniably the foremost prophet and the most eloquent missionary of the

American faith in the twentieth century. He represented all that was best in the American tradition, and called upon his fellow citizens to live up to the very highest ideals of the tradition that had given birth to the country. To that end he exhorted Americans to be, like their spiritual forefathers during the days of the Revolution, "those creative dissenters who will call our beloved nation to a higher destiny, to a new plateau of compassion, to a more noble expression of humaneness . . . Giving our ultimate allegiance to the empire of justice, we must be that colony of dissenters seeking to imbue our nation with the ideals of a higher and nobler order."[37] A better expression of his role as a missionary, and, indeed, of America's role as a missionary in the world, can scarcely be found.

ENDNOTES

[1] Quoted in Stephen B. Oates, *Let the Trumpet Sound: The Life of Martin Luther King* (New York: Harper & Row, 1984), p. 280.

[2] Quoted in David L. Lewis, *King: A Critical Biography* (New York: Praeger Publishers, 1970), p. 256.

[3] From Martin Luther King's "I Have a Dream" speech, in Francis L. Broderick and August Meier, eds., *Negro Protest Thought in the Twentieth Century* (New York: The Bobbs-Merrill Company, Inc., 1965), p. 403–405.

[4] Although the term *Negro* was widely used during the fifties and sixties (and still is), the term *black*, a more recent and conventional usage, will be employed here.

[5] Ralph Ellison, *Invisible Man* (New York: New American Library, 1947), p. 7.

[6] The following discussion of Jim Crow is derived from C. Vann Woodward's excellent study, *The Strange Career of Jim Crow* (New York: Oxford University Press, 1966).

[7] Any good constitutional casebook contains discussion of these and similar legal restrictions. See, for example, Martin Shapiro and Rocco J. Tresolini, *American Constitutional Law* (New York: Macmillan Publishing Co., 1975), pp. 515–81, esp. pp. 530–34, and *passim*, for relevant case materials.

[8] Quoted in Charles E. Silberman, *Crisis in Black and White* (New York: Random House, 1964), p. 132. The quote is from Gunnar Myrdal's noted study, *An American Dilemma: The Negro Problem and Modern Democracy* (New York: Harper & Row Publishers, 1944).

[9] Kenneth B. Clark, *Dark Ghetto: Dilemmas of Social Power* (New York: Harper & Row Publishers, 1965), p. 81.

[10] Quoted in Silberman, *Crisis*, p. 36.

[11] There were, of course, many cases dealing with the civil rights of blacks between 1896 and 1954, several of which had a direct bearing on the separate-but-equal doctrine. The Brown case is usually taken as the most significant, although several others, such as: *Sweatt* v. *Painter* (1950), clearly led up to it. See Shapiro and Tresolini, *American Constitutional Law*, pp. 515–81; and John R. Schmidhauser, *Constitutional Law in American Politics* (Monterey, Calif.: Brooks/Cole Publishing Company, 1984), pp. 443–52.

[12] There are a few biographies of Martin Luther King, Jr. The one consulted here is the recent work by Stephen B. Oates, *Let the Trumpet Sound*, and the following account is drawn largely from it. I also used David L. Lewis, *King: A Critical Biography*, published just two years after King's death, as well as the books written by King himself, indicated in the following notes. For a good, recent account of the Civil Rights movement as a whole,

see Harvard Sitkoff, *The Struggle for Black Equality: 1954–1980* (New York: Hill and Wang, 1981).

[13]Quoted in Oates, *Let the Trumpet Sound*, p. 68.

[14]Martin Luther King, Jr., *Stride Toward Freedom: The Montgomery Story* (New York: Harper & Row Publishers, 1958), p. 63. Most of the following summary is taken from this book.

[15]Quoted in Oates, *Let the Trumpet Sound*, p. 71.

[16]King, *Stride Toward Freedom*, p. 137.

[17]Ibid., p. 224.

[18]Martin Luther King, Jr. *Why We Can't Wait* (New York: Harper & Row Publishers, 1963).

[19]Ibid., pp. 83–84.

[20]Quoted in Oates, *Let the Trumpet Sound*, p. 256.

[21]Quoted in Lewis, *King*, p. 354.

[22]Sidney Mead, "The Nation with the Soul of a Church," in Russell E. Richey and Donald G. Jones, eds., *American Civil Religion* (New York: Harper & Row Publishers, 1974), p. 60.

[23]Robert Bellah, "Civil Religion in America," in Richey and Jones *Civil Religion*, p. 40.

[24]See the discussion, with documents, in the excellent text by George C. Bedell, Leo Sandon, Jr., and Charles T. Wellborn, *Religion in America* (New York: Macmillan Publishing Co., Inc., 1975). The reference to Herberg is on pp. 20–21.

[25]Cited in Bellah, "Civil Religion," p. 28.

[26]Ibid., p. 22.

[27]Quoted in Bedell, Sandon, and Wellborn, *Religion in America*, fn. 45, p. 50.

[28]Quoted in Bellah, "Civil Religion," p. 34.

[29]Richard Hofstadter, ed., *Great Issues in American History*, Vol. I (New York: Vintage Books, 1958), p. 396.

[30]Martin Marty, "Two Kinds of Civil Religion," in Richey and Jones, *Civil Religion*, pp. 139–57.

[31]Ibid., p. 145.

[32]Ibid., p. 147.

[33]Martin Luther King, Jr., *Where Do We Go From Here: Chaos or Community?* (New York: Harper & Row Publishers, 1967), pp. 98–99.

[34]King, *Why We Can't Wait*, p. 78.

[35]Quoted in Broderick and Meier, *Negro Protest Thought*, p. 403.

[36]King, *Where Do We Go From Here?* p. 51

[37]Ibid., pp. 157–58.

BASICS OF MARXIAN THOUGHT

6

INTRODUCTION

"The philosophers," noted Karl Marx in the eleventh of his famous Theses on Feuerbach, "have only interpreted the world, in various ways; the point, however, is to *change* it."[1] This is one of the most frequently cited comments that Marx ever made. Indeed, few doctrines have had as much influence upon the course of twentieth-century politics as Marxism. Marx's followers have changed the world in dramatic ways, all claiming to be inspired by his philosophy. But whether the changes wrought in Marx's name would have met his approval is, of course, an entirely different matter. More importantly, the extent to which modern Marxists can legitimately attribute their actions to the main tenets of Marxian philosophy is an issue that has received enormous attention by Marxists and non-Marxists alike. This is the subject of our concern.

Naturally, a philosophy that has generated as much controversy and commentary as Marxism cannot be dealt with in great detail in the present context. However, there are certain basic Marxist doctrines that must be understood in order to deal intelligently with twentieth-century political developments. These include Marx's views on history, economics, revolution, and the role of the proletariat—the working class—in modern societies. Probably the most famous and certainly the most widely read summary of his ideas is contained in the *Communist Manifesto,* which he coauthored with Friedrich Engels in 1848. But an even more concise presentation appeared in the opening lines of a document he wrote about a decade after manifesto, the preface to a work entitled, *A Contribution to the Critique of Political Economy.* Its significance as perhaps the best summary statement of the entire Marxian corpus necessitates our quoting it rather extensively:

> In the social production of their life, men enter into definite relations that are indispensable and independent of their will, relations of production which correspond to the definite state of development of their material productive forces. The sum total of these relations of production constitutes the economic structure of society, the real foundation, on which rises a legal and political superstructure and to which correspond definite forms of social consciousness. The mode of production of material life conditions the social, political, and intellectual life in general. It is not the consciousness of men that determines their being, but, on the contrary, their social being that determines their consciousness.[2]

As many of the basic elements of Marxian thought are contained in this paragraph, it is important to outline what Marx had in mind.

THE ECONOMIC FOUNDATION OF SOCIETY

Probably Marx's most significant contribution to modern social analysis was his conviction that throughout history, economic behavior, the manner in which societies produce goods and services—the "mode of production," in his terms—was the foundation of all other social relationships. In other words, the ways that people make a living, whom they work for and the relationships they have with their employers, what they produce and the tools they use on the job, their working hours, the details and routines of the laboring process, and so forth, determine everything else that they do. In short, economics is fundamental and everything else is derivative. Thus, politics and government, art, religion, family relationships, moral convictions, the legal and administrative organization of society, the ways people think, act, spend their free time (if they have any), and how they approach the world—"forms of social consciousness" generally—are of secondary importance. Such things are part of what Marx called the "superstructure" of society that arises from its economic foundation. Marx's position on these matters is usually referred to as *historical materialism*.

Marx's development of historical materialism led him to some other important conclusions about human nature, society, and the state. For instance, Marx insisted that the superstructure of any society cannot be understood, and in fact really should not be taken seriously, apart from the mode of production employed in that society. He felt strongly that it is a foolish waste of time to consider all the assorted shenanigans of kings and princes, for instance, or the petty morals, rituals, religious observances, and habits of thought generally of various social classes throughout history, without looking *first* at the economic structures that are the foundations of such things. To take seriously what people thought and said about themselves throughout history was, in his terms, to "share the illusion of the epoch." Marx had withering contempt for those who failed to see this point, and believed, with justice, that he was the first to grasp fully the actual basis of all forms of behavior of society.

INDIVIDUAL, NATION, AND STATE

Naturally, Marx's position about the economic foundation of society had particular relevance to analyses of the modern national state. It is fair to say that Marx had little use for either the nation or the state. For instance, answering the charge that communists intended "to abolish countries and nationality" generally, he replied simply that "the working men have no country."[3] Indeed, when the proletariat takes state power from the bourgeoisie in the advanced industrialized countries, he expected that international exploitation and "the hostility of one nation to another will come to an end."[4] His views about the state were similar. He saw it as part of the superstructure, of course, but more than that, the state was a means of oppressing the rest of society by the ruling class. In the hands of the bourgeoisie it was "but a committee for managing the common affairs of the whole bourgeoisie."[5] Its character would not change under proletarian control—it would still be an instrument of oppression—but this time the oppressed would be the former oppressors, and their disappearance from society would also make the state unnecessary. The state would eventually, in Engels's famous phrase, "wither away." As this prediction was derived from Marx's understanding of social class and history, it is important to deal with that next.

SOCIAL CLASS AND HISTORY

Explaining the economic foundations of society was important to Marx in other ways as well, especially as it informed his understanding of social class. What is a social class? Marx defined it in two ways, objective and subjective. According to the first method, a social class is understood by reference to its members' relationship to the means of production. In short, one either owns the means of production or works for those who do. However, the second way of defining social class is in some respects even more important, especially as it became a vital issue affecting revolutionary tactics of the Russian Bolsheviks under Lenin's leadership, and party policy during Mao Zedong's rule in China. Members of the proletariat must become aware of themselves as a separate class before they can act collectively as an historical force. In short, the proletariat must develop what Marx referred to as *class consciousness,* which he assumed was the product of many year's of social and economic development. His studies of history convinced him that the "objective conditions" of a society's economic stage guaranteed the eventual development of class consciousness for the oppressed members of society.

The importance of Marx's emphasis upon the role of social class throughout history can hardly be understated. Indeed, he began the first section of the *Communist Manifesto* with some of the most famous lines he ever wrote: "The history of all hitherto existing society is the history of class struggles."[6] Marx continued with a brief reference to historical examples of class antagonisms throughout history—"freeman and slave, patrician and plebian, lord and serf, guildmaster and journeymen, in a word, oppressor and oppressed."[7] This bifurcation of society continued to the present age, which was divided between the bourgeoisie—the capitalist owners of the means of production—and the proletariat, those who sold their labor to the capitalists for wages. But the relationship of oppressor to oppressed remained. More than that, in Marx's view, during his day it was worse than ever before.

The reason for this had to do with what Marx regarded as the "distinctive feature" of his epoch, the *simplification* of class relations under capitalist rule: He felt that the activities of the bourgeoisie forced everyone into either one class or the other—there was practically nothing "left over" or in between the two antagonistic classes. Now, Marx was careful to give great credit to the bourgeoisie for vastly expanding the efficiency and productivity of the modern industrial mode of production and spreading its methods of economic organization throughout the world. But he also felt these activities would result in the ultimate demise of capitalists as a class and their replacement by the proletariat. The reason was that capitalist methods eventually become self-defeating. The obsessive drive for profits results in the increasing exploitation and misery of the workers who supply their labor to the vast enterprises built up by the capitalists. When the proletariat finally becomes conscious of itself as a separate class, it will revolt, overthrow the capitalists, and establish itself as the sole ruler of a new, classless society. Marx expected this to happen in his lifetime, and in the most industrially advanced countries. He also believed that revolution would be the midwife for the new age to come.

REVOLUTION AND STAGES OF DEVELOPMENT

Probably no matter raised more practical concerns among the followers of Marx than the tactics that they should employ against the bourgeoisie as capitalism developed and became more "ripe" for overthrowing. Unfortunately for them, Marx spent an enormous amount of time explaining the workings and describing the faults of capitalism, and on occasion spoke about communist party tactics in a democratic capitalist society. In the *Communist Manifesto,* he also provided a list of actions that the proletariat should undertake after assuming power, some of which ended up being remarkably prescient. But the specifics of the stages of historical development that should *follow* the revolution received comparatively little attention on his part. Moreover, when he did talk about these matters, he sometimes used phrases that required much more detailed explanations than he gave, such as "revolutionary dictatorship of the proletariat" or the "revolution in permanence." As a result, his postrevolutionary historical projections provided little practical guidance for communists who had to cope with the harsh realities of wielding power. As we shall see in the case of the Soviet Union especially, decisions were often made on the basis of existing political necessities more than upon anything Marx had to say.

Marx did, however, address himself to the postrevolutionary scenario sufficiently to enable observers to make at least some comparisons between what he envisioned and what actually happened, in the Soviet Union, China, and in other places. In his *Critique of the Gotha Program,* for instance, Marx stated that "between capitalist and communist society lies the period of the revolutionary transformation of the one into the other. There corresponds to this also a political transition period in which the state can be nothing but *the revolutionary dictatorship of the proletariat*" [his emphasis].[8] In other words, the sequence outlined seems to be: capitalism—proletarian revolution—dictatorship of the proletariat—communism. The third item in this series refers to the first "phase" of communism, to use Marx's term, and is marked by various "defects," by virtue of having "just emerged after prolonged birth pangs from capitalist society."[9] Among these defects is included, for example, the application of the old bourgeois notion of "right," which results in an unequal distribution of the social product. This too, of course, would pass when society enters into the "higher phase of communist society," which he described in ringing terms as embodying the principle, "From each according to his ability, to each according to his needs!"[10] In short, Marx felt that societies still had to go through some conflicts before achieving the ultimate, historical goal of full communism.

Since Marx associated these conflicts with the "first phase" of communism, his views on the dictatorship of the proletariat acquired great importance in the twentieth century, especially after the successful Marxist revolution in the Russian Empire. Probably the best source for his views about this stage of historical development is contained in his commentary on the events of the revolution in France in 1870–1871, in the wake of the French defeat in the Franco-Prussian war. A revolutionary workers' organization known as the Paris Commune was formed, and it ruled that city for a few months before being crushed by loyalist troops. Engels's introduction to Marx's review was very clear about the meaning of the dictatorship of the proletariat: ". . . do you want to know what this dictatorship looks like? Look at the Paris Commune. That was the Dictatorship of the Proletariat."[11] And as Thomas Sowell has pointed out, those who are accustomed to the lurid meanings associated with this term in the twentieth century are in for a real shock. Marx systematically praised what he saw as the Commune's endorsement of universal suffrage, freedom of speech, thought, and religious beliefs, and renunciation of militarism.[12] It is true that Marx did not shy away from using violence, but he also felt that proletarians were more likely victims than the bourgeoisie—which in fact was the case when the Commune was destroyed. But the important point is that Marx did not associate the dictatorship of the proletariat with wanton terror and bloodshed—precisely those things identified with it in this century. He seemed to look upon it more as a transitional stage to the arrival of full communism.

COMMUNISM AND THE END OF ALIENATED LABOR

Full communism is the "second phase," then. Unfortunately, Marx devoted even less time outlining the details of life in that advanced stage of history than he did to the dictatorship of the proletariat. The sorts of things he had in mind were usually embodied in a few cryptic references scattered here and there throughout his writings, such as the comment already cited. He did, however, provide some glimpses of life in a fully developed communist society, and these have intrigued scholars of Marxism almost as much as his critique of capitalism, perhaps because they are so few in number. Probably the best source of his ideas is some documents he wrote in the 1840s, which were not actually published until nearly a century later, and then given the title, *Economic and Philosophic Manuscripts of 1844*. These fascinating writings contain some of the best materials Marx ever wrote on what actually was the center-piece of his concerns about labor in a capitalist society—the fact that it involved workers in the process of *alienated labor*. It is no exaggeration to suggest that Marx found alienated labor to be the most repulsive aspect of life under capitalism, a system, in his view, in which it developed in the most vicious ways.

What is alienated labor? In Marx's words: "the fact that labour is *external* to the worker, i.e., it does not belong to his essential being; that in his work, therefore he does not affirm himself but denies himself, does not feel content but unhappy, does not develop freely his physical and mental energy but mortifies his body and ruins his mind." [his emphasis].[13] In other words, alienation occurred in the *act* of producing, according to Marx, and it resulted in persons who became dehumanized in the process; that is, reduced to the status of things or mere animals who carried out no more than life's basest functions—eating, sleeping, procreating, and so forth. Marx couldn't stomach forced labor of any sort, and he devoted most of his professional life after 1850 to describing its horrors under the capitalist mode of production, especially in his masterpiece, *Das Kapital*. Throughout his analysis he always assumed that work should be a noble, uplifting, and expressive projection of individuals' human nature. He condemned the division of labor in capitalist economies on the same basis, in that it forced people to focus their energies upon only one sphere of activity, to the exclusion of everything else.[14] It was his conviction that free, spontaneous creativity was the essence of human behavior, as well as the highest expression of what it meant to be a human being. But capitalism denied this to people, or restricted it to a very few. And although Marx concluded that as an economic system it was inevitably doomed by the forces of history, there is no question that he also passed a moral judgment on capitalism as a most oppressive and exploitative system of economic and social organization.

Marx's position on alienated labor is cited here for the purpose of drawing attention later to some stark contrasts with the developments in the Soviet Union and the People's Republic of China. Although Marx may have presented an ideal impossible for any society to attain, it is still true that the various socioeconomic systems in the world, communist ones included, may be evaluated at least to a degree in terms of the extent to which they have developed in the ways Marx expected or hoped for. One of the grand ironies of history is that it has been in those societies claiming to be Marxist, and not capitalist, that forced labor has been the most extensively and brutally practiced. But this is only to say that many other *isms* besides the parent Marxism developed in the wake of his views about the course of history in capitalist and socialist societies. And two of these, Stalinism and Maoism, are our concern in the chapters that follow.

ENDNOTES

[1] "Theses on Feuerbach," in Robert C. Tucker, ed., *The Marx-Engels Reader*, 2nd ed. (New York: W. W. Norton & Company, Inc., 1978), p. 145.

[2] "Marx on the History of His Opinions," in Tucker, *Marx-Engels Reader*, p. 4.

[3] *Manifesto of the Communist Party*, in Tucker, *Marx-Engels Reader*, p. 488.

[4] Ibid., p. 489.

[5] Ibid., p. 475.

[6] Ibid., p. 473.

[7] Ibid., pp. 473–474.

[8] *Critique of the Gotha Program*, in Tucker, *Marx-Engels Reader*, p. 538.

[9] Ibid., p. 531.

[10] Ibid.

[11] *The Civil War in France*, in Tucker, *Marx-Engels Reader*, p. 629.

[12] See especially Thomas Sowell, *Marxism: Philosophy and Economics* (New York: William Morrow and Company, 1985), pp. 143–64.

[13] *Economic and Philosophic Manuscripts of 1844*, in Tucker, *Marx-Engels Reader*, p. 74.

[14] There is a passage in *The German Ideology* in which Marx comments that it should be possible for a person to do one thing in the morning, another in the afternoon, and something else during the evening, without being forced to have any of the activities undertaken be a dominating influence in one's life. See *The German Ideology* in Tucker, *Marx-Engels Reader*, p. 160.

JOSEPH STALIN

Founder of the First Marxist State

7

Stalin . . . is an unprincipled intriguer who subordinates everything to the preservation of his power. He changes his theories according to whom he needs to get rid of at any given moment. *Nikolai Bukharin*[1]

You know what Stalin is? Hitler plus Asia. *A former prisoner in one of Stalin's labor camps*[2]

. . . if he had a pistol in his hands and all his opponent had was a knife, he would only attack when his opponent was sleeping. *Adolph Hitler*[3]

I have never met a man more candid, fair, and honest. *H. G. Wells*[4]

Stalin is the outstanding mediocrity in the Party. *Leon Trotsky*[5]

Comrade Stalin, having become secretary-general, has boundless power concentrated in his hands, and I am not sure whether he will always be capable of using that power with sufficient caution. *Lenin*[6]

There is a dogmatic Marxism and a creative Marxism. I stand on the ground of the latter. *Joseph Stalin*[7]

INTRODUCTION

In December 1929 the fiftieth birthday of Joseph Stalin was celebrated as one of *the* social events of the century in the Soviet Union, rivaled only, perhaps, by the commemorations of the Bolshevik victory in the Russian Civil War or the ritualistic observances of Lenin's stature as the greatest revolutionary in history. But the adulation normally reserved for the departed leader of the Bolsheviks was exceeded enormously by effusive expressions of hero worship accorded to the new, undisputed leader of the Soviet Empire. Stalin was honored as Lenin's most faithful disciple, companion, and adviser; he was touted as a great revolutionary in his own right; he was celebrated as a courageous war hero, a dauntless builder of socialism, and, indeed, one of the most brilliant theorists of Marxist doctrine who had ever lived. These gushy accolades were accompanied by an extravagant display of pomp and ceremony in a public festival, very carefully orchestrated by party members who knew well how to please their boss. A cult of personality had been born.

Most of this was undeserved, in 1929, at least. In fact, those who staged the whole thing realized that the record did not really justify such an elaborate celebration, although Stalin's self-image required it. Up to that time Stalin had been understood among most party members as a sort of veteran, hardworking journeyman who applied himself with great vigor to all those tasks associated with the various careers he undertook during his long life in politics. He was, in short, the Bolshevik version of a practical politician—ruthless, but effective. It was true that some party notables—Leon Trotsky, for instance—had been discredited under Stalin's rule, and no longer exercised much influence. But this was part of the rough-and-tumble politics to which every Bolshevik had become accustomed. Now that the leadership struggle was over, the expectation was that the future would be an approximate extension of the past, that the general secretary would continue to function as the practical politician, guiding the fortunes of the party and the country on a sensible course of economic and social development.

Stalin, however, had other ideas. Indeed, he intended to carry the leadership legacy of Lenin to far greater heights than any of those around him dared to imagine in 1929. Thus the praises heaped upon him at his birthday celebration figured more as a projection into the future than as an accurate reflection upon the past. In short, Stalin fully intended to add himself to the hagiology of the notable Russian leadership of the past, in the mold of such figures as Ivan the Terrible and Peter the Great, as well as Lenin the Revolutionary. Stalin planned to become a great founder of the new Soviet state.

Strictly speaking, of course, Stalin derived his ideological inspiration from Marx and Lenin, two giants in the revolutionary tradition. Karl Marx was the principle figure, in that he supplied most of the sacred texts that explained the meaning of political existence, in terms that could be universally applied. Lenin's principle contribution was to show how Marxian theory could be applied to acquire power in a backward, preindustrialized country, such as Russia in the early decades of the twentieth century. But it was Stalin who actually built the world's first socialist state in the names of Marx and Lenin, and it was Stalin who imparted his own name to the model of politics that has since become known throughout the world: Stalinism. Further, the policies pursued in Soviet Russia under his leadership have been reenacted throughout the world in those countries that have been influenced by the Soviet experience. In short, Marx supplied most of the philosophical concepts, Lenin inspired the dream and imparted a legend, but it was Stalin who informed the reality of modern, Soviet-style communism. No founder has had such lasting, contemporary influence in international and domestic affairs as Joseph Stalin.

What happened to Stalin the pragmatist, Stalin the party functionary, Stalin the practical politician? Actually, Stalin's career as a practical politician, at least in domestic affairs, was over by the late twenties, a point that was recognized by his more perceptive opponents. However, as we shall see, he remained rather pragmatic in the conduct of foreign affairs. In fact, although Western leaders often saw it otherwise, the foreign policy of Stalin was in several respects marked by very prudential considerations; it was his *domestic* policy that can be described as adventuristic. In short, there are actually two aspects of Stalin's career that bear analysis: Stalin as the practical, Bolshevik politician, which explains his rise to power as well as his conduct of foreign affairs after 1930; and Stalin the founder, the role he assumed in creating the modern Soviet state. Our main purpose here, of course, is to demonstrate Stalin's leadership role as a founder, and most of our attention will be focused on this. But it is important to note that he was more than that. Indeed, it was Stalin acting as the practical politician exercising his very considerable abilities in power politics, both in domestic and foreign policy areas, that enabled him to undertake the far greater role of a founder.

STALIN AND PRACTICAL POLITICS

The Rise of Stalin

Stalin was different from other Bolshevik leaders in at least two respects.[8] First, while many had middle- or even upper-class backgrounds, Stalin's origins were distinctly more humble. He was born in

1879 in a small town in Georgia, a province in the old Russian Empire. His parents were poor, his father died in a drunken brawl when Iosif (his Georgian name) was only eleven, and he attended local schools until the turn of the century, at which point he decided to become a professional revolutionary.[9] This often involved some harrowing escapades involving the authorities, numerous brushes with death, as well as frequent arrests, incarcerations, and sentences of exile to the farthest reaches of the empire. From all of these he managed to escape except one, his last exile, which was also the longest and most distant from central Russia. In fact, Stalin probably would have languished in exile indefinitely had it not been for the fall of the Russian monarchy in early 1917, which resulted in the release of all political prisoners. He quickly left for European Russia, where he could join other Bolshevik leaders in continuing the revolution against the provisional government, which had temporarily replaced the fallen monarchy.

Here Stalin was at a disadvantage. The reason for this derived from the second thing that made him different from other leaders in the party: his lack of speaking abilities and his relatively meager academic credentials. The party led by Lenin was distinguished by claiming the allegiance of many first-rate intellects, several brilliant orators, and numerous flamboyant personalities—of which Lenin himself was the leading example. But Stalin had none of those qualities. He spoke in a weak voice, with a thick Georgian accent, and seemed rather more like a member of the rank-and-file than an important party leader. In fact, as Isaac Deutscher put it in his biography of Stalin, "what was striking in the General Secretary [the party post Stalin assumed in the early twenties] was that there was nothing striking about him."[10] Leon Trotsky, the brilliant organizer of the Red Army and probably the brightest light in the party next to Lenin, held Stalin in even less esteem, branding him as the "personification of the bureaucracy."[11] And he wondered: how could such a plodding, colorless individual rise to a position of authority in the party, much less constitute a threat to anyone?

Actually, he was among the first to find out. True, Stalin's role in the events from 1917 to 1922 was not very great, and he did not distinguish himself as a very effective military commander. In fact, in terms of glory, glamour, and credit, the Russian Revolution and the civil war that followed it were basically a show run by Lenin and Trotsky. By contrast, Stalin's strong suit centered upon mastering the intricacies of administrative politics in the Bolshevik Party. By the end of the civil war, he was a member of every important decision-making office in the party, save one—the Secretariat. And this coordinating body did not really become important until his appointment to it in April 1922; then he made it important. The Secretariat became a board of directors for assorted Central Committee departments, which collectively managed party affairs. In addition to this, Stalin was a member of the Politburo (political bureau), the executive committee of the Central Committee, which set the broad outlines of party policy. He also belonged to the Organizational Bureau, which was in charge of personnel appointments. This was an absolutely crucial post, as the Bolshevik method of determining administrative appointments, which nominally looked like "election" from lower to higher, actually proceeded in the opposite direction: the higher body determined the composition of the lower bodies by approving all candidates for their positions. Thus the flow of authority in the party went from top to the bottom. And Stalin was on the top.[12]

This was an excellent place to be, given the important controversies he was engaged in throughout the twenties, and with opponents who could be deadly. In addition to Lenin, who had assumed nearly legendary status while he was still alive, these included Trotsky, the Red Army Commander; Nicolai Bukharin, a respected economist, whose ideas inspired those of both Lenin and Stalin; Lev Kamenev, a respected crony of Lenin's; and Grigori Zinoviev, a prime figure in the Communist International and head of the all-important Petrograd Soviet. Lenin was the first to go, although not by Stalin's machinations. In fact, Lenin attempted to make some last-ditch arrangements to have Stalin removed from his post as general secretary, but he died before he could act upon them. His "last testament" contained devastating criticisms of the general secretary, suggesting that his "rudeness" and vicious temperament disqualified him from continuing in his post. Stalin's personality defects might be an "insignificant trifle," Lenin concluded, but still could assume "decisive significance" from the standpoint of maintaining good relations among party members.[13]

He was absolutely correct. The meaning of this "insignificant trifle" became fatally clear to Stalin's opponents during the struggles over party leadership following Lenin's death. Stalin was able to engineer Trotsky's downfall by 1926. Kamenev and Zinoviev also fell into disrepute shortly afterward, and Bukharin lasted until 1929. In each case, Stalin's meticulous attention to the minutiae of administrative politics over the years had enabled him to outmaneuver his opponents and literally have them voted out of power in the party hierarchy. He had honeycombed the party apparatus with men of his own choosing, and neither the fervid eloquence of Trotsky nor the weighty erudition of Bukharin made any difference in generating political support. Joseph Stalin, the earthy Georgian, that "strange man who evidently preferred bureaucratic drudgery to politics," had bested them all.[14]

However, it would be a mistake to assume that the only reason why Stalin prevailed over his opponents was because of his superior organizational skills. There is an important sense in which he was simply closer to the rank and file in the party, a great many of whom by the mid-twenties had had their fill of dazzling revolutionary orators. Among the many examples that illustrate this point is his behavior at Lenin's funeral ceremony, in 1924. Stalin may have been an unprincipled intriguer, to use Bukharin's phrase, but he was still able to strike many responsive chords among the ordinary people with his simple, heartfelt, and emotional expression of grief and gratitude. He never had to fake his humble origins or simulate crude mannerisms to generate sympathetic responses at such occasions. In that sense he was genuine.

Other party leaders were at a disadvantage in this respect. In fact, there was always something a bit ridiculous about the high-powered cerebral outpourings of the overintellectualized Bolshevik leaders when they reflected upon their native land, and upon the basic habits, needs, and longings of its people. But Stalin had no such awkwardness about these things at all. Indeed, as James Billington has pointed out, Stalin was much closer to understanding the basic needs and psychology of the peasants, the "crude mentality of the average Russian," to put it bluntly, than most of his serious competitors in the party, who, as we have noted, tended to have middle- or upper-class backgrounds.[15] Stalin's background was as rough as his manners, but it often served him well.

This was also the case in foreign affairs, although Stalin's success came mostly by reacting prudently to events rather than by trying to manipulate them from behind the scenes. In that respect, foreign policy was inherently more frustrating to Stalin than domestic policy, because it was not possible for him to exercise the sort of control that he enjoyed within Soviet boundaries, especially after 1930. Thus, he was forced by circumstances to exercise caution toward other countries as a Soviet leader. In short, Stalin's role as the practical politician continued in the area of foreign policy at the same time that it had practically ended in domestic politics.

Stalin and Soviet Foreign Policy

Stalin's approach to foreign relations during the twenties was in keeping with Lenin's policy, which was to promote revolution everywhere.[16] To this end, Lenin established the Comintern (Communist International) in 1919. Its threatening and rather self-serving proclamations were a source of constant exasperation for foreign leaders. The policy of the Comintern was to declare the Soviet Union as the leader of proletarians all over the world, and to state that Communist parties in all countries owed their first allegiance to Moscow. This made good ideological sense to the Russian Bolsheviks and certainly seemed consistent with what Marx had said about working people having no country. But it also put communists everywhere—except in the USSR, of course—in the position of being subversive. And since Russia was the only country where a Marxist revolution had actually succeeded, the Soviet government had in effect declared a sort of nonshooting war against every state that contained significant numbers of communists.

Stalin was too pragmatic to allow this policy to continue when it conflicted with the interests of the Soviet state, which it did, dramatically, after Hitler's rise to power after 1933. In fact, he was perfectly willing to put matters of ideology aside if the governments of Europe could just come to some common agreement about how to deal with the Third Reich. The fact that they could not, actually reflected ideological inflexibility on the part of British and French leaders, who could not quite bring themselves to deal seriously with the Soviet government. But Stalin had no qualms at all about whom he would deal with or on what terms. Accordingly, he instructed Comintern members in 1935 to stop trying to make life miserable for their capitalist hosts, and to try instead to encourage building a common front against the fascists. Unfortunately for the Soviets, continued Western capitulation to Hitler during the thirties convinced Stalin that their main interest was simply to turn the German dictator eastward, against Soviet Russia. The Munich Agreement in September 1938, to which the Soviet Union was not a party, reinforced this feeling. During the year that followed, Stalin continued to try dealing with the West to counter Hitler's moves against Poland. But when that failed he simply concluded that they were all cowards and frauds, and that it was far better for him to deal with Hitler directly. At least the führer and he shared a common contempt for the Western democracies.

The main result of Stalin's pragmatism, Western temporizing, and Hitler's eagerness to secure his eastern flank was the Nazi-Soviet Pact, which was signed on August 23, 1939. By its terms the parties agreed to be neutral in the event that one of them became involved in a war with another country. In actuality it guarded Hitler's flank and assured him that the Russians would not complicate matters while Germany dealt with Poland and the West, in that order. By a secret protocol Stalin and Hitler agreed to divide Poland after the capitulation of the Polish government. When the war actually broke out, in September 1939, Stalin quickly claimed this booty, as well as the Baltic states—Estonia, Latvia, and Lithuania. In late November, after failing by previous diplomatic methods to extract some territorial concessions from Finland, the Soviet Union attacked that country and engaged the Finns in a short conflict that proved to be a major embarrassment for the Red Army. Peace was concluded in March 1940. Also in the spring of that year, Stalin ordered the occupation of Bessarabia, a strategically important province in northern Rumania. Finally, in 1941 he concluded a five-year treaty of neutrality with Japan, a move designed to secure the long eastern border of the Soviet Union.

In making these arrangements Stalin showed himself to be a very deft practitioner of international power politics, and surprisingly free of ideological bias. The point of all these moves, of course, was to avoid a direct and potentially fatal confrontation with Germany, at least until the Soviet Union had built up its strength sufficiently to counter the frightfully developing might of the Third Reich. Stalin probably felt that a conflict with the Nazis would occur sooner or later, but for him it was always better later than sooner. Of course, for Hitler it was the other way around: better sooner than later. Stalin's miscalculations in this respect very nearly cost him and the Soviet Union the war. According to an estimate cited by A. J. P. Taylor, he was warned no less than seventy-six times in the early months of 1941 about the impending German attack.[17] The problem was that many of these warnings came from Western sources, which Stalin distrusted for what he considered the most excellent reason: that the West was not interested in the safety or welfare of the Soviet Union. Under normal circumstances he was probably right, but the war brought upon them all a terrible foe that could only be defeated by a concerted effort.

Once that was accomplished, Stalin reverted to his earlier strategy of doing his utmost to safeguard the security and interests of the Soviet Union. The problem was that from the standpoint of the Western democracies, this strategy looked distinctly aggressive. In fact, the postwar situation from a Western perspective appeared as threatening as the prewar years. In the half decade after the war, all of Eastern Europe had fallen under Soviet domination, Communist insurgents were threatening Greece and Turkey, and Soviet troops remained in Northern Iran (until 1946).[18] The Cominform, a noisy, updated version of the Comintern, was established in 1947. The following year saw the closing of access routes for Western powers across the Soviet Zone in Eastern Germany, forcing the United States to keep West Berlin supplied by air. China fell, or was "lost," to communist forces in 1949; in 1950 a Soviet-supplied army in North Korea invaded the South. In short, Stalin seemed intent on practicing power politics in a most heavy-handed fashion. To Western eyes, he quickly began to look like a Russian version of Hitler—like "Hitler plus Asia." The swastiska had been replaced by the hammer and sickle.[19] In short, the Cold War had begun.

Which side was more responsible for actually starting it has been the subject of intense scholarly debate ever since. But from the Soviet point of view, Stalin acted like any responsible, practical statesman concerned about protecting the national interest of his country. Consider, for instance, the things he did *not* do. He did not take over Finland, which was formerly a part of the Russian empire and more recently an ally of Germany. Surely he would have been justified in doing that! But the Finns could be left alone so long as they stayed neutral and didn't cause any trouble. He did not punish Tito's defection from the communist fold in 1948 by an invasion of Yugoslavia; nor did he become more belligerent when the Greek communists were crushed with the help of American aid under the Truman Doctrine. But then, he was just being true to his word. After all, didn't he and Prime Minister Churchill agree during the war that Greece was to be 90 percent within the Western sphere of influence, while Yugoslavia should be split on a 50-50 basis? And unlike the treacherous Western leaders, whose constant promising and postponement of a second front during the war so greatly increased Russian casualties, he kept his word.[20]

But what about the rest of Eastern Europe? The Americans and British were always whining about that area, as if it had any real strategic value to them. It is true that the Soviets now controlled the region, but they did not in fact end up with a very good deal. Much of it was as nearly devastated as European Russia; only Poland had suffered more. They got back some provinces from Poland that were populated by Byelorussians and Ukrainians. They also held on to Bessarabia, but that had been part of the old empire anyway. True, there was that occupation zone in Germany. But the Soviet hunk of Germany was the least industrialized part of the Reich. The Western allies ended up with the three-quarters of Germany that had most of the population and industrial base—by far the richest and most useful part. And they hadn't really borne the brunt of the war!

Moreover, there were other areas that Soviet troops just stayed away from, such as China. Aside from providing some weapons—many of them from captured Japanese stocks—and a few advisers, Stalin offered minimal help to the Chinese Communist Party during its long conflict with the imperialists. Certainly he showed little enthusiasm for their victory. In fact, Mao Zedong was snubbed by the Soviet leader at least as often as he was helped by him. Soviet troops had occupied Iran, but left in 1946. In fact, the Red Army did not move into any country that it had not already occupied by the end of World War II. There was the Korean incursion, true; but that did not involve Soviet troops, only Soviet equipment. Besides, the southern half of the peninsula had been fairly definitely declared outside the American defense perimeter by the

American secretary of state. Allowing the North Koreans to unite the country looked like a fast, inexpensive way to pick up some additional territory. How was Stalin to know that the Americans would act the way they did, by engineering a United Nations military intervention? So it could be argued that Stalin was fooled by that one. But then, he was dealing with irrational and unpredictable Americans, and not with Russians.[21]

Naturally, the details surrounding American-Soviet relations during this most crucial period are beyond the scope of our present inquiry. The main argument here is that Stalin's actions can be understood by reference to his earlier behavior as a practical politician, determined to secure the borders of the Soviet state. In this he must be judged as successful, certainly if measured by prewar standards. Of course, no leader of a country that has been invaded as often as Russia ever feels totally secure. But none had done as well as Stalin in practicing the sort of power politics necessary to reduce the possibility of an invasion in the future. In fact, in all of his activities as a practical politician, none had more impact upon the flow of events in the world than his conduct of foreign affairs.

While all this was going on, of course, Stalin assumed the role of a founder in the domestic realm. This also had international significance, as Stalin's activities as a founder had a tremendous impact in all those countries that came under the influence of the Soviet state. To these countries the term *Stalinism* has a vivid and distinct meaning, as it does for the citizens of the Soviet Union. It is to the work of the general secretary in "founding" Stalinism that we now turn.

THE RULE OF STALIN

Preparatory Stage: The Policy Debates of the Twenties

Stalin's radical policy initiatives of the thirties were made against the background of the intense debates during the earlier decade about the course of economic development the country should take. Indeed, the political opposition he faced during this time was all defined in terms of this issue. But in economic terms the positions all derived at least in part from Lenin's wartime leadership and policy recommendations before he died. Two of these, War Communism and the New Economic Policy (NEP), were directly the result of his efforts. A third one developed more or less as a reaction to the NEP, and was identified with Trotsky's so-called "left opposition" in the early twenties. The "right opposition" of the late twenties, represented in the political debates by

Nicolai Bukharin, was actually a defense of the NEP, which had been the official policy since 1921. Bukharin was also the intellectual godfather to Stalin's celebrated "Socialism in One Country" idea, but the economic and political content of this was not made clear until the general secretary unleashed his "Revolution From Above" in the thirties.[22] Each of these positions now needs some brief explanation.

War Communism. Although this policy has some theoretical justification, War Communism was mostly a product of the desperate improvisations made by the Bolsheviks during the Russian Civil War.[23] It involved terror, mass coercion, forcible grain requisitions from the peasants, and a totally centralized decision-making process designed to exact unquestioned obedience. In short, it was a brutal command system oriented to the accomplishment of a single goal—winning the war. It worked, of course, but it also left an intensely militarized party in charge of a devastated and totally exhausted country. Lenin realized that continuation of this policy would probably have threatened the legitimacy of Bolshevik rule. There were some uprisings against this rule in Russia, and one of them, which involved a revolt of sailors and workers at the naval base at Kronstadt, deeply unnerved the Bolshevik leadership. Thus, by the time of the Tenth Party Congress, in March 1921, there was considerable commitment to the idea that some change was in order.

These immediate circumstances were complicated by a much deeper problem, of which every Bolshevik was aware. Russia was "underdeveloped," to use a modern term. With the country's defeat in World War I at the hands of the Germans, and the agonies of the civil war fresh in mind, many leading party members felt that the country should be built up quickly, simply for its own protection. Clearly, Soviet Russia would get little help from abroad, especially if there was continued chaos and brutality at home. What everyone needed was domestic order and tranquility—some peace and quiet, in other words—and Lenin proposed measures at the conference that were designed to get precisely those things. Together they were known as the New Economic Policy.

The New Economic Policy. Lenin's proposals repudiated War Communism as something that had been forced upon the party by the circumstances, and embraced a "reformist," or gradualist, approach to economic development. Instead of engaging in some crash economic-development program that could lead to unknown traumas, the party should prepare itself for the "temporary expedient" of tolerating policies that stretched into the indefinite future the realization of socialism's goals. He recommended that the forcible grain requisitions from the peasants be dropped in favor of a fixed tax in kind, allowing them to reap some profits from the production beyond what they had to supply to the state. Large investment in heavy industry would of course be encouraged, but in an economic system that allowed generally for "petty-bourgeois," capitalist exchanges. "The important thing," Lenin insisted, "is to give the peasants an economic incentive" to produce, something nobody had enjoyed in Russia for some time. All this was to give the Soviet Union some breathing space to develop more or less as it would by "natural" economic forces.[24]

The NEP was the official policy of the regime for about eight years. Stalin defended it against Trotsky's "left opposition" in the early twenties, and Bukharin formed a "right opposition" to defend it against Stalin in 1928. In the former case, Trotsky's views were interpreted by Stalin as more radical than those of Lenin—hence the label. That is, Trotsky wanted the Soviet state to push aggressively for more vigorous economic growth than what many felt the NEP would allow, at least as they understood Lenin's explanations of it. It appeared especially that he called for "squeezing" the peasants—taxing them heavily to gain capital for industrial investment—more than Lenin would have felt was prudent. To this Stalin reacted—and Bukharin supported him—with pious shock, arguing that the master's policies for steady, nondisruptive development should not be subverted. Of course, by the end of the twenties that is exactly what Stalin himself intended to do, and to an extreme that Trotsky never contemplated. This also put Bukharin on the conservative side as a member of the right opposition to the changed policies of Comrade Stalin. In fact, he ended up as the last real defender of the NEP.

Socialism in One Country.   Although this doctrine clearly had economic content, its principle orientation and main appeal were political in nature. In fact, in purely economic terms it was naïve, at least as Stalin understood it in the middle twenties. It is best seen against Trotsky's more realistic internationalist understanding of economics, which gave due credit to the importance of world economic patterns. Indeed, Trotsky did not take issue with Socialism in One Country "so much as socialism in a separate country which pretended to develop in disregard for the world economy in general."[25] Trotsky also maintained that the building of socialism in Russia could not in the final analysis be completed without complementary socialist revolutions throughout the world. This seemed to make sense in terms of Marx's views on the subject, but it was poor politics. Against it Stalin argued that socialism was possible in one country, regardless of what else was going on anywhere in the world, and the best way to demonstrate this simply was to do it. This was his "creative Marxism," his special contribution to Marxist theory and practice.

More than that, Socialism in One Country constituted a Soviet declaration of independence, a bold assertion of the "autonomy of the Russian national revolutionary process," in the words of Robert C. Tucker.[26] It was also conceptually simple, capable of wide interpretation, and easily adapted to the uses of propaganda and sloganizing. Further, it allowed Stalin to claim some intellectual distinctiveness in the party as a leader with a program; in short, the doctrine gave him identity. But for millions of Russians, these things meant little when seen against the enormous sacrifices that he would wring from them in its name.

The Stalin Revolution

The War Against the Nation.[27]   Stalin's role in the founding of the modern Soviet state began in the context of his last political fight of the twenties, against the right opposition that formed around Nicolai Bukharin. In 1929 the regime experienced its third straight season of failing to meet the grain requirements for the cities, and Stalin's patience with the Russian peasants as well as with the NEP had run out. In a speech given at the end of that year he stated simply that the work of "socialist construction" could not be based upon two different modes—large-scale, concentrated industry in the cities, and "the most scattered and backward, small-commodity peasant farming" in the countryside.[28] This made no economic sense to him at all, especially as the NEP policy didn't seem to be working anymore. This was enough reason for the state to get tough with the peasants.

However, probably the most compelling reason for dealing harshly with the farmers had little to do with economics. Stalin was among many in the party leadership who never really accepted Lenin's policy of accommodation with the Russian peasantry. It made sense enough in the short run, perhaps, when the country was recovering from war and revolution; but the short run, in his view, was coming to an end. And continuing to gloss over the matter somehow by referring to the peasants as "rural proletarians," as Lenin did, fooled nobody. Indeed, it is only a slight exaggeration to suggest that to a Marxist mentality the Russian peasantry constituted the theoretical equivalent of the Neanderthal man. Peasants were an embarrassing legacy of a backward past. Trying to "cooperate" with them as a "temporary expedient" never sounded very Bolshevik anyway, and certainly did not sound convincing now. Moreover, Stalin saw the matter in terms of a test of wills—his versus that of the peasants. It was a power struggle involving a class that in the final analysis had to be overcome if the Soviet Union were to advance. This he accomplished, although at enormous costs in human suffering and in agricultural production.

The first type of cost—the toll in lives and suffering—can barely be appreciated by simple reference to the numbers of people involved. In all, some five to six million—no one knows for sure—perished during the collectivization drives over the course of the first Five Year Plan. Many millions more than that were killed by the famine that blighted the Ukraine during the early thirties. The process of collectivization itself was brutal nearly beyond description. People were beaten, murdered, or starved to death as local party members, aided by toughs from the cities, bludgeoned the peasantry into the collective farms. The Kulaks, a category of supposedly better-off farmers, were stripped of their possessions, deported, resettled, sent to work camps, or simply shot. Many "dekulaked" themselves by getting rid of their goods and fleeing to the cities. Others committed suicide. In terms of scale, the collectivization campaign in the Soviet Union was rivaled in human suffering only by the holocaust during World War II.[29]

The economic costs were high as well. In fact, production in agricultural commodities actually declined from the precollectivization years. In some areas this decline was staggering. The livestock population (horses, cattle, pigs, and sheep) was cut roughly in half between 1928 and 1934.[30] Horses were supposed to be replaced by tractors, but tractor production, like every other category of industrial output, fell far below official projections. In some cases, the goals of the first Five Year Plan were not met until the 1960s.[31]

Regardless of official projections, however, industrial development proceeded at an impressive rate. The most conservative Western estimates of Soviet economic growth from 1928 to 1940 show a doubling of output. This is obviously not as spectacular as Soviet claims for this period, which put the increase on the order of five or six times the 1928 figures, but it was still an impressive achievement.[32] Certainly it came at the right time, allowing the Soviets to meet and then greatly surpass the military output of the Nazi Germany in the forties. And after the war the Soviet Union was able to stand face-to-face with the United States, the foremost power in the world. That is, in an incredibly short amount of time, Stalin founded the modern Soviet Union, a country that was able to compete with the first-class industrial and military powers of the day.

While all this was going on, Stalin also set himself the task of founding a new party in his image. The result was The Terror of the thirties, a series of horrible and bloody purges that penetrated to every corner of Soviet political and economic life. How the country managed to survive this, forced collectivization and industrialization, and the ravages of World War II as well, remains truly one of the marvels of the twentieth century.

The Purges.   Purges of party members were not a new experience for the regime when Stalin came to power. Under Lenin's leadership the party had relied upon the purge as a device to weed out incompetence and "opportunism," or simply to get rid of inconvenient or obnoxious opposition. Although this did not always mean "liquidating" the "undesirable elements," it often did, particularly during the civil war. But Stalin's purges were different from anything that had gone on before, in terms of their magnitude and intensity. And they occurred during a period when the traumas of forced collectivization and industrialization were being experienced by the population. Against this horrific background, the purges amounted not only to additional "excesses" on the part of the regime, but to what Alec Nove has termed "excessive excesses."[33] No nation had ever undergone such an experience.

The process started out slowly and gained in intensity, reaching a dramatic climax with the so-called "show trials" of 1936–1938. The first trials involved some engineers who were accused of "wrecking"; that is, of the deliberate destruction of equipment and materials. Actually the charges were based upon actions that usually involved simple industrial accidents. But Stalin did not believe in "accidents"; he charged the victims with deliberate attempts to destroy the development of socialism in the USSR. In fact, in the following years, tens of thousands of individuals were accused of all sorts of nefarious deeds and of belonging to numerous conspiratorial groups, usually directed by enemies from abroad, especially Trotsky. And they permeated every niche and cranny of the Soviet Union: the economy, the military, and—horror of horrors—the party itself. Based upon the extraordinary nature of the charges against the accused, one would have to conclude that the Soviet Union contained a vast network of spies and saboteurs. But thanks to Comrade Stalin and the efficiency of his secret police, they were all rooted out, forced to confess their sins in public trials, and sentenced to death or to the infamous labor camps.[34]

What is one supposed to make of all this? Certainly the charges against the accused bore no relationship to reality. In fact, their enormous fraudulence numbs the imagination. In his excellent study of the Communist Party of the Soviet Union, Leonard Schapiro commented about one of the more complicated alleged plots by saying that if the charges about the conspiracy were actually true, "it is beyond the bounds of all probability that such a conspiracy should have failed."[35] Yet the Soviet press regularly belched out frenzied reports of utterly fantastic plots devised by a multiplicity of devilish groups, all insanely intent upon wrecking the USSR, and all found out in the end. "It is not easy," a saying went, "to fool Comrade Stalin." In a macabre sense that was true. Stalin, the instigator of these enormities, was fooled by none of them. On the contrary, he knew exactly what was going on and why.

So what was he trying to accomplish? The explanations of this vary. Nicolai Bukharin, who observed the purges from the sidelines until his own life was claimed by them, suggested that Stalin was aware of strong undercurrents of discontent in the party against his rule, and wanted to put an end to them as completely as he could.[36] Further, Stalin felt that the "Old Bolsheviks" of Lenin's party had served their purpose, and he wanted to get rid of them and remake the party in his own image. Lenin had led them all in an atmosphere of sterling speeches, highly charged intellectual exchanges among party members, policy criticisms and defenses, elaborate debates over the direction the party should take, *ad nauseum*. Stalin simply felt that those days were over. He was never very comfortable with those things anyway, and at all events he needed builders, and not critics. After all, states do not talk or debate their way into greatness; they must struggle to achieve it. And Stalin regarded himself as the undisputed leader of that struggle.

Indeed, understanding the conception that Stalin had of himself as a leader, as a self-conscious founder of something new, is of crucial importance in comprehending his actions. Again, the absorbing research of Robert C. Tucker is indispensable. He suggests that Stalin saw himself in the tradition of some of Russia's most famous—or infamous— czars, especially Ivan the Terrible. Indeed, his own secret police was "quite consciously" modeled after the *oprichnina*, the terrible instrument of oppression used by the ruthless monarch to keep the Russian nobility in line.[37] When Stalin created its modern counterpart for use against the Communist Party, he deliberately attempted to go further than Ivan did, by using it to destroy what he felt were his *potential* enemies—of which number there was no limit—as well as those who were a more immediate threat. And when he was finished, the party and the country it ruled under his leadership were totally "cleansed" of any opposition. Both were completely the creative results of his founding.

Indeed, by the end of the thirties Stalin had founded a social and economic order that responded with merciless speed to his every whim. By the end of the forties this was true for a large portion of Europe as well. Throughout the Soviet realm all roads led to Stalin; everything he ordered was carried out, and nothing that he forbade was allowed. Perhaps the best way to express the incredible extent of his domination over the land he ruled is to recite some biblical verses that probably were familiar to the former theology student from Tiflis: "I am the vine, you are the branches. He who abides in me, and I in him, he it is that bears fruit, for apart from me you can do nothing. If a man does not abide in me, he is cast forth as a branch and withers; and the branches are gathered, thrown into the fire and burned."[38]

Stalin's Last Years

The war years provided a temporary respite from the rigid social controls exercised by the Soviet government over the population. From summer 1941 to the spring of 1945 the nation was engaged in the task of dealing with the terrors inflicted by a foreign enemy instead of those carried out by its own government. After the war most expected a return to "normalcy," in the sense of a more relaxed social and economic environment. But Stalin's intentions were entirely different. Soon after the war he made the dismal announcement that there was to be a return to prewar policies. That meant more Five Year Plans, continued collectivization of agriculture, renewed emphasis upon heavy industry, redoubled efforts to build the military—now that the United States was the main enemy—and so forth. In short, nothing had changed; life was to go on the way it had before—which was miserable.[39]

For everyone except him that is. But who would have the incredible courage to tell the general secretary that he ruled over a devastated land, with "an enslaved, miserable, poverty-stricken population, with an economy best described as state-monopoly capitalism, and with a political system of a fuhrerist, police-state variety,"[40] when he was convinced that Soviet civilization was distinctly "superior to any non-Soviet social order"?[41] Who was to tell Stalin that the Western capitalist countries were not on the verge of collapse, that capitalism showed signs of increasing vitality, and that war and revolution were not just around the corner for most places in the world?[42] And who could possibly be bold enough to suggest to the aging autocrat that most party members lived in a state of muted but continuous terror, and that under his leadership the Soviet Union had become the most fraudulent enterprise on the face of the earth? In short, who was to tell Comrade Stalin the truth?

This was a life-threatening proposition at best. It was rendered infinitely more complicated by the realization on the part of everybody around him that the general secretary was becoming increasingly bizarre in his old age. For instance, he wiled away time by dabbling in assorted academic areas, including philology. He issued "authoritative" pronouncements about human motivation that made many Soviet psychologists silently grind their teeth.[43] Worst of all, in the fall of 1952, he "uncovered" yet another "terrorist" plot. It supposedly involved a group of doctors who were under instructions from abroad to engage in assorted "wrecking activities" by killing off some key personnel in high places. The similarities between the accusations in this affair and the prewar orchestrations of the secret police were all too apparent, and gave rise to very real terrors that another purge was on the way. Fortunately, to the immense relief of everyone involved, in the following spring Stalin died before the matter could be seriously pursued.[44]

After the party suffered some brief tremors, it began the unfamiliar task of selecting a new leader for the Soviet Union. The country was considerably different from the one bequeathed to his comrades by Lenin. In fact, neither the party nor the country that it ruled were very Leninist anymore, except in name, perhaps, and in theory. It was a Soviet Union that had been transformed from a semifeudal backwater of European affairs into a world-shaking superpower. It was a Soviet Union that had been founded by Joseph Stalin.

STALIN THE FOUNDER

There is a bittersweet story told in the Soviet Union that concerns Lenin's revival after fifty years in the grave. A miracle drug is invented that restores life to the dead. Felix Dzerzhinski, a Polish communist who was one of Lenin's close associates, is given the drug first. After he comes back to life he resolves to see Lenin right away, assuming that the great Bolshevik has also been revived. When he comes to Lenin's grave, however, he discovers that the glass-enclosed case that contained Lenin's body is empty. A note is left behind in Lenin's handwriting, and it reads as follows: "To whom it may concern. I have looked around and am leaving at once for Zurich [the place of his last exile before the revolution]. We must begin all over again."[45]

Is this how Lenin would have reacted to Stalinist Russia? Would he have felt that all of his previous work had come to naught, or had been twisted by his now equally famous successor? Of course, the story must be discounted at least somewhat, given the fact that Lenin himself was guilty of all the practices that Stalin carried out on a much grander scale. And Lenin has never been officially denounced by Soviet leaders, as Stalin was by Nikita Krushchev in his famous 1956 speech. But even many Western scholars have tended to look upon Lenin and Stalin in different terms, especially in the relationships that each had to Marx.[46] Thus, in order to appreciate more fully Stalin's role as a founder, these relationships must briefly be explored. As we shall see, both of them contributed significantly to the Marxist legacy, chiefly by applying what each felt were Marxist principles to situations that Marx never seriously considered. But our main task is to show that Stalin's interpretations and applications of both Marx's and Lenin's ideas made him one of the twentieth century's most influential founders. In short, we shall argue the simple proposition that Stalin founded Stalinism.

Lenin and Marx

Lenin's contributions to Marxism had lasting significance for twentieth-century politics. For our present considerations, one of the most important centered upon his development of some of Marx's often vague notions about the relationship between the communist party and the proletariat. Lenin insisted that the proletarian revolution could only be led by a disciplined corps of professional revolutionaries. He and his fellow Bolsheviks noted with despair that the working class did not automatically develop "class consciousness," as Marx had said it would. On the contrary, on its own the proletariat attained no more than a "trade union consciousness," which only resulted in demands for such relatively unimportant things as improved working conditions, higher wages, and the like. Consequently, it had to be led by a dedicated group of committed Marxists—the vanguard of the proletariat—whose purpose it was to ensure that workers would carry out their historical, revolutionary mission. It seemed that the success of the Bolsheviks in Russia provided stunning evidence for the validity of his views.

However, potentially the most beneficial contribution of Lenin was also the most short-lived. He demonstrated how Marxist theory could be applied to the conditions of a less-industrialized society, such as that of czarist Russia, by advocating a pattern of economic development that, for a short time, anyway, was quite successful. As we have seen, the pattern of development outlined by Marx saw socialism as emerging naturally from a fully developed capitalist system after a proletarian revolution. Following that was the first phase of communism, associated with the rule of the revolutionary dictatorship of the proletariat, and then full communism. Marx believed that the first phase of communism would involve ridding society of the last vestiges of its capitalist past. But when Lenin applied this scheme to Russia he assigned a different mission to the phase involving the dictatorship of the proletariat, making its principal task the construction of the necessary economic preconditions for the development of a mature, industrialized society. Historically, this crucial time period corresponds to the New Economic Policy enacted in 1921, and consisted of "building socialism." That is, the economic base of the country had to be built up to the point that put it in the correct relationship to the "superstructure" that Marx said theoretically derived from it. In short, Lenin's "creative Marxism" consisted of making a revolution *before* conditions actually warranted it from the standpoint of economic development, and then letting the society progress economically in the direction Marx had said it should, but under the rule of the Communist Party, not capitalists.

Lenin's successors were left with more ordinary tasks of administering "Leninist Marxism" in the Soviet Union. Not everyone was pleased with that role, and in the end Stalin rejected it completely. By the end of the twenties he saw the NEP as simply a temporary affair, and not a serious expression of Lenin's real views. This is also how Trotsky and the left opposition argued in the early twenties, although in place of the NEP they did not anticipate anything like what Stalin ended up doing. With these considerations in mind, one can only ponder how much different things might have been if Lenin had lived to the age of seventy-three instead of Stalin.

Stalin and Marx

In many respects Stalin derived his Marxism from Lenin's teachings, but by the end of the twenties he was in the position to apply his own definitive understanding of Marx's philosophy. Certainly many of his policies seemed to follow Marx's prescriptions, as outlined in the *Communist Manifesto,* for instance. In that document Marx provided a list of ten measures that would be undertaken by the proletariat after the revolution, most of which involved a vast expansion of state power over the economy. These included the abolition of private property and rights of inheritance, centralization of credit and means of communication in the hands of the state, and the extension of industrial methods of production to agriculture, to cite just a few. Stalin did all these things, and carried them to extremes that many Bolsheviks felt unwise. Marx also felt it would take some time to expunge old bourgeois methods of commercial exchange to the point that capitalists would simply disappear as a class. Stalin took this a step further by labeling whole categories of people as members of "dying classes," such as the kulaks, for example, and then having them murdered or sent to labor camps by the million. But the fact that he explained all of his policies in Marxist terminology left the impression that the Soviet state was not actually doing anything that could not somehow be traced to what Marx had said.

However, there were at least three ways in which Stalin's activities as a founder constituted major departures from Marxist theory. The first involved his complete reversal of the relationship between politics and economics as originally understood by Marx. That is, while Marx asserted the primacy of economics over politics, for Stalin it was the other way around—he used his position of unrivaled political leadership to dictate economic policy. Indeed, few were more determined than he in using the raw political power of the state to achieve economic ends, as demonstrated dramatically by his forced industrialization and collectivization policies. In carrying these out he actually stood both Marx and Lenin on their heads. While Marx said that the state was part of the "superstructure" of society, and Lenin seemed inclined to have the communist-ruled state allow economic development to take place without extensive intervention (the NEP), Stalin brutally used the state-as-superstructure to build its own economic foundation. In short, Stalin as founder applied Marx's teachings and Lenin's interpretations in a highly selective fashion to build the world's first socialist state.

The second significant departure involved Stalin's fervid embrace of nationalism, which was illustrated by both his foreign and domestic policies. Marx, of course, insisted that workingpeople had no country, and foresaw that proletarian revolutions in the advanced industrial countries would occur at approximately the same time. Indeed, after World War I his followers fully expected the revolution in Russia to be followed by complementary revolutions in other European countries. Since this didn't happen, the Bolsheviks were forced to consolidate their position in the Soviet Union, largely for the sake of ensuring their own survival. But the theoretical projections of Marx lingered in the minds of many among the Russian Marxists, particularly Leon Trotsky—and he suffered for it. Stalin did not object to Marxist internationalism in principle, but being of an eminently practical bent, he felt that working people had to show their allegiances to *someplace,* and that place happened to be the Soviet Union. And as we have seen, nearly everything Stalin did in terms of Soviet foreign policy was subordinated to the interests of the Soviet state.

Thus, when it was in the interests of the Soviet Union to encourage subversive activities in foreign countries by Comintern officials, Stalin approved it. But when it became more important to curry the support of Western countries for a united front against Hitler, he just as quickly put ideology aside and ordered a change in policy. Further, Stalin's domestic policies clearly had international significance, as he was convinced that a weakened Soviet Union would not be able to survive in a second confrontation with Germany. In fact, few policies were more fiercely directed to serving the interests of the Soviet state than Stalin's Socialism in One Country. Clearly, the socialist motherland had to be strong in order to fend off its powerful capitalist enemies, whom Stalin was convinced were out to destroy the Soviet Union. This also had the effect of putting the Soviet government in a state of war against many of its own citizens, a situation that Lenin had wanted to avoid, if possible. His early death, combined with Stalin's victories over his competitors in the twenties, made such a war inevitable.

The third way that Stalin departed from Marx centers upon the extraordinary brutality of the means he used to build the world's first Marxist socialist state. Marx, as we have seen, was most repulsed by what he felt were the inhuman working conditions forced upon workers by capitalists. Forced labor, in short, was repugnant to him. But in the country fashioned in his name by Stalin, forced labor became the norm. Indeed, the forced labor camps of Stalin's Russia were simply a more extreme version of the labor situation that existed generally in the Soviet Union. It is only a slight exaggeration to say that under Stalin's rule practically everybody worked under conditions of duress; the only truly free, creative, and spontaneous worker in the entire Soviet empire was Stalin himself. Perhaps, then, had Marx also been administered the life-giving potion, he would have joined Lenin in Zurich, or at least spent more of his time in London criticizing *socialist* regimes, and not capitalist ones, for brutally exploiting workers.

Stalin and Lenin

Stalin's departures from Leninism were similar in some respects to his departures from Marx. First, he emphatically embraced Russian nationalism, something that would have been particularly galling to Lenin. While Lenin hoped to adopt a policy of enlightened tolerance toward all the national minorities in the old empire, Stalin vigorously attempted to Russify everything in the Soviet Union. National history was rewritten to emphasize the importance of Russian contributions; Russian inventors and explorers were singled out for praise; Russian language was made mandatory; Russian accomplishments were glorified in every conceivable way, especially in the Great Patriotic War (World War II). Indeed, the Russian outlook on the world was so completely adopted by Stalin that some observers feel his nationality had more influence upon his behavior than his Marxist ideology.[47] In short, Stalin wanted to be not only a great Marxist leader, but especially a great *Russian* leader, one who "out-Ivaned" Ivan the Terrible, a leader whose name would ring forever in the annals of Russian history. It is safe to say that he succeeded.

He succeeded also in distinguishing himself from Lenin by the manner in which he carried out certain Leninist policies and the way he operated as the leader of the Communist Party. Nothing illustrates the first matter more vividly than Stalin's practice of War Communism. The principal difference between the two leaders lies not in the methods used—which were brutal beyond description in any case—but in terms of scale and duration. What to Lenin was a temporary expedient that could in some respects be justified as his application of the Marxian

dictatorship of the proletariat became for Stalin the defining characteristic of his regime. The relentless war against the peasants, the ceaseless
emphasis upon heavy industrial development at the expense of everything else, and the terror of the thirties were all policies carried out by
a person who was simply indifferent to the sorts of constraints that
would have influenced a man like Lenin. As noted by Boris Souvarine,
"what had existed under Lenin was carried by Stalin to such extremes
that its very nature changed."[48] In short, War Communism is not just a
particular aspect of Stalinism; it *is* Stalinism.

Stalin's leadership of the Communist Party was also distinctive, and
contrasts sharply with that of Lenin. The party of Lenin consisted of a
combination of hardheaded and sometimes brutal tactics married to a
sincere belief in the superiority of communism as a philosophy that
genuinely provided the key to historical and social truth. Lenin was
deservedly considered the first among equals by his cohorts. But even
when he got his way, he had to go through an exhausting process of
persuasion for the rest of the party to go along with him. The "other
equals" still had to be cajoled, pleaded with, manipulated, threatened, or
whatever, but their views and wishes had to be respected and taken into
consideration. The point is that they were also members of a ruling
structure that centered upon the primacy of a group of leaders as the
decision-making agency for the entire society.

All that was changed by Stalin. The effect of the purges during the
thirties was to transform completely the relationship between the leader
and the party. If Lenin could be considered as first among equals, Stalin,
by the end of the thirties, had no equals. He never had to "persuade"
anyone. He was temperamentally—and perhaps intellectually—unsuited
to that task but at all events, by the end of the thirties it was only
necessary for him to "make a suggestion," and it was acted upon
immediately. This clearly had its costs as well, and they were enormous.
By the time Stalin was done purging Lenin's party of the "old Bolsheviks," he had transformed it to an atomized mass of individuals largely
bereft of ideals, and aware only of the awesome potential and consequences of the raw exercise of political power. The philosophical
idealism of the party had simply been burned out by terror. Of course,
in the normal course of things it was bound to become less fervent
anyway, because most people cannot maintain revolutionary fervor
indefinitely. But without question much of the corrosive cynicism that
infects party members today in Soviet Russia is the result of Stalin. In
this sense, the Communist Party of the Soviet Union is the product of his
founding, not Lenin's.

Another product of Stalin's founding resulted from his long years
as undisputed ruler of the Soviet Union. Stalin's totalitarianism, like that

of Adolf Hitler, rested fundamentally upon a view of the world that, in the arresting characterization of Hannah Arendt, was fictitious.[49] In order to cover up the harsh facts surrounding his collectivization and industrialization drives, Stalin ordered the regime to engage in spectacular propaganda campaigns. This practice reached ridiculous extremes during the purges, primarily for the purpose of lending some credibility to the outrageous charges against the accused, and generally to his assault upon the Communist party. But the long-term effects of this practice, certainly one of the most striking legacies of Stalin's rule in the Soviet Union, was to destroy the integrity of language as a vehicle for expressing truth about the actual state of affairs in the real world. In short, under Stalin's rule the Soviet state became, and remains today, an extravagant and adamantly unapologetic liar. In fact, Stalin himself admitted as much in a comment he once made about Soviet diplomacy: "Words have no relation to action—otherwise what kind of diplomacy is it? Words are one thing: actions another. Good words are a mask for concealment of bad deeds. Sincere diplomacy is no more possible than dry water or wooden iron."[50] But such candid admissions rarely find their way into the Western press.

This frank assertion about the function of Soviet propaganda has been substantiated by careful observers of the press in the Soviet Union. For instance, in his fascinating study of the media in the Soviet Union and Eastern Europe, Paul Lendvai concludes that its basic function is to cover up the vast differences between what these societies are and what their leaders pretend them to be.[51] Numerous Western visitors have come to the same conclusion, often to their own surprise. Hedrick Smith, for example, said that he had thought Orwellian "double-think" was simply the product of a novelist's imagination, or at most something that had used to exist, but was now gone. "So I was hit doubly hard by the number of intellectuals who privately agonized over how routinely they practiced double-think and how pervasive was the practice."[52] There is also tremendous irony in this development, in light of what Marx said numerous times about not taking at face value what individuals or states proclaim about themselves. Nowhere does this apply more than in the Soviet Union. It is in this sense that the *real* Russia, the one issuing from the realities of everyday life, is not the one that is depicted in official accounts. Official, party-approved Russia, the one founded by Stalin and reported in official publications, exists in the world of Soviet propaganda.

Stalin, the Founder of Stalinism

The differences between Stalin and Lenin were significant enough to suggest Lenin probably would have ruled differently, had he lived longer. In fact, our brief consideration of the left and right oppositions to Stalin also suggests that the course of Soviet history would have been dramatically different if a Trotsky or Bukharin had been at the top instead of Stalin. Of course, it is also true that someone else with Stalin's personality and priorities could have taken over the leadership. That was the difficulty of the party system under Lenin. It was not structured in such a way as to prevent this from happening; nor did it contain sufficient safeguards against abuses in order to minimize the worst effects of a Stalinlike leadership. Probably it was inevitable that a single person eventually would take the reins of power, but it was not inevitable that the person in question would be Stalin.

The fact that it was, means that Lenin most likely would have returned to Zurich, had he awakened and looked around the Soviet Union today. Perhaps, however, while musing in the comforts of that city, he would not have been totally displeased with what he saw of modern Russia. Behind the pompous boasts, party rituals, the questionable statistics, and the fictitious explanations, there exists the hard truths of the modern Soviet Union that Stalin built into a superpower. He found Russia a backward, semifeudal society, upon which the weight of centuries past seemed to render impossible any hopes for a better future. If he did not himself create that better future, Stalin certainly laid the groundwork for his successors to build upon. And this groundwork was an impressive achievement. No nation ignores or snubs the Soviet Union today. No nation can seriously entertain the possibility of defeating the USSR in war. Although much progress needs to be made, Soviet citizens are generally better off today than they ever have been. That too ultimately is a product of Stalin.

And, of course, Stalinism is the product of Stalin. Without question, regardless of his departures from various aspects of Marx's teachings, he founded the most significant and influential application of Marxism in the twentieth century. The harsher features of Stalinism have been softened over the years, but most of the basic outlines of the system he created remain in place. And as Marshall Goldman and others have pointed out, the Stalinist model has shown amazing tenacity and resistance to change.[53] Whether or not it will ever change in significant ways is a matter of conjecture. Probably it would take a new founder, one of Stalin's caliber, to affect the country as much as he did. At this writing it appears that Mikhail Gorbachev is making genuine efforts to realign Soviet domestic policies in ways that are more conducive to an open society. He has freed some political dissidents, most notably Andrei Sakharov;[54] called for genuine elections involving competing candidates at local levels in Soviet politics; and has dropped some aspects of what Robert J. Kaiser has termed "the Soviet Pretense," by encouraging more discussion and openness *(glasnost)* about the real problems facing the Soviet regime.[55] But he is faced with a serious problem that Stalin was able to overcome because of his methods of ruling and because he was its principle creator—the Soviet bureaucracy. Thus, Gorbachev and his successors will still have to work within the confines of the system created by Stalin, which continues to involve many people who see the world as Stalin did. Indeed, it is the Stalinist *system* that has been Stalin's most significant and permanent legacy. And it is this, perhaps, that informs the lament of the poet Yevtushenko, who once cried: "We carried him out of the Mausoleum. But who will carry Stalin out of the heirs of Stalin?"[56]

ENDNOTES

[1]Quoted in Robert Daniels, "The Struggle with the Right Opposition," in Robert Daniels, ed. *The Stalin Revolution* (Lexington: D. C. Heath and Company, 1972), p. 27.

[2]Quoted in Anton Antonov-Ovseyenko, *The Time of Stalin: Portrait of a Tyranny* (New York: Harper & Row, 1981), p. 255.

[3]Ibid., p. 264.

[4]Quoted in Adam Ulam, *Stalin: The Man and His Era* (New York: The Viking Press, 1973), p. 359.

[5]Quoted in Robert C. Tucker, *The Soviet Political Mind* (New York: W. W. Norton, 1971), p. 106.

[6]Lenin wrote this on December 25, 1922, and the quote is taken from Robert C. Tucker, ed., *The Lenin Anthology* (New York: W. W. Norton, 1975), p. 727. Lenin dictated a series of notes in preparation for the upcoming party congress in April, and he rendered his opinion of various party leaders, Stalin included. In a continuation of this note written on January 4, 1923, he recommended Stalin's removal from his post as Secretary-General.

[7]Quoted in Robert C. Tucker, *Stalin as Revolutionary* (New York: W. W. Norton, 1973), p. 175.

[8]For an account of the origins of the factions Bolshevik and Menshevik, see Leonard Schapiro, *The Communist Party of the Soviet Union*, 2nd ed. (New York: Vintage Books, 1971), pp. 37–55.

[9]For an account of Stalin's youth, see, especially, Tucker, *Stalin as Revolutionary*, pp. 64–144. See also Antonov-Ovseyenko, *Time of Stalin, pp. 232–55*.

[10]"The Leader and the Party," in Daniels, *Stalin Revolution*, p. 7.

[11]"Soviet Bonapartism," in Daniels, ibid., pp. 189–98. For more of Trotsky's comments about Stalin, see *The Age of Permanent Revolution*, ed. Isaac Deutscher (New York: Dell Publishing, 1964), pp. 150–62.

[12]Isaac Deutscher especially stresses the importance of Stalin's administrative posts in his rise to power. See Deutscher, "The Leader and the Party," in Daniels, *Stalin Revolution*, pp. 3–14. See also Schapiro, *Communist Party*, pp. 180–200; and Ulam, *Stalin*, pp. 18–82. For an account of the Russian Revolution see Robert Daniels, *Red October* (New York: Charles Scribners Sons, 1967). For treatments that focus upon Stalin's role, see Tucker, *Stalin as Revolutionary*, pp. 181–239; and Ulam, *Stalin*, pp. 114–92.

[13]For Lenin's criticisms of Stalin's personality and conduct, see the documents contained in Tucker, *Lenin Anthology*, pp. 728–46.

[14]Ulam, *Stalin*, p. 208.

[15]"The Legacy of the Russian Past," in Daniels, *Stalin Revolution*, p. 165.

[16]For treatments of Soviet policy in the interwar period see Alvin Z. Rubinstein, *Soviet Foreign Policy Since World War II* (Cambridge, Mass.: Winthrop Publishers, 1981); Joseph L. Nogee and Robert H. Donaldson, *Soviet Foreign Policy Since World War II* (New York: Pergamon Press, 1984); and A. J. P. Taylor, *The Origins of the Second World War* (New York: Fawcett Crest Books, 1961).

[17]A. J. P. Taylor, *The War Lords* (New York: Penguin Books, 1978), p. 103.

[18]A good survey is found in Zbigniew K. Brzezenski, *The Soviet Bloc*, rev. ed. (Cambridge, Mass.: Harvard University Press, 1967). See also Hugh Seton-Watson, *From Lenin to Khrushchev* (New York: Praeger Publishers, 1980).

[19]Among the many reviews of this crucial period, see, for instance, Louis Halle, *The Cold War as History* (New York: Harper & Row, 1967), which also contains some fascinating autobiographical references. Military evaluations of Soviet power during the postwar period are found in Thomas W. Wolfe, *Soviet Power and Europe: 1945–1950* (Baltimore: Johns Hopkins University Press, 1970), pp. 1–73.

[20]This informal agreement was the result of some bargaining between Churchill and Stalin in the fall of 1944. Most accounts of the war contain some reference to this episode. See, for instance, James MacGregor Burns, *Roosevelt: The Soldier of Freedom* (New York: Harcourt Brace Jovanovich, 1970), p. 537, which is particularly interesting, given FDR's dislike of such sphere-of-influence, power-politics behavior. Burns also suggests (p. 374) that the continued postponement of the second front was "perhaps the most determining single factor" in beginning the cold war.

[21]The remarks were made by Secretary of State Dean Acheson in a speech on January 12, 1950. See James A. Nathan and James K. Oliver, *United States Foreign Policy and World Order*, 2nd ed. (Boston: Little, Brown, 1981), p. 118: Acheson stated that the American "defensive perimeter runs along the Aleutians to Japan and then goes to the Ryukus . . . [then] . . . runs from the Ryukus to the Philippine Islands." Adam Ulam points out that "the American reaction to the North Korean invasion on June 25 must have been one of the greatest surprises of Stalin's life." Adam Ulam, *The Rivals: America and Russia Since World War II* (New York: Random House, Viking ed., 1971), p. 171.

[22]For a treatment of Bukharin's influence upon the Bolsheviks' economic theories, see David S. McLellan, *Marxism After Marx* (New York: Harper & Row, 1979), pp. 115–30.

[23]For relevant documents, see Tucker, *Lenin Anthology*, pp. 423–61.

[24]Ibid., p. 509–10; note especially the comments on pp. 503–33, pp. 707–14.

[25]McLellan, *Marxism*, p. 125.

[26]Tucker, *Stalin as Revolutionary*, p. 380.

[27]This term comes from Ulam, *Stalin*, p. 289.

[28]"The Socialist Drive," in Daniels, *Stalin Revolution*, pp. 54–55.

[29]An excellent account is found in the Smolensk Archive. This consists of some party documents that were captured by the invading Germans in 1941 and fell into the hands of the Western Allies after the war. An excerpt from this source is Merle Fainsod, "Collectivization: The Method," in Daniels, *Stalin Revolution*, pp. 95–106.

[30]Alec Nove, "Economics and Personality," in Daniels, Ibid., p. 64.

[31]For a gripping account of this process, see Roy Medvedev, *Let History Judge*, trans. Colleen Taylor (New York: Vintage Books, 1973), pp. 71–109.

[32]For data on this, see Harry G. Shaffer, "Soviet Economic Performance in Historical Perspective," in Samuel Hendel, ed., *The Soviet Crucible* (Belmont, Calif.: Wadsworth, 1980), pp. 295–305; and Alec Nove, *Stalinism and After* (London: George Allen & Unwin, 1981), pp. 41–48.

[33]"Economics and Personality," in Daniels, *Stalin Revolution*, p. 63.

[34]Alexander Solzhenitsyn estimates that the total number of victims of communist rule in the Soviet Union is 66 million. This covers the period from the October Revolution to 1959. See *The Gulag Archipelago Two* (New York: Harper & Row, 1975), p. 10. Many find this astronomical figure hard to accept. Another estimate, made by Soviet geophysicist Iosif Dyadkin, puts the figure at between 13 and 23 million people killed by the Soviet

government during peacetime. See Jan Prybyla, "The Economic Crisis of State Socialism: Its Philosophical and Institutional Foundations," *Orbis,* Winter 1983, p. 880.

[35]Schapiro, *Communist Party,* p. 429.

[36]"The Crackdown on the Party," in Daniels, *Stalin Revolution,* pp. 138–45.

[37]Tucker, *Soviet Political Mind,* p. 181.

[38]John 15:5–6. These are the words of Jesus.

[39]Ulam, *Stalin,* p. 630; and see Tucker, *Soviet Political Mind,* pp. 173–202.

[40]Tucker, Ibid., p. 234.

[41]Quoted in Ibid., p. 187.

[42]E. Varga, a distinguished Soviet economist, published a work in 1946 that said many of these things, and was severely censured for it. See the account in Schapiro, *Communist Party,* p. 537.

[43]Tucker, *Soviet Political Mind,* p. 143–73.

[44]For treatments of these years, see, especially, Schapiro, *Communist Party,* pp. 548–51; and Ulam, *Stalin,* pp. 700–741.

[45]Recounted by Robert Kaiser, *Russia: The People and the Power* (New York: Pocket Books, 1976), p. 140.

[46]For an excellent review of the literature on this matter, see Stephen F. Cohen, "Bolshevism and Stalinism," in Robert C. Tucker, ed. *Stalinism* (New York: W. W. Norton, 1977), pp. 3–30.

[47]See, for example, Robert G. Wesson, *Soviet Foreign Policy in Perspective* (Homewood, Ill.: The Dorsey Press, 1969), p. 400.

[48]Quoted in Cohen, "Bolshevism and Stalinism," in Tucker, *Stalinism,* p. 14.

[49]Hannah Arendt, *The Origins of Totalitarianism* (Cleveland: The World Publishing Company, 1958). See Part Three.

[50]Quoted by Brian Freemantle, *KGB* (New York: Holt, Rinehart & Winston, 1982), pp. 41–42.

[51]*The Bureaucracy of Truth* (Boulder, Colo: Westview Press, 1981), p. 21.

[52]Hedrick Smith, *The Russians* (New York: Ballantine Books, 1976), pp. 383–84. Of all the treatments of life in the Soviet Union, the accounts of journalists have been the most interesting and perhaps also the most perceptive. In addition to Smith's book, see also Robert Kaiser, *Russia: The People and the Power* (New York: Pocket Books, 1976), and David K. Shipler, *Russia: Broken Idols, Solemn Dreams* (New York: Penguin Books, 1984).

[53]Marshall Goldman, *USSR in Crisis* (New York: W. W. Norton, 1983). See also Timothy J. Colton, *The Dilemma of Reform in the Soviet Union* (New York: The Council of Foreign Relations, 1984); and Seweryn Bialer, *The Soviet Paradox* (New York: Alfred A. Knopf, 1986).

[54]Although any freeing of dissidents is an encouraging sign, for a contrary view of its significance, see Dimitri K. Simes, "Gorbachev: A New Foreign Policy?" in *Foreign Affairs,* 65, no. 3 (1987), pp. 477–500.

[55]Robert C. Kaiser, "The Soviet Pretense," *Foreign Affairs,* 65, no. 2 (Winter 1986–1987), pp. 236–51.

[56]Quoted in Paul Lendvai, *The Bureaucracy of Truth* (Boulder, Colo.: Westview Press, 1981), p. 129. Yevtushenko took a more optimistic view in a 1987 interview. See "A Poet's View of *Glasnost,*" *Time,* February 9, 1987, pp. 32–33.

MAO ZEDONG
Revisionist

. . . a man of tireless energy, and a military and political strategist of considerable genius. (American Journalist *Edgar Snow* on Mao Zedong, after interviewing him in 1936.)[1]

Mao Tse-Tung's thought is an everlasting universal truth . . . Every sentence of Chairman Mao's works is a truth, one single sentence of his surpasses ten thousand of ours. *Lin Piao,* Defense Minister during the Great Proletarian Cultural Revolution.[2]

"I won the Empire on horseback!" said the Emperor. "Why should I bother with the Classics?"

"You may have won it on horseback," replied the scholar Lu, "but can you rule it on horseback?" (Record of the Grand Historian on the Emperor Han Gaozi, 202–195 B.C.)[3]

The whole of the opposition's error lies in this, that being bound to "guerrillaism" by traditions of a heroism that will never be forgotten, they will not understand that those days are over. *Lenin*[4]

I stand for the theory of permanent revolution . . . In making revolution one must strike while the iron is hot—one revolution must follow another, the revolution must continually advance. *Mao Zedong*[5]

INTRODUCTION

In a recent biography of Mao Zedong, Ross Terrill relates an interesting story about an incident that occurred during Mao's youth. He was a schoolboy of ten at the time, and, like all schoolboys, was required to memorize faithfully and then repeat the lessons assigned to him by the teacher. Mao couldn't stomach this routine. He especially hated the ritual that required the student to walk to the teacher's desk and dutifully parrot to the class some assorted gems of wisdom gleaned from the classics of Chinese literature. Once, when it was his turn, he refused to do so. His reason for not conforming was simple enough: if the teacher and the whole class could hear him well enough from where he was sitting, why should he leave his seat? The teacher was outraged, and ordered the stubborn youth to follow the traditional practice. Mao decided to meet his antagonist halfway. He dragged his chair to the front of the classroom and glared at the teacher. His open defiance was met with an enraged pull at his sleeves in an effort to get him to stand up. Mao tore himself from the teacher's grasp and stormed out of the school. When he returned three days later, he noted with satisfaction that he was treated with a bit more respect after that. Mao Zedong had won his first revolution.[6]

Many others were to follow. From his teenage years as a frustrated youth defying an imperious father to his dying days as ruler of China's one billion people, Mao Zedong was constantly leading revolution. He rebelled against his father, family, school officials, and friends. He railed against governments, party dignitaries, and foreign ideologues who insisted that they knew more about China than he did. He fought against imperialists, capitalists, foreign invaders, domestic subversives, intellectuals, leftists, rightists, and Confucious. He battled the armies of Chiang Kaishek, Imperial Japan, Harry Truman, and assorted warlords too numerous to mention. In the end he beat them all, and accomplished what many felt was an impossible task—the unification of China under the banner of Communism and the rule of a single government.

For all that, he was vilified as a "revisionist" by those assumed to know best about such matters, the rulers of Soviet Russia. In fact, the term *revisionist* was one of the kindest things ever said by the inspirational leaders of world communism about Mao Zedong. Mao himself preferred to be remembered as a great teacher of the Chinese people, and, through them, of the rest of the world. There is some justification for both titles. Using the Soviet application of Marxist theory as a reference point, there is no question that Mao considerably revised some important doctrines and practices of Marxism-Leninism to make them fit better the conditions in China. More than that, he demonstrated to the Soviets an alternative revolutionary model, one actually with far

144

greater application in the world of peasant-based underdeveloped countries than the Soviet model. Thus, both designations are correct. Mao taught the followers of Marx and Lenin to revise their revolutionary doctrines in ways that had more worldwide significance than either Marx or Lenin ever imagined.

These matters are best understood by tracing the stormy life of Mao and his long journey to power in China. We shall then briefly treat the main events surrounding his rule, and conclude with some comments about the most important ways in which Mao can be regarded as the twentieth century's greatest revisionist.

MAO'S REVOLUTIONARY TRAIL

Mao's rise to power occurred in an era when China was being wracked by continuous civil war and foreign intervention. China's political history in this century is extremely complicated, and only its main features can be outlined here. Our discussion will thus be confined to commenting briefly upon the most important participants in China's political development, and how each fared, from the fall of the Manchu dynasty in 1911 to the ultimate triumph of the Communists in 1949.[7]

The Warlords

For at least three millenia China was ruled by a succession of dynasties headed by an emperor. The last one, the Manchu dynasty, was also one of the weakest, and in 1911, after a long series of humiliations inflicted by foreign powers, finally collapsed. It was succeeded by a regime that attempted to maintain centralized rule over all of China, but this lasted only until 1916. It was followed by about two decades of decentralized rule centered upon the various regions of the country governed by local political and military leaders—the warlords. These individuals ruled their provincial domains with considerable independence from outside authorities, raising their own armies, levying their own taxes, and generally governing as they saw fit. In fact, the strength of some warlords and the near absence of central government after 1916 made it difficult for many to see how China could ever again be reunited. The fact that it eventually was, reflected the ruthless determination on the part of the warlords' principal antagonists—the Kuomintang and the Chinese Communists.

The Kuomintang

The Kuomintang (KMT)—the Chinese Nationalists—was the name later given to an organization that was originally formed during the dying days of the Manchu dynasty in an effort to reform it. Its founder and main leader was Dr. Sun Yat-Sen, and his principal concern was to restore order and provide a strong, centralized government in China in the chaotic conditions of the early decades of this century. But by the 1920s the country's desperate political situation finally forced him to accept help from the Communist International (Comintern), which he hoped would provide assistance and training for nationalist troops. He was also instructed by Comintern officials in Moscow, who had their own priorities, to make an alliance with the newly formed Chinese Communist Party (CCP). This was an attempt to present a "united front" against China's enemies, and it became particularly important after 1931, when Japan invaded Manchuria and began its long and immensely destructive war on the Chinese mainland. But actually the Soviets were more interested in uniting Chinese efforts against the Japanese than the Nationalists or Communists. Indeed, most of efforts of the latter two groups—until the Japanese invasion—were expended in trying to destroy each other. For many years, neither was able do do that, and Sun's dream for a united and prosperous China seemed as remote as ever.

The Chinese Communists and the Road to Victory

The Chinese Communist Party (CCP) actually began as an informal Marxist study group, but was formally organized in 1921 directly as the result of Lenin's efforts to provide Comintern direction to Marxist groups beyond the borders of the Soviet Union. For about the first decade and a half of its existence, its principal officers were chosen by and received their instructions from the leadership in Moscow. Like the KMT officials, Chinese Communists were directed to cooperate with Sun's organization in efforts to bring some order to China's chaotic political situation. They were also given instructions in political tactics to operate like the KMT and the Bolshevik Party in Russia, which was to concentrate their strength in the urban areas and act essentially like a worker-based political movement. In this fashion, political control would spread from the cities outward, based upon the standard Marxist assumption, as well as the Soviet experience, about the function of an urban proletariat in the conduct of revolutionary activities.

There were several things wrong with this strategy. For one thing, China was even more primitive in industrial development than the Russian empire was before its revolution, and basing a mass political movement upon the tiny Chinese urban proletariat did not seem to make much sense. Certainly there was no shortage of oppressors in China, but most of these came in the form of landlords, warlords, and foreign invaders. Secondly, following the instructions of foreign advisers who were unaware of Chinese conditions or who chose willfully to ignore them quickly produced deep resentment among many in the Chinese Communist Party, especially Mao Zedong. In fact, Mao's stubborn resistance to the steady procession of Bolshevik "experts" coming from the USSR practically guaranteed him the status of an outsider and renegade within the CCP, as we shall see. Finally, "cooperating" with the KMT in carrying out such ideas became not only foolish, but nearly suicidal. In short, if communism were to succeed in China, it had to develop in terms peculiarly relevant to Chinese conditions, and not according to the script laid down by various outside "authorities."

No one was more aware of this than Mao Zedong. Indeed, as we have already noted, he had been battling authorities of various stripes long before he became a committed communist.[8] Born of peasant parents in 1893, Mao made his mark early in life by resisting his father's authority, revolting against the institutionalized education he had to endure, and participating in the rebellion that toppled the Manchu dynasty in 1911. In the following decade he continued his formal schooling, but still managed to inspire various sorts of rebellious activities—workers' strikes, subversive newspapers, dissident "study groups," and the like—against provincial authorities. But he also spent a good deal of time traveling, studying, and writing. In fact, although extremely intelligent and well read, Mao was mostly self-educated, and by the time the CCP had its first meeting, in Shanghai in 1921, he had developed firm views about the world of Chinese politics and his place in it. He saw himself as the next most important self-made man in Chinese history—there were only two before him(!)—and the intensity of his feelings on China's anguished political situation was so well known that he was referred to as that "lunatic Mao."[9] It was a nickname well earned.

Naturally, being regarded as an egomaniac and a lunatic is hardly conducive to good relations with one's colleagues. At various times between 1921 and the escalation of Japan's war against China in 1937, Mao was regularly denounced by CCP leaders, stripped of his positions in the party (he later got them back), put under house arrest, blamed for all the misfortunes that fell upon the armies under his command for following orders he received from above, and publicly reprimanded for his unorthodox political views. To make matters much worse, when not being harrassed by internal CCP disputes, he and his People's Liberation Army (PLA) were being chased all over China by Chinese Nationalist Forces. The fact that he was able to survive all these things is a testament to his extraordinary courage and resourcefulness.

More than that, his survival required the prudent application of a set of political doctrines that Mao developed himself and tested under the most strenuous conditions. It is true that he gave lip service to the standard Marxist views about the role of an urban proletariat carrying out a revolution, but his heart was never really in it.[10] A more characteristic statement of his views is contained in a remarkable document entitled, "Report on an Investigation of the Peasant Movement in Hunan," whch appeared in 1927. He explained that if one were to assign ten points of emphasis to the execution of a revolution in China, three would go to the urban and military elements, and seven to the peasants—the poor peasants especially. Indeed, Mao insisted that "without the poor peasants there would be no revolution. To deny their role is to deny the revolution. To attack them is to attack the revolution. They have never been wrong on the general direction of the revolution."[11] His other writings reinforced this view, particularly those dealing with the conduct of Communist troops toward the common people of China. Always respect them, Mao intoned; gain their support, and China will be behind you.[12] It was this advice that eventually gained him victory and rule over all of China.

Before 1949, however, this prospect seemed ridiculously remote. After the death of Sun Yat-Sen in 1925, the control of the KMT fell in the hands of General Chiang Kai-shek, who was determined to rid the party of communists. Accordingly, he ordered a bloody massacre of workers and CCP leaders in Shanghai in 1927, which brought that city under his control. In the following years Chiang's armies relentlessly pursued Mao in efforts to destroy him completely and unify China under KMT rule. Mao's forces successfully dodged, weaved, and meandered their way out of the Nationalists' grasp, in spite of often having to follow orders from CCP leaders that very nearly resulted in their destruction. By 1934, however, Mao had run out of options. Chiang's fifth "extermination campaign" against his base in Jiangxi left Mao with almost no room to maneuver. Faced with annihilation or surrender, he chose a third alternative—retreat. Under constant KMT harrassment, the PLA evacuated its provincial base and engaged in what has since been referred to as the Long March.

This journey, which began near the end of 1934 and ended in October of the following year, has attained legendary significance in the history of the CCP and modern China. It was excruciating beyond description. Mao's soldiers went through some of the most formidable terrain in China, and were forced to endure sickness, starvation, and obstacles of every sort imaginable—bitter cold, withering heat, swamps, forests, mountains, and frequent attacks by Nationalist forces. However, there were some positive aspects. First, Mao learned valuable lessons in the art of guerrilla warfare, mostly from the primitive tribes his forces encountered along the way—"the best fighters we ever had to face," he admitted respectfully.[13] Second, his status as a military and inspirational leader among Chinese Communists was greatly enhanced. Finally, after the march ended, in North Central China, Mao was in the position for the first time in years of being relatively secure from all of his enemies. He took advantage of this opportunity to read, write, and give lectures at an academy he founded in Shensi province. None of these things, of course, would have happened if Chiang hadn't driven his army away from its base in southern China.

His most significant accomplishments in the years immediately following the Long March were in the areas of scholarship and politics. First, he made several very important contributions to Marxist theory and practice with writings on military tactics and philosophy. The main force of his arguments was to lend a peculiarly Chinese interpretation to the problems of revolutionary war, the application of Marxism in predominantly peasant societies, and the events that had taken place in China since the turn of the century. "Strategic Problems in China's Revolutionary War" appeared in late 1936; "Strategic Problems in the Anti-Japanese Guerrilla War" came out in 1938, as did "Protracted War." Two of his most important philosophical writings, "On Practice," and "On Contradiction," appeared in 1937, and have retained their status as significant contributions to the corpus of Marxist-Leninist sacred writings.[14] By the end of the decade Mao had established himself as a Marxist theoretician of the first rank.

It was a status that set Mao apart from the Soviet advisers who continued to pour over the borders into China in the thirties, in attempts to run the Chinese revolution from Moscow. Mao found it increasingly difficult to treat them with any respect, especially as their abundant learning was not based upon sufficient experience— or *any* experience, from his point of view—that seemed relevant to the Chinese situation. By contrast, Mao argued convincingly that his own learning—indeed, all learning—had come from experience. In his lecture, "On Practice," probably his most important one, he stated simply that "if you want to know the taste of a pear you must change the pear by eating it yourself."[15] That, of course, was what made Mao so different from practically all of his opponents in the CCP, and especially those from the Soviet Union—he had actually *tasted* the pear; his political advisers from across the borders had simply *theorized* about it. It was a cardinal principle of Mao's thought that "all knowledge originates in direct experience."[16] And his experience had taught him that "the Sinification of Marxism," he wrote in 1939, involves "making certain that in all of its manifestations it is imbued with Chinese peculiarities . . ."[17] Clearly, intimate acquaintance with these "peculiarities" was something at which he excelled.

He also excelled at building up CCP control over the region he occupied in central China, which was his second major accomplishment during the late thirties and early forties. By the middle of 1941 the Soviets were involved in a fight for their national survival, and Stalin had his hands full without worrying about trying to direct the Chinese Communists. Chiang's forces were fighting the Japanese, and this left Mao with a relatively free hand in northern China. Most of his efforts were to consolidate and expand his rule, and they paid off handsomely. The one secure base in Shensi in 1937 had grown to nineteen bases by 1945, in areas containing some 90 million–100 million Chinese.[18] Moreover, the Seventh Congress of the CCP, held in 1945, was a complete victory for Mao. He was elected to the new office of Chairman of the Chinese Communist Party, a position that he held until his death. In perhaps the most fitting riposte to a quarter-century of Comintern interference, Mao's "thought" was officially enshrined as the guiding ideology of the party. Finally, an elaborate cult of personality surrounding his ideas and leadership, which was to grow to grotesque proportions in the years to come, began to develop. Mao and Maoism had finally arrived.

Before it could rule over all of China, however, Chiang Kai-shek and the Chinese Nationalists had to be dealt with. It first appeared that Chiang, who had the support of both the Soviet Union and the United States, would have an easy victory, and that the country would shortly be unified under his rule. Of course, nothing of the sort happened. After fighting a rearguard action for two years after the end of World War II, the PLA went on the offensive and began a drive that would bring the Chinese Communists ultimate victory. Chiang's early successes were deceptive; the Nationalists' social base—still the cities, the middle classes, and the landlords—was too narrow in a giant country where most the population consisted of poor peasants. Of course, these were the very people whom Mao relied upon to feed his growing regiments, the people at the foundation of his theory of revolution. And these were the people who, under Mao's leadership, crushed the armies of Chiang Kai-Shek on the mainland by the end of the decade, and sent their remnants into exile on the island of Taiwan.

In 1949 the Chinese Communists accepted the surrender of two hundred thousand Nationalist troops in Peking and took over the city. In October Mao proclaimed the birth of the People's Republic of China, and with it, the end of years of domination by China's foreign and domestic oppressors. A new era had begun.

CONTINUING THE REVOLUTION: MAO IN POWER

The First Decade of Maoism

The most distinctive feature of Mao's leadership over the reunited China was his inability to adjust successfully to the challenges of ordinary governance. Practical politics under conditions of peace is often a tedious affair by any standard, but it was especially so for a man of Mao's temperament. He reacted by attempting to keep revolutionary zeal alive with numerous projects for the economic and social reconstruction of China. The fact that none of these was successful did not deter him from continuing to initiate new programs. Indeed, Mao's revolutionary activities continued unabated until his death. He won the empire on horseback, as the ancient Chinese saying went, but, unfortunately for millions of Chinese, tried to rule it on horseback as well.

This manner of rule encountered serious obstacles, from ordinary citizens as well as from CCP cadres (political officials of all types) and intellectuals. The early land-reform efforts resulted in some thirty-five million landlords in China being dispossessed, with perhaps two or three million losing their lives in the process.[19] Ordinary farmers received about half an acre apiece from this redistribution, but were quickly "persuaded" to give this up to join agricultural cooperatives. Yet these failed dismally, and by the middle fifties were being abandoned en masse. City dwellers fared no better. Foreign trade was drastically reduced in an effort to make China self-sufficient. In the evening, lights were turned off; neighborhoods were required to establish their own factories; "counterrevolutionaries" in the cities were shipped off to hard labor in the country or faced summary execution. Even the cadres were affected by being forced to adopt Mao's ascetic life-style. Reduce the toasts at party functions, Mao admonished; no birthday celebrations, minimum applause at CCP meetings, and no "self-glorification" by naming places after people.[20] In short, no one in China escaped the influence of Chairman Mao.

Of all his efforts to reconstruct the Chinese social, intellectual, and economic landscape, probably none were as traumatic as the "Hundred Flowers" campaign, and the "Great Leap Forward," which came in the later fifties. The first followed an attempt by Mao to institute "thought reform" among intellectuals soon after he came into power, and it had a chilling effect upon the Chinese cultural and academic environment. The Hundred Flowers campaign—based upon a passage drawn from an ancient Chinese saying, "Let a hundred flowers bloom, let a hundred schools contend"—was designed to counteract that, at least somewhat. Accordingly, all Chinese were encouraged to be independent and speak their minds. Voice of America radio broadcasts were allowed, journalists were unleashed to write what they wanted, intellectuals were encouraged to speak out, and even some of Chiang Kai-Shek's old speeches were dusted off and released. For a brief, shining period in the early history of the People's Republic of China (PRC), freedom of thought and speech flourished.

It didn't last long. Amidst all this blossoming, the most common growths, from Mao's standpoint, were weeds. In fact, the country was overgrown with them, all tending to the same conclusion: China had been put into a cultural, economic, and intellectual straightjacket by the Communist government, and most people were simply tired of it, especially the creative types—entrepreneurs, artists, academics, and writers. Faced with a chorus of dissent, Mao wasted no time in reacting. Declaring that "any word or deed at variance with socialism is completely wrong," he gave a speech in early 1957 in which he explained an important distinction.[21] There is a difference between "contradictions" among the people, on the one hand, and those between the people and their enemies, on the other.[22] The first could be tolerated, whereas the second could not. Intellectuals and others who did not understand this and who spoke out for freedom of expression ended up cleaning up toilets or sweeping floors. In fact, any "contradiction" that Mao found threatening to his rule or to that of the CCP he labeled as a contradiction between the people and their enemies—"class" enemies, who somehow always mysteriously sprang up whenever there was an opportunity to do so. The Hundred Flowers campaign provided many opportunities for precisely that, and the result was the elimination of many anti-Maoist weeds.

Mao's second grand effort at reform focused upon China's economic organization, and had the aim of achieving great increases in production—a Great Leap Forward (GLF) in economic development. Mao gained approval for his plan from the Central Committee in May 1958, and spent the rest of the year trying to whip up enthusiasm for it in the country. The basic plan called for stuffing China's vast population into 24,000 "people's communes," an economic building block for all areas of life—industry, commerce, education, and government.[23] Mao was convinced that great things could be accomplished with these units by application of willpower, unflagging determination, and relentless commitment to revolutionary change. Accordingly, he made grandiose predictions about the future. Steel output would rise by 800 percent, he said. Cars would be produced in great abundance; Great Britain would be surpassed, as would the Soviet Union and, yes, even the United States (in fifteen or twenty years, or so)! We Shall Create a New Heaven and Earth for Man, read one wall poster, many of which were designed by the Chairman himself. In summary, Mao was convinced that the Great Leap Forward was to be unlike anything ever seen by mankind.[24]

He was right about that, but wrong about the direction the GLF would take. In economic terms, China went *backward,* not forward. The Gross National Product of China declined by a quarter from 1958 to 1962; per-capita income was down by a third, and total industrial production was off by 40 percent.[25] Steel production, the standard measure for industrial power, declined by a third. To make matters worse, famine blighted many provinces. Rations went below starvation level, and people resorted to eating tree bark, algae, leaves, and animal feed. PLA regiments foraged the mountains and forests on hunting expeditions for fodder of any kind. And to add to their miseries, for three years after the GLF began, the Chinese suffered from all manner of natural disasters, including drought and floods, which retarded economic production in every category.[26] Obviously, much of this was owed to the bad weather, but the poor economics greatly complicated efforts to cope with nature's devastations.

Mao spent the next half dozen years defending himself against attacks from party leaders who had grown weary of his assorted bloomings and leaps. Deng Xiaoping, who was destined ultimately to succeed Mao, quietly grumbled that "a donkey is certainly slow, but at least it rarely has an accident."[27] He also estimated that the GLF set back China's development by at least five years. Liu Shaoqi, a prominent leader ultimately to be purged by Mao, was even harsher. He blamed 70 percent of the economy's dismal performance on man—actually, *one* man; by implication, Mao Tse-Tung—and 30 percent on nature.[28] Perhaps the most serious challenge came from the defense minister, Peng Dehuai, who accused Mao of economic dilettantism, among other things, and got himself dismissed from office for his efforts. He was replaced by Lin Piao, who remained in the post during the next series of upheavals, and who was also the centerpiece of a spectacular but unsuccessful attempt to oust Mao from office a decade later. Clearly, Mao's opposition in the wake of the Great Leap Forward was serious.

Mao responded to his critics in his typically vigorous fashion. He did engage in some "self-criticisms," but this was more to elicit sympathy than really to admit that he had done anything wrong. In fact, Mao had few qualms about admitting his error in assuming that, for instance, backyard furnaces for producing steel were the way to socialist cornu-copia. But he never would back down from his fundamental assumption about the importance of keeping one's revolutionary batteries recharged by "returning to the people" and "learning from the countryside." He had always loathed the cities, felt that his brain was emptied the longer he stayed there, and insisted that the "socialist revolutionary spirit" existed only among the masses of Chinese peasantry. Thus, what was really needed, he explained to the Central Committee in December 1963, was a new movement in "socialist education." China's problems could be solved by self-discipline, "correct thinking," and renewed commitment to revolutionary goals. In short, next to maintaining the spirit of revolution in the country, nothing else really mattered.

Mao weathered the storm of criticism and by the mid-sixties was ready to move again. His standing as spiritual leader of China's continuing revolution was heightened with the publication of a small pamphlet known as the "Little Red Book," consisting of quotations from Chairman Mao. It was to take on monumental significance in the execution of his next revolutionary endeavor: the Great Proletarian Cultural Revolution.

The Great Proletarian Cultural Revolution

The conclusion that Mao drew from the policy failures of the previous years was exactly the opposite of those made by nearly everyone else in the ruling circles of the CCP. Most felt that caution and stability were the order of the day, but Mao took this as evidence that the Communist Party itself needed to be reformed. It had become clogged with bureaucratic thinking, he felt, and subverted by counterrevolutionary tendencies. The "capitalist roaders"—those who had developed capitalist attitudes over the years—had to be purged from the party. Indeed, anyone who failed to show a sufficiently revolutionary outlook had to go. To cleanse the party of such types, he needed allies. But who? Lin Piao, the defense minister, could be trusted. His slavish commitment to Mao was unsurpassed by anyone. Who else? Young people, students by the million—they could carry out the job. All that was needed was to tap their native rebellious nature, stir them to heights of revolutionary frenzy, and use them to teach all who had been sitting on their hands for the past decade and a half the true meaning of the Chinese revolution. Such were the purposes and means of the Great Proletarian Cultural Revolution.

It was under way by the middle of 1966, with Mao's declaration that "to rebel is justified." That clarion call sent millions of young people, frantically waving their little red books containing the "thoughts of Mao," off on a destructive frenzy that has few parallels in modern history. "Don't be afraid of disorder," they were told; concentrate on the "four olds": old ideas, old culture, old habits, old exploiting classes—get rid of them all; "smash the old world to pieces."[29] Cultural objects of immense value were destroyed, temples were razed, the homes of intellectuals were gutted, and non-Marxist literature was burned as the Red Guards (as they were called) ravaged their way through China. Fox

Butterfield, a reporter for the *New York Times* who visited China several years after Mao's death, in 1976, recounted that "almost all the Chinese I met had been compelled to throw away valued books, records, or paintings, to placate bands of fanatic Red Guards who ransacked their homes looking for decadent 'bourgeois' or 'feudal' culture. Most of China's leading writers, musicians, and artists were imprisoned or forced to stop their creative work for over a decade."[30] Indeed, one of the main effects of the Cultural Revolution was to destroy an enormous amount of Chinese culture.

It also greatly debilitated the country's technical-economic base. The battle cry was that it was better to be red than expert, and as a result, tens of millions of jobs were outlandishly mismatched with people's skills. Administrators were sent to the countryside to learn the fine arts of pig tending; skilled surgeons plowed fields, while barely competent medics were put in charge of complex surgical procedures. College professors cleaned stables and students graded teachers—when schools were open, that is—and some one hundred million Chinese ended up illiterate as a result. Many others lost their loved ones, their reputations, or their lives, especially those whom Mao wanted to get rid of. For instance, Liu Shaoqi's forty-five years of service with Mao were not sufficient to prevent his downfall. He and others at the top, such as Deng Xiaoping, were forced to go through humiliating "self-criticisms," and wear dunce caps while being dragged through the streets by hordes of screaming youths. Scores of top CCP officials and army commanders were purged from their positions. In short, the Cultural Revolution left no one untouched, regardless of social standing, in the People's Republic of China.

By the middle of 1967 Mao had had enough, and decided to put an end to the process. But he had to pay a heavy price. The army finally had to be given the task of rooting out the Red Guards from the factories, schools, offices, and farms, and sending the "little devils" back to their homes in the cities. They were burned out and sullen—probably the worst victims of the tragedies they had inflicted upon China at Mao's bidding. However, perhaps an even greater blow for the revolution, at least from Mao's standpoint, was the fall of Lin Piao near the end of 1970. This was because Piao, who had nearly exhausted the Chinese vocabulary—not an easy thing to do—in his extravagant praise of Mao, had also become a prominent public figure in his own right. Piao had raised himself by elevating Mao, and seemed more interested in exploiting the symbolic significance of the Chairman than in supporting Mao's policies. Mao suspected the Piao was actually trying to engineer his downfall, and, in a confused affair that ended with Piao's death in an "accidental" plane crash, managed to end that threat to his position. The wiley Mao, even in his seventies, was still able to protect himself.

Mao's Last Years

The demise of Piao was very costly for Mao, as it required further purging of officials in the party and the PLA. It was messy, too. Five members of the Politburo, the top ruling elite, died violently, and numerous senior members of the army were forced out of the country. Lin Piao himself, who of course had been built up considerably during the previous ten years, now had to be "rebuilt downward" for public consumption, and totally disgraced. The tattered image of the CCP received another drubbing. Purge after purge of top leaders, many of whom had only recently enjoyed enormous political status, only served further to discredit the country's governing apparatus.[31] Indeed, one of the major tasks of the post-Mao leadership has been to restore the prestige of the party leadership in the PRC.

Mao's decline in his last years made that job more difficult, partly because his political support was waning, but also because his policies remained erratic. Part of the price he had to pay for the anti-Piao coalition was to accept the return of the formerly disgraced Deng Xiaoping, temporarily at least, as a member of the party in good standing. This lasted until 1976, when Deng was again denounced, this time for being a "capitalist roader"—meaning, as he commented sourly, that "you're doing a good job"—and stripped of his party posts.[32] Near the very end of his life, Mao even had to fend off a challenge to his rule by his wife, who had a well-deserved reputation as a notorious schemer. In spite of it all, he still managed to instigate a mini-cultural revolution that involved criticizing Confucius and revering the concept of the dictatorship of the proletariat. He saw Nixon after the Watergate incident ended his presidency, and wondered how such a trivial episode could have unseated the leader of the most powerful country in the world; after all, he said, everyone knew that Americans love to fuss with tape recorders! He also saw some of Nixon's relatives—Julie Nixon Eisenhower and her husband, David—whom he greeted as old friends, with as much enthusiasm as his frail body could muster. As the last year of his life wore on, that wasn't much.[33]

Mao's physical decline was even more dramatic than his political demise. By the early summer of 1976 it was clear that he had not much longer to live. He was extremely weak, and barely able to control the lolling of his head from one side to another. His jaw hung open to one side, giving him a dazed, zombielike appearance. He scrawled cryptic instructions that had to be deciphered by his attendants, who then had to figure out what he meant by them. What, for instance, was one supposed to make of the order, "Act according to the principles laid down"? Unfortunately, Mao had changed his mind so often, with his on-again, off-again revolutions, that it was impossible to deduce from the many policy and personnel shifts just what he wanted to be continued, and what he wanted changed. On another occasion he also said, "Help Jiang Qing" (his wife). Pray tell, help her do what? Take over his job (a doubtful instruction), carry out a self-criticism (more likely), change her ways, or leave him and the PRC alone after his death? At one point he even made reference to his imminent appointment with Karl Marx; an obvious, if unusual, reference to his coming death. A Westerner could only wonder about what sort of after-death scenario Mao had in mind, given the vigorous atheism of Marx and his master pupil in question.[34]

Whatever his ultimate destiny, Mao Zedong departed from this earth on September 9, 1976. A week of national mourning was proclaimed, and a million people flocked by the Gate of Heavenly Peace in Peking in ceremonial observance. One month later Jiang Qing and three of her companions were in jail, after a bungled attempt to take over the reins of power. This was actually the first round in a succession struggle that would last until Deng Xiaoping returned to consolidate his position as the new ruler of post-Mao China. In the meantime millions of Chinese contemplated their fortunes in a China that would not, for the first time in the twentieth century, contain a Mao Zedong.

MAO THE REVISIONIST

Mao Zedong had one of the most remarkable and influential lives of any political leader in the twentieth century. His primary influence, of course, was on China. But it was a China that served as a vast laboratory for the testing of Marxist-Leninist principles under conditions very different from those envisioned by Marx. It is true that Lenin was forced by the primitive conditions in Russia to grapple with the peculiarities of dealing with a predominantly agrarian society. But neither he nor Marx nor any of their followers really knew much about China. Mao did, of course, and proceeded to revise Marxist-Leninist principles in a fashion that added yet another-*ism* to the family of modern political ideologies: Maoism. And Maoism means revisionism.

Mao can be regarded as a revisionist in two ways: first, with regard to his interpretation of some of Marx's principal ideas, and second, in relationship to the Bolshevik experience in Russia. In practice, these two things often merge, as the Soviets regarded their experience with Marxism as the benchmark to assess all other Marxist revolutions. We shall respect this interpretation by looking at Mao's revisionism to a large extent from a Soviet-Marxist perspective. Thus, we can say that Mao's revision of Marxist theory involved (1) his understanding of the place of

the peasants in carrying out revolution; (2) his emphasis on the importance of willpower in conducting revolutionary tasks; (3) his approach to
revolution, extending it indefinitely into the future, and; (4) his definition of class. Perhaps most irksome to the Soviets, however, were Mao's
revisionist positions with regard to: (5) matters of military strategy and,
finally, (6) the place of China in the world. We shall discuss each of these
matters in turn.[35]

The Peasant-Centered Revolution

First and foremost in importance and chronology was Mao's
insistence that no revolution could be carried out without the peasants'
playing the central role. This departed significantly from Marx's view, of
course, and from the Soviet experience as well. In fact, most of the time
neither Marx nor his Bolshevik followers in Russia could disguise their
contempt for peasant farmers. Most Bolsheviks heartily sympathized
with Marx's sneering remark in the *Communist Manifesto* about "the
idiocy of rural life," and felt that anything worthwhile in the world was
the product of urban life. More than that, from the standpoint of theory
and practice it was clear that a Marxist revolution must involve an
uprising of the urban proletariat in an industrial society. To this idea
Lenin added the crucial point about revolutionary tactics, in that the
proletariat should be led by a small group of dedicated professional
revolutionaries—the vanguard of the proletariat. But he still insisted
upon the central place of the urban proletariat in the conduct of the
revolution. The rural dwellers took their direction from the cities.

To Mao it was the other way around. One could just have easily
referred to "idiocy of urban life," according to his priorities. In fact, he
hated the cities, and felt that they were quite hopeless. He believed that
they contained all sorts of contemptible and nonrevolutionary sorts of
characters—intellectuals, bureaucrats, and the like—and that what everybody needed from time to time was the invigoration that comes from
living and working with the masses in the country. Most importantly,
from the theoretical standpoint of who should lead the revolution,
considering from what source it should draw its primary support in
terms of people, power, and inspiration, the peasants were unquestionably at the center of his system. True, Mao gave lip service to
Marxist-Soviet dogma. Often he had no choice, and at all events he
wanted "the freedom to say one thing, think another, and do a third
if local conditions so dictated," in Dennis Bloodworth's terms.[36] As we
have seen, his peasant-centered outlook continued after the revolution
as well, which is why the focus of so much Maoist social experimentation was on the countryside. In short, intellectually, tactically, and

temperamentally, Mao drew his inspiration from the countryside, not the cities.

Human Will Over "Objective Forces"

Mao departed from the Marxist script also in his emphasis upon the effectiveness of human will in accomplishing great historical tasks, as opposed to relying upon "objective forces" in history that assumedly function independently of conscious designs. Indeed, Marx felt that even the greatest leader should not consciously be able to alter in any significant way the inevitable "march of history," as this is essentially a function of a society's economic development. Of course, the development of communism in the Soviet Union and elsewhere has taken place as a result of enormous efforts of will, of individuals determined to achieve particular goals, regardless of the "objective conditions." But the dogma remains the same. The unpredictability of individual initiatives arising from the masses has made human will an object of suspicion among Soviet Marxist theorists. They have always been uneasy with "spontaneity," largely because of its uncontrollable nature.

Clearly, Mao distrusted spontaneity as much as any Russian Marxist. When the cultural revolution developed in unpredictable and dangerous ways, for instance, he turned it off. But he also started it. And he started the Great Leap Forward, as well, along with other smaller efforts in social and economic engineering. Certainly none of these would have developed because the conditions were somehow historically "ripe" for change; on the contrary, his opponents argued that the opposite was usually true. For example, when Mao wanted to collectivize the peasantry in the fifties, he was faced with the opposition of Liu Shaoqi, who felt that such a move made no sense without the requisite agricultural machinery. Get the tractors first; then collectivize, he felt. Shaoqi lost the argument, and later his life. Mao insisted that human willpower could make up for what was lacking in machinery. As we have seen, he was wrong. Not only was Chinese agriculture set back significantly, but Mao's policies also generated a great deal of conflict. Yet, for him, conflict was to be expected. Indeed, endless conflict was the rule of the universe.

Endless Revolution

In 1957 Mao wrote one of his most famous pieces, "On the Handling of Contradictions Among the People," in which he asserted that everything develops through struggle, including Marxism. This is even true after the revolution that brings into being the socialist state. "What is correct," he stated, "always develops in the course of struggle with what is wrong . . . Such struggles never end. This is the law of development of truth and it is certainly also the law of development of Marxism."[37] Mao's brand of Marxism involved unending struggle between truth and untruth, with no final victory of the former in sight. Indeed, he felt that every six or seven years, new "demons and monsters" would surface, and society would have to go through some serious struggles to overcome them. The main point of the various domestic upheavals he instigated—especially the cultural revolution—was to rekindle the fighting spirit in the minds of the people, to keep revolutionary struggles going indefinitely. To Mao the primary meaning of political existence was to engage the whole society in endless revolution.

But that is not exactly what Marx believed. For Marx, revolutionary struggle was the midwife that brought forth a new historical stage; and in the last stage of them all, full communism, there would be no more struggle. True, it would take some conflict to rid society of its bourgeois elements—the "first phase" of communism—but even this would eventually come to an end. Ultimately, all of mankind would live together in peace and harmony, when communism was fully developed.[38] In the classless society of the future, the basis of all struggle, class conflict, would no longer exist. That is, the "objective conditions" would make any further struggle impossible. Mao, by contrast, believed that social struggles had origins in sources other than class conflict. This is the fourth major aspect of his revisionism.

Maoist Definition of Class

We have seen that Marx understood social class according to two criteria; first, in terms of the class members' relationship to the means of production, which eventually generates, second, class members' *awareness* of themselves as belonging to a group with distinct characteristics, interests, and goals. Mao's approach to social class concentrated primarily on the second aspect of Marx's definition. In fact, few things about Maoism are more blatantly revisionist than his view that, among significant numbers of people, one's ideological outlook can exist independently of one's class background. Certainly, social class was not ignored; indeed, during Mao's rule, many people were hounded because of their *parents'* class standing, especially during the cultural revolution. This was because the Red Guards assumed that the bourgeois mentality of suspect classes had contaminated the children. But to Mao, communism and capitalism were best understood in terms of one's attitude, regardless of social standing or family background. That is why, a decade and a half after the communist victory in China, he insisted that the Communist Party itself was poisoned with those who had capitalist outlooks—the so-called "capitalist roaders." Thus, adopting the correct class attitude became a matter of constant diligence, requiring frequent "purifications," "self-criticisms," and reinvigorations of revolutionary enthusiasm. Clearly, his views about endless struggle were closely linked to his understanding of social class.

There was also a streak of adventuristic mischief in his outlook. Mao once declared that "life should have some complication, otherwise it would be too monotonous."[39] In a more serious vein, he seemed to think that a life free of conflict was spiritually barren. In fact, much of what he did to China was the result of the sheer boredom that attends ruling in a society that is not at war. From this standpoint, it probably would have been better for the country if he had stepped down after 1949. For nearly a quarter century after the revolution he forced the Chinese to fight when there was no one left to fight, except perhaps those who felt further upheaval was senseless. In fact, of all the aspects of Mao's revisionism, his commitment to endless struggle against all those with the wrong class attitudes was probably the most destructive.

Maoist Military Strategy

The last two aspects of Maoist revisionism are significant for military affairs and foreign policy. The first one concerns the tactical, military implications of this doctrine about the peasant-led revolution. To understand it requires brief reference to the sources in Chinese history that inspired Mao's military decisions during his long struggle for power, as well as to the instructions from Comintern advisers that he chose *not* to follow. Against this background it is clear that Mao was a revisionist from a Soviet point of view largely because he was Chinese, and not European.

The military strategy of Mao's forces during China's long civil war was modeled after the rules contained in Sunzi's *Art of War,* a Chinese manual of combat.[40] Sunzi, who lived during the fifth century B.C., theorized that battles are won, not by frontal assaults, but by indirection and deception. Undermine your enemy's morale, the sage advised; appear strong when you are weak and weak when you are strong, so as to goad your enemy into making disastrous attacks. Ambush him, wear him down with endless pursuit, strike hard when he is weak and demoralized, get him to doubt himself. Sunzi also counseled, most importantly, that it was not dishonorable to withdraw, particularly when it is prudent to do so. One must always be flexible, elusive, and clever; avoid the heavily armed cities; hit the enemy where he is weak. Speed, mobility, concentrated force at crucial places—these are the ingredients for ultimate success, said the fifth-century expert on military affairs. All of this, of course, amounts to perfect advice for twentieth-century guerrilla warfare. Mao understood Sunzi well and referred to him often. This is why he asked, with justified indignation; what Bolshevik, schooled in the arts of frontal warfare in European conditions, could possibly understand the Chinese genius for succeeding under very different circumstances, where the European dogma made no sense?

In fact, the advice he received from the Cominterm officials in the CCP often verged on the snobbish, to Mao's very great disgust. For instance, while Mao was operating from his various mountain bases, he usually received some patronizing criticism for his practice of rounding up assorted local bandits and other disaffected bums, and turning them into soldiers for his army. He was simply following a perfectly Chinese pattern, which in this case traced its ancestry to a certain Liu Bang, whose dynasty began in 210 B.C. Liu was a very interesting character, who began in life as an ordinary peasant. He was extremely resourceful and clever, and succeeded by guile and boldness in overthrowing the Qin dynasty with a group of ruffians and hills-men he recruited from the countryside. He then founded his own dynasty, and it lasted for some four hundred years—not bad for a country boy with no formal training in military dogma.[41]

Mao was a country boy too, and his role model was none other than the illustrious Liu Bang. Like the master, he put his bastions of military strength, not in the cities, but in such places as the towering peaks of Chingchang mountains. There he too collected an odd assortment of individuals—disaffected peasants, random ruffians, ne'er-do-wells, and "declassed" persons of various stripes—to form, in the manner of Liu Bang, his own army. And, of course, he operated like Liu Bang as well— much to the consternation of his Comintern advisers. Disperse your army into roving bands of soldiers, they told him; harrass the enemy when he ventures out from the cities. Or meet the enemy with massed attacks in a good, proper, set piece European style. But don't put military bases in mountains, caves, and whatnot—whoever heard of such a thing? Mao did, of course. And after suffering through numerous military disasters by following irrelevant instructions, he responded in a fashion in which Liu Bang and Sunzi would have been proud: he simply ignored it.

China as the Revolutionary Role Model

Perhaps the most direct challenge to Soviet authority that derived from Mao's revisionism was his insistence upon asserting China's leadership as the role model for revolutionary activities throughout the world. The reasons for Mao's position were based upon his personal experience, as well as upon considerations of national pride. On the first matter, he certainly had little reason to feel cordial toward the Soviets, as their continued bad advice during the twenties and thirites had nearly got him killed. Moreover, after the revolution Stalin revealed little sympathy for supporting China's economic development. Mao was finally able to extract some aid from the communist giant, but it was considerably less than what the Soviets were doing for their Eastern European clients, and nowhere near what the Americans were doing for Western Europe. In short, Stalin's attitude toward the CCP remained cautious.

But if Stalin was bad, Nikita Khrushchev, his successor, was even worse. Khrushchev did manage to increase Soviet aid to China, but his other policies were cause for grave concern. For instance, his "de-Stalinization" campaign in 1956 was deeply unnerving to Mao; what if some of his colleagues got the same idea about him? Moreover, Khrushchev engaged in all sorts of "revisionist" policies, from his point of view, such as promoting "peaceful coexistence" with the United States. How could anyone in his right communist mind declare peaceful coexistence with the main foe of socialists everywhere? The only conclusion that Mao could draw from all this was that Khrushchev was not a good Marxist.

This was the same conclusion that Khrushchev drew about Mao. More than that, he felt that the Chinese leader was mentally unhinged. Mao was accustomed to referring to the United States as a "paper tiger," for instance; Khrushchev had to remind him prudently that this paper tiger had nuclear teeth. No matter, replied Mao. If it came to nuclear war, half of the human race might be lost, but the other half would emerge victorious and the whole world would be socialist. Of course, the half that remained would probably be Chinese, not Russian. That thought may have caused the burly Russian leader to wonder if peaceful coexistence with the United States was somehow preferable to friendly antagonism with the People's Republic of China. By the early sixties Mao was entertaining similar thoughts, feeling that the Russians were even worse than the United States. The rift between the two finally resulted in the Soviets' calling back their advisers and ending the technological assistance they had been providing. This left the Chinese in charge of completing the various gargantuan construction projects that the Russians were so good at building, and caused the delay in developing their own atomic bomb. But the Russian departure also put the Chinese totally in charge of their own affairs. And it served to clarify Mao's world view.

What was the world according to Mao? It was this: the world is divided into two camps, the revolutionary and the counterrevolutionary. Into the latter group fell the Soviet Union, the United States, and all those countries in their respective spheres of influence. The former group included China and virtually all the rest of the world, an enormous area comprising most of Africa, Asia, and Latin America. In fact, Mao considered the revolutionary situation in the world as an extension of the revolutionary experience of China. The industrialized, counterrevolutionary countries represented the cities, and the vast Third World, with its hundreds of millions of peasants, represented the countryside. China was at the center of this revolutionary group; it was the base in the world countryside fighting against the forces of counter-revolution in the global "cities." Mao assumed, with justification, that the Chinese experience in revolution was far more relevant to the world situation than that of the Soviet Union, especially given the number of underdeveloped countries in the world. Naturally, the global role model and inspirational leader for these countries was the People's Republic of China.

But China's weakness and Mao's preoccupation with domestic affairs kept him from acting seriously upon his world views. There was also considerable opposition to his anti-Soviet policies, many of which centered upon the political coalition led by Lin Piao. One may also wonder just how serious he was in his denunciations of the two superpowers, particularly the United States, given Nixon's two visits in the 1970s. Indeed, Mao was probably flattered by the first visit, because of Nixon's attempt to use his good services to influence the North Vietnamese. The fact that the effort failed, indicated to both the limits of Chinese influence in the world, even on a close neighbor. In short, the role model that Mao provided in international affairs was far more relevant to the conduct of guerrilla warfare than it was to China's image as a significant world power.

CHINA AFTER MAO

In his 1978 text on China, Lucian Pye commented that "it would be impossible to exaggerate the role of ideology in China today. Unques-tionably it is far more important there than in the Soviet Union or in any other socialist country."[42] This was certainly a valid judgment at the time. There is a Chinese saying that "he who has once been bitten by a snake, jumps at a piece of string."[43] All of China had been bitten by the Maoist snake, and, even after his death, was not sure when it might strike again. This gave Mao's successors the gargantuan task of trying to restore the confidence of the Chinese people in the country's ruling apparatus. The Maoist snake had to be replaced by Deng Xiaoping's donkey. It would not be an easy task.

However, giant strides have been made during the decade since Mao's death. The consolidation of Deng Xiaoping's rule in China has brought with it significant changes in the country's ruling apparatus and, most importantly, its economic policies. These changes have been noted with enthusiasm by close observers of China; from the United States, especially. Harrison Salisbury, while he was "Retracing Mao's Long March"—the title of a recent essay—found a China very different from the one bleakly presented by close observers of the Maoist era.[44] What did Salisbury see? "I don't know much about Chinese hearts," he reported, "but I think that Deng Xiaoping and his new economic policy have swept the rural masses like nothing since the revolution itself."[45] Everywhere he went Salisbury found the countryside bustling with the enthusiasm and vigor of private enterprise, as a result of Deng's deliberate effort to decentralize economic decision making and encourage private initiative. In short, the diminutive Deng, who was named *Time* magazine's Man of the Year in 1985, appears to be guiding China on a path of change as far-reaching as, but greatly more beneficial than, the ceaseless upheavals inflicted upon the country by Mao.[46]

But Deng's policies have generated some conflict as well—especially in terms of ideological justification. Naturally, after denouncing capitalism for a half century, Chinese leaders cannot say now that it is fine, that it works, and that socialism—at least Mao's variety—is a disaster. Instead they prefer to call the new economics the "responsibility system." However, at the same time a front-page editorial in a December 1984 issue of the *People's Daily*—the voice of the CCP—declared that it is "naive and stupid" to adhere to Marxist dogma in the area of economic modernization. Considering that the main import of Marx's philosophy—as he saw it, at least—was precisely in the field of economic development, this is an absolutely stupendous thing to say.[47] Of course, even Mao admitted that Marx could be criticized. But being gradually debunked is another matter. And regardless of how the Chinese qualify their comments about Marx (by saying, for instance, that only "some" of his doctrines are obsolete), that is exactly what it appears they are doing. Probably Deng Xiaoping, always the practical man, has the best approach to these matters of ideology and definition: it doesn't matter what color the cat is, he once said, as long as it is able to catch the mice.

Clearly, Deng's resourcefulness goes beyond giving apt definitions. As a result of recent decisions made by CCP officials, the economic reforms practiced in the countryside are now being applied to the cities. This means that the approximate market conditions that have prevailed in agriculture since 1978, which involved decontrol of many prices and more local decision-making, are being applied to stateowned urban enterprises as well. The overcentralization of China's economy has been declared "irrational." However, in political terms, the advances have been less impressive. In December 1986, a number of massive demonstrations took place, involving disaffected students as well as some of China's most prominent intellectuals, who together called for instituting more democracy in China's governing apparatus. Deng's regime reacted with a firm, although generally nonviolent, response. But the incidents precipitated a party shake-up that resulted in the advance of several political hard-liners, along with the demise of at least one prominent party official, Hu Yaobang, widely perceived as the ultimate successor to Deng. Thus, Deng's tolerance for political liberalization to accompany the economic reforms clearly has limits. Still, in a typical Maoist fashion, the economic reforms were applied to the countryside first, then to the cities, where the demonstrations took place. In terms of economic policy, it seems that at the moment, at least, Deng's multicolored cats are catching a great number of mice. It also seems that China, with or without Mao, is destined to be revisionist. The question remains as to whether or not this revisionism will include genuine political reforms as well.

ENDNOTES

[1]Quoted in Dick Wilson, *The People's Emperor: Mao: A Biography of Mao Tse-Tung* (Garden City, N.Y.: Doubleday and Company, 1980), p. 189.

[2]Ibid., p. 432.

[3]Quoted by Dennis Bloodworth, *The Messiah and the Mandarins: Mao Tse-Tung and the Ironies of Power* (New York: Atheneum, 1982), p. 83.

[4]Ibid., after the title page.

[5]Quoted in Wilson, *People's Emperor*, p. 356.

[6]Ross Terrill, *Mao: A Biography* (New York: Harper Colophon Books, 1980), pp. 9–10.

[7]For an account of China's complicated political history during this time, see Richard C. Thornton, *China: A Political History 1917–1980* (Boulder, Colo.: Westview Press, 1982), pp. 3–127. There are also a number of splendid introductory texts on Chinese politics, such as James C. F. Wang, *Contemporary Chinese Politics: An Introduction*, 2nd ed. (Englewood Cliffs, N.J.: Prentice-Hall, 1985); and James R. Townsend and Brantly Womack, *Politics in China*, 3rd ed. (Boston: Little, Brown, and Company, 1986).

[8]There is a fair number of good biographies of Mao. Probably the most notable ones include Edgar Snow, *Red Star Over China* (New York: Grove Press, 1971), a work that was first published in 1938; Stuart Schram, *Mao Tse-Tung* (Baltimore: Penguin, 1968); and the work of the dean of American Sinologists, John King Fairbank. Professor Fairbank's lifelong experience with China studies, along with a brief review of his immense scholarly output, is dealt with in one of his most recent books, *Chinabound: A Fifty-year Memoir* (New York: Harper & Row, 1982). The biographies consulted here were completed after Mao's death in 1976, and include the works of Wilson, Bloodworth, and Terrill, cited earlier. For a good listing and an excellent introduction to the politics of China, see Lucian W. Pye, *China: An Introduction*, 2nd ed. (Boston: Little, Brown, and Company, 1978).

[9]Quoted in Wilson, *People's Emperor*, p. 89.

[10]See, for example, his essay, "Analysis of Classes in Chinese Society," in Anne Fremantle, ed., *Mao Tse-Tung: An Anthology of His Writings* (New York: New American Library, 1962), pp. 51–59.

[11]Quoted in Wilson, *People's Emperor*, p. 114.

[12]Ibid., pp. 132–35. This advice comes from the Chingkangshan Program (named after the Chingkang Mountains, where he was when he wrote it). See the account, "The Struggle in the Chingkang Mountains," in Fremantle, *Mao: An Anthology*, pp. 60–74.

[13]Quoted in Wilson, *People's Emperor*, p. 177.

[14]All of these writings, or excerpts thereof, are contained in Fremantle, *Mao: An Anthology*. See also the collection edited by Stuart Schram, *The Political Thought of Mao Tse-Tung* (New York: Frederick A. Praeger, 1963).

[15]Fremantle, *Mao: An Anthology*, p. 205.

[16]Ibid.

[17]Schram, *Political Thought*, p. 114.

[18]Bloodworth, *Messiah and Mandarins*, p. 68.

[19]This is Bloodworth's estimate, p. 103.

[20]Wilson, *People's Emperor*, p. 299.

[21]Quoted in Ibid., p. 346.

[22]This address was later expanded upon and published as "On the Correct Handling of Contradictions Among the People." See Fremantle, *Mao: An Anthology*, pp. 264–97.

[23]Wilson, *People's Emperor*, p. 361.

[24]See especially Terrill's account in *Mao*, pp. 262–66.

[25]Wilson, *People's Emperor*, p. 386.

[26]Bloodworth, *Messiah and Mandarins*, pp. 178–79.

[27]Quoted in Terrill, *Mao*, p. 269, footnote.

[28]Bloodworth, *Messiah and Mandarins*, p. 182.

[29]Quoted in Ibid., pp. 207–208.

[30]Fox Butterfield, *China: Alive in the Bitter Sea* (New York: The New York Times Book Co., 1982), p. 18.

[31]On the Lin Piao incident, see especially Terrill, *Mao*, pp. 347–52.

[32]Quoted in Terrill, Ibid., p. 416.

[33]For Mao's last years, see especially Ibid., pp. 382–93.

[34]This account is based upon Ibid., pp. 417–20.

[35]For treatments of Mao's thought, see Arthur A. Cohen, "Maoism," in Milorad M. Drachkovitch, ed., *Marxism in the Modern World* (Stanford, Calif.: Stanford University Press, 1965), pp. 164–91; Arthur A. Cohen, *The Communism of Mao Tse-Tung* (Chicago: University of Chicago Press, 1964); Harold C. Hinton, *An Introduction to Chinese Politics* (New York: Praeger Publishers, 1973), pp. 88–112; Pye, *China*, pp. 189–213; and especially Dick Wilson, ed., *Mao Tse-Tung on the Scales of History* (Cambridge, England: Cambridge University Press, 1977).

[36]Bloodworth, *Messiah and Mandarin*, p. 49.

[37]In Fremantle, *Mao: An Anthology*, p. 286.

[38]There is, of course, in Marx the concept of the revolution in permanence, which he mentioned in an 1848 speech before the German workers in the Communist League. This notion has always been troubling to Marxist scholars, but probably too much significance has been attached to it. Marx called for permanent revolution in the context of communist workers being faced with a recently successful petty- bourgeois revolution. Under these circumstances he advised that the revolution keep going until "all more or less possessing classes have been forced out of their position of dominance." This is rather different from Mao's beliefs that the revolution must continue to maintain the purity and fervor of the revolutionary approach to life. See Marx and Engels, "Address to the Central Committee to the Communist League," in Robert C. Tucker, ed., *The Marx-Engels Reader* (New York: W. W. Norton & Company, Inc., 1978), pp. 501–11. The quote is from p. 505.

[39]Quoted in Wilson, *People's Emperor*, p. 338.

[40]Bloodworth, *Messiah and Mandarins,* pp. 44–46.

[41]Ibid.

[42]Pye, *China,* p. 190.

[43]Cited in Bloodworth, *Messiah and Mandarins,* p. 299.

[44]Harrison Salisbury, "Retracing Mao's Long March," in the *New York Times Magazine,* November 18, 1984, pp. 42–47, 50–60, 54–66. For excellent earlier appraisals of China in the wake of Mao's rule, see Simon Leys, *Chinese Shadows* (New York: Penguin Books, 1978); Steven W. Mosher, *Broken Earth: The Rural Chinese* (New York: The Free Press, 1983); and Fox Butterfield, *China: Alive in the Bitter Sea* (New York: The New York Times Book Co., 1982).

[45]Salisbury, "Mao's Long March," p. 46.

[46]See the excellent review in *Time* magazine, "Man of the Year: Deng Xiaoping," January 6, 1986, pp. 24–69.

[47]In addition to the article cited in the preceding note, for accounts of China surrounding Deng's modernization policies, see, for instance, the following reports in *Time:* "Capitalism Comes to the City," October 29, 1984, p. 47; "Lower Profile for Mother-in-Law," December 3, 1984, p. 42; "Marx is Dead—Long Live Marx," December 24, 1984, p. 35; "It Cannot Harm Us," January 14, 1985, pp. 36–37; and an article by Stuart Schram, "Economics in Command? Ideology and Policy Since the Third Plenum," *China Quarterly,* no. 99 (September 1984). Recent editions of *Current History* also contain excellent assessments. See "The People's Republic of China, 1985" *Current History,* 84, no. 503 (September 1985); and "The People's Republic of China, 1984," *Current History,* 83, no. 494 (September 1984).

ADOLF HITLER
Founder and Destroyer

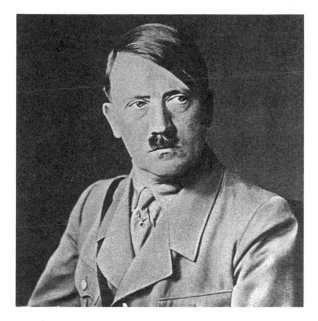

He was a scrubby little rogue . . . *Paula Hitler,* Adolf's sister[1]
. . . he lacked self-discipline, being notoriously cantankerous, willful, arrogant and irascible . . . (one of Hitler's teachers in Linz, Austria)[2]
An Austrian charmer. *Frau Popp,* Hitler's housekeeper in Munich[3]
Hitler's power is not political; it is magic. *Dr. Carl Gustav Jung*[4]
That Germany, in the hour of her greatest need, brings forth a Hitler—that is proof of her vitality. *Houston Stewart Chamberlain*[5]
In principle and doctrine, Hitler was no more wicked and unscrupulous than many other contemporary statesmen. *A. J. P. Taylor*[6]
. . . we are forced to consider Hitler . . . not as a personal devil, wicked as his actions and philosophy may be, but as the expression of a state of mind existing in millions of people, not only in Germany but to a smaller degree in all civilized countries. *Walter C. Langer,* author of a secret wartime psychological analysis of Hitler[7]
I shall never survive the defeat of my people. *Adolf Hitler,* November 1939[8]

INTRODUCTION

In December 1924 Adolf Hitler was released from jail. He had served only a portion of a sentence imposed upon him for his conviction in leading an unsuccessful uprising against the Bavarian government.[9] His failure cost him a year in prison and the virtual disintegration of the movement he had been leading against the authorities in Bavaria. He came back to a party in organizational disarray and utter despondency. During his absence the National Socialist German Workers' Party—the Nazis—had been reduced to a contemptible menagerie of factions, all sniping at one another with petulant impotence. Many of his friends were still in confinement, while others were outside sulking. The Sturmabteilung, the private army that served party needs by keeping order at meetings and instilling martial qualities into new recruits, was in a pitiful state, frittering the time away with useless activities in assorted "sports clubs." The remaining members of the party had gone back to a more-or-less normal existence, helped immensely by the return of a stable political and economic environment. In short, the Nazi movement appeared to be shattered beyond repair. The future for it and Adolf Hitler looked bleak.

Then Hitler spoke. In February 1925, at a crowded hall in Munich, he made his first major speech after his release from prison. His audience was varied, consisting of party members and sympathizers, but included nonmembers as well, along with a considerable number of skeptics and political opponents. Regardless of their predispositions, everyone in the audience had entered the hall in an expectant, although somewhat contentious and challenging, mood. But after being exposed to the alluring tones of the Führer's voice, they all left feeling rejuvenated and filled with hope. Hitler had put them under his spell. John Toland describes the scene:

> Cries of "Heil!" rang out. Women wept as the crowd pressed from the rear, climbing onto the chairs and tables. Men who had been bitter enemies surged to the platform and shook hands, some of them unable to restrain tears . . .[10]

Such was the effect of Adolf Hitler. He accomplished in one speech what none of his followers had been able to produce over the course of one year during his absence in prison. In a single flash of oratorical brilliance, Hitler silenced his critics, moved the party to unity under his leadership, and infused it with purpose and vitality again. He succeeded in demonstrating that the Nazi Party and everything it stood for were simply unthinkable without him.

In terms of ideological leadership, Adolf Hitler was probably the most total founder of the twentieth century. He founded Nazism, the

Nazi Party, and the Third Reich, an enterprise that demonstrated dramatically all the major characteristics of modern political ideologies. Nazi hagiology was simple; although there were numerous figures leading up to Hitler, there was no question that he was the founder and the central figure of the ideology. Further, he supplied the most noted sacred text, *Mein Kampf,* and this explained thoroughly the meaning of political existence for Germans and non-Germans as well. Indeed, most of Hitler's speeches were devoted to explaining to Germans who they were, how they fit into the grand scheme of history, what their national mission was, and why it was justified. He was at the heart of everything associated with Nazism.

For all that, Hitler's role as a founder did not actually involve the creation of any ideas that were new or unfamiliar to the German people. He was a synthesizer of ideas, not an innovator. His originality as a founder consisted of forging together some powerful themes in the German philosophical and historical experience and investing them with the extraordinary dynamism of his own personality. These themes were all familiar ones: anti-Semitism, geopolitical expansionism, and German nationalism inspired by the notion of Germanic, or "Aryan," racial superiority. To these elements Hitler added only one, anti-Bolshevism, which he explained in terms of the other three. The result was Nazism, a powerful mix of ideological precepts that Hitler raised to a fever pitch and unleashed on a path of destruction that engulfed the German people and nearly the whole civilized world as well. While its separate components are all intelligible apart from one another and Hitler, the *combination* of ideas, practices, and institutions known as Nazism is not. It and the Third Reich are inconceivable without Adolf Hitler.

Thus, it is important to explore the special character of Hitler's personality in order to understand the reasons for his rise to power in Germany. First, however, we shall treat the historical and philosophical roots of Nazism, and then survey Hitler's remarkable political career as founder and ultimately the destroyer of the Third Reich. We shall conclude our treatment with some brief comments about the impact of this most remarkable ideological leader upon events in twentieth-century politics.

HISTORICAL AND PHILOSOPHICAL ROOTS

Statism

The origins of the statist ideology so dramatically epitomized by Adolf Hitler derive from the religious upheavals that occurred during the Reformation, when the state replaced the church as the ultimate

repository of political authority throughout Europe.[11] This development was the logical and historical outcome of the attack made against
the Catholic Church by Martin Luther (1483–1546). Luther, who began
his career with the intent to reform, insisted that the vast array of
administrative and political powers wielded by the Church could not be
justified in spiritual terms. After all, he argued, the true church really
consisted of the invisible body of believers, which by definition could not
be subject to the temporal authority of the Roman Church. Further, he
believed that the state was as much an instrument of God as the Church,
and therefore deserved to be obeyed, as well, under nearly all circumstances. Certainly evil rulers will be punished, he stated, but that is the
prerogative of God, and not man. Therefore, the most that any person
could do in the face of oppressive political authority, Luther concluded,
was to offer passive resistance. The result of Luther's attack on Church
authority, and generally the effect of Reformation thinking in Germany,
was to strengthen the authority of the state against any conceivable rival.

The role of the state in German affairs was augmented further by
the horrible wars that took place on German soil over the course of the
next 100 years. In one of these, Luther himself made a contribution.
When he heard about a revolt of some peasants in Southern Germany
against the rule of their arrogant nobles in 1524–1525, he was filled with
rage, and demanded that no mercy whatsoever be shown to the rebels.
Luther got his wish, with a vengeance, but far worse was to come. About
a century after the suppression of the peasant uprising, a series of
religious conflicts known as the Thirty Years War broke out all over
Germany. By its end, one-third to one-half of the population had been
killed, and all German lands suffered devastation even beyond that
inflicted by Allied forces during World War II. The conclusion drawn
from these events was clear and lasting, and no one needed to convince
Germans about the necessity of a strong temporal authority to maintain
peace, order, and stability. Indeed, anything was preferable to risking
the unbridled destruction unleashed by war. One's civic duties involved
discipline, civil order, and allegiance to the state—in short, obedience.

This outlook also found powerful expression in a long line of
distinguished German statesmen and philosophers, some of whom are
considered giants in the history of Western civilization. Immanuel Kant
(1724–1804), for example, certainly one of the stars of the Enlightenment, insisted that it was "the duty of the people to bear any abuse of the
supreme power even though it should be considered unbearable."[12] He
went on to assert that a single ruler was justified in taking actions counter
to the wishes of the majority of the people, provided he had in mind the
general welfare. This line of thought was carried even further by Georg
Friedrich Hegel (1770–1831), another influential thinker in the German

tradition. Hegel virtually identified individual freedom with conformity to the will of the state. "In considering freedom," he declared, "the starting point must not be individuality," but rather the "ethical whole" that constitutes the state. In fact, against the background of the grand, history-making actions on the part of the state, "single individuals are only moments." In a flourish of rhetorical excess, Hegel even proclaimed the state as "the march of God in the world."[13] A stronger statement on behalf of state authority can scarcely be imagined.

German statism was carried forward to the twentieth century by such thinkers as Heinrich von Treitschke (1834–1896), one of the more notable figures who glorified the German Reich. A year before the German Empire was proclaimed in 1871, Treitschke summarized four centuries of German political reflections about state authority by asserting flatly that "theoretically no limits can be set to the functions of the state."[14] It is the "instrument of civilization," he declared; a "moral community" dedicated to the positive "improvement of the human race." Further, the state should not shrink from violence to achieve its noble aims. Indeed, he praised the "moral majesty" of war as a means of testing the stamina and worthiness of a nation. This was a conviction expressed by many in Germany on the eve of the First World War. While an Englishmen, Norman Angell, confidently demonstrated the impossibility of war in an enormously popular book called *The Great Illusion* (1910), the best brains in Germany were devoted to the task of proving precisely the opposite. In fact, one of them, Friedrich von Bernhardi, of the German general staff, not only declared that war was inevitable, but that it was desirable and a "biological necessity" as well.[15] And as the guns of August, to use Barbara Tuchman's expression, wreaked their awesome destruction on European battlefields in 1914, the first year of that terrible war, German statism and German militarism were being discussed in the same breath.[16]

The Leadership Principle

In 1870 Otto von Bismarck, the great Prussian leader and principle architect of German unification, remarked that "a statesman cannot create anything himself. He must wait and listen until he hears the steps of God sounding through events; then leap up and grasp the hem of His garment."[17] Nothing summarizes better than this the role of leadership in the development of Germany since the time of the Reformation. From Luther to Hitler, German lands had been forged together into states by ambitious leapers and graspers. Many of them, like Hitler, often grasped more than they could hold on to, but that never discouraged other German leaders throughout the nation's history from continuing to try. Thus, seen against the background of German national development, Adolf Hitler was far from unique. Quite the contrary, he followed a long and often bloody tradition of political opportunists. For instance, the formation of the Prussian state came about as a result of the remarkable initiatives of Frederick the Great during the eighteenth century. Of course, Bismarck, through a combination of boldness and duplicity, was the statesman mainly responsible for the creation of the German Empire in 1871. And like Hitler, they each succeeded in imposing their particular stamp upon the inhabitants.

What made Hitler so very different from his predecessors was his rationale—the body of thought that he drew upon to justify his activities as leader of the German state. That is, he was informed not only by the legacies of statism and the leadership principle, but also by a sort of secular religion of a peculiarly German kind that is usually referred to as "Volkish thought." It convinced him and the Nazis that the Germans were different, that they were superior, that they were the "master race," whose mission on earth was to safeguard their "racial purity," propagate themselves, and extend their dominance over inferior peoples. More than anything else, this made Nazi Germany unlike any other regime that had ever come to power in Germany—or indeed in any other place on earth.

Racism

The idea of German national distinctiveness had origins that actually were not terribly sinister. It is usually traced to the work of Johann Fichte (1762–1814), who, like his great contemporary, Hegel, was interested in justifying the creation of a greater German state, but only as the defender of Germanic national values. This was not an unreasonable position, considering the humiliations suffered by the various German states during the Napoleonic era, which influenced Fichte and a great many German thinkers. They were all, in fact, inspired by the extraordinarily successful example of France, the most vigorous national state in the world. Fichte was among many observers who concluded that in order for nations to prosper, or even to survive, they had to be united by common national values and ruled by a single national state.

Although Fichte never succumbed to the racial superstitions that motivated the Third Reich, he clearly laid the intellectual groundwork for the development of ideas that contributed more directly to Nazi beliefs. Without question the most important of these was the Volkish thought, which gained enormous vogue in Germany during the latter part of the nineteenth century. The Germanic concept of the Volk is not exactly translatable into a single English word; perhaps the most accurate rendering is captured by the phrase, "people-tribe-group." This entity was considered to have an "essence" or a common "soul," and one's membership in it implied a mystical union with one's fellows, who collectively participated in communication with God. Further, the person-Volk-universe-God nexus was considered a unity, which was bound together by spiritual "forces" that flowed through each element of the mixture, connecting them all to one another. The "Germanic faith" was the summary expression for these ideas, which were popularized in German lands by such thinkers as Paul de Lagarde and Julius Langbehn.[18]

From a contemporary standpoint, it is not easy to understand how so many Germans could be committed to the Germanic faith, that "bond of unity" for all Germans. However, prior to the time when Germans were politically united, the common "soul" that presumably bound them all together probably acted as a substitute for the more tangible experience of living within common political boundaries. But none of this would have mattered at all if there hadn't been such an ominous, dark side to the Germanic faith. The fact that there was had terrible consequences for the twentieth century.

To understand these it is necessary to see what the Volkish writers valued and, more importantly, what they were reacting against. Considering the historical period when their ideas became most influential—the generation before World War I—it would seem that there was really something ridiculous about the whole Volkish phenomenon. When Germany was a mighty empire and rapidly becoming the most powerful state in Europe, the Volkish writers were looking *backward,* not forward. Indeed, they idealized what they felt were happier, less complicated times in the past, when most Germans lived off the land and were governed by hundreds of petty feudal principalities. Volkish artists concocted fantastic visions of rural landscapes populated by strong tillers of the soil, or panoramic displays of young, virile bodies bathing in sunlight on the stone hardness of some exposed precipice. All this was very quaint, perhaps; but one can reasonably ask just what on earth any of it had to do with the powerful industrial Germany that was developing before their eyes.

The answer is that the Volkish writers had no use at all for this new Germany, and actually were rather repulsed by it. In fact, the de Lagardes and Langbehns of the late nineteenth century were frankly traumatized by the modern world and by secular values generally. The new, powerful industrial state was just an awful, alien thing to them; it was a materialistic, dirty, and spiritless behemoth, a place where people didn't know who they were or where they belonged. That is why the

Middle Ages, with its orderly delineation of ranks and its social stability, had so much appeal. It was a time when the virtues of nobility, loyalty, and bravery were familiar; when great deeds were performed against the backdrop of woods and mountains and streams and rivers, all under the purifying brilliance of sunlight. But in modern Germany all this had changed, all the ancient virtues had been forgotten, nature was being despoiled, and all the gods had left; or rather, said Friedrich Nietzsche, one of the most anguished observers of his day, they had been driven out. And now people were left alone with a spiritless world of machinery and functions and factory smoke and nothing to believe in. The Germanic faith gave them something to believe in, something to enable them to cope with all the frightening uncertainties of modern life.

It also gave them someone to blame for the hideous aspects of modernity—the Jew. Why the Jew? Because Jews, more than any other group, were identified with all the things in the modern world that Volkish writers despised. And their distinctiveness as a separate religious group made them easy targets for believers in the Germanic faith. More than that, Volkish writers stressed what they felt were the inherent blood differences between Germans and Jews. Physical characteristics were considered decisive; Jewish physiognomies were presented in outrageous caricatures, depicting a typical member of the Jewish "race" as a swarthy, slightly obese, shifty-eyed goblin with a long nose and thick lips. This was the extreme opposite of the Volkish vision of Aryan purity and goodness, which was presented in terms of the sturdy and muscular, blue-eyed, blond youth, working the soil in environments fully suggesting a purity reminiscent of the Garden of Eden. By vivid contrast, the Jews were presented as urban creatures, who performed functions associated with the modern, secular world. They were hateful in every respect to all true members of the Volk.

During the time that Hitler lived in Vienna, from 1907 to 1913, racist propaganda against Jews had reached a feverish pitch. The literature that the young Hitler absorbed during his stay there had come to the following conclusions about Germans, Jews, and the way the world worked:[19] the course of world history has been determined by the eternal conflict between two races, the Aryans (interestingly, this was originally just a linguistic term) and the Jews. The former was the source of all the progress that civilizations had attained in the world; the latter, usually depicted in biological and hygenic terms as "vermin," "parasites," "poison," or "filth," was the source of all that was vile, ugly, and bad—of everything, that is, that retarded the health of societies. Moreover, any admixture of blood between the two races was always degenerative, and contributed to the demise of civilization. On the other hand, boundless glories awaited those nations that solved their "Jewish problem," thus permitting the superiority of the Aryan genius to attain its natural heights. In short, only the strongest and best deserved to survive.

Thus, it is clear that the "master race" idea was not something invented by Hitler. By the time he began his political career in Munich soon after World War I, the conviction that the Germans—considered the closest to being pure Aryans—were superior was widely if somewhat ambiguously believed by nearly all Germans, within and outside the Empire. Certainly it is true that Volkish ideas permeated every part of German society— its ruling elites, musical and artistic circles, the educational establishment especially, and the military. Of course, German racism existed in the context of the more directly relevant political concepts already discussed; namely, statism and the leadership principle. And with millions of Germans in the habit of singing, *"Deutschland, Deutschland uber Alles,"* which translates roughly as, "Germany, Germany, over All," many Europeans, and not just Jews, had every reason to feel uneasy about the intentions of the German government.

It is entirely possible that none of these things would have been pushed to the extreme limits they actually reached in Hitler's regime. It is also possible that the connections among them would not have been made. Of course, some relationships were logically and historically grounded: statism with the leadership principle, and Aryan superiority with anti-Semitism. But one still could suppose that without World War I, without Hitler, without the postwar turmoil and humiliation that came from being defeated in war—in short, without the events that occurred between 1914 and 1933, the beliefs we have discussed might have remained in the more or less undeveloped state they had before World War I.[20]

They did not, of course; Hitler put them all together. That is what made him the most dramatic and devastating founder of the twentieth century. Indeed, without the unique driving force of his personality, "the phenomenon of the German dictatorship," concludes Karl Bracher in his excellent study of the Nazi regime, "could not have come to pass."[21] This is because it was Hitler as founder who brought together the various themes of the German philosophical and political traditions to form something new. It was Hitler as founder who carried these themes to their logical, extreme, and horrible conclusions, thus creating the ideology of Nazism. And it was Hitler as founder who led the political movement that put this ideology into practice and set it on a path of destruction and conquest that has few parallels in history. With the main themes of the German historical and philosophical background in mind, it is now our task to see how he did these things.

HITLER AS A FOUNDER

Hitler and the Rise of Nazism

Hitler was born on April 20, 1889, in Austria, and spent most of his boyhood years living in small towns in that country.[22] His academic performance was generally mediocre, but he showed some promise as an artist, and to that end he applied for admission into the Vienna Academy of Fine Arts in the fall of 1907. After failing twice to pass entrance examinations, he drifted downward to the depths of Vienna society over the course of the next six years. He left for Munich in 1913, and when the war broke out in the following year he joined a Bavarian regiment. For four years Hitler served with exceptional distinction as an infantryman on the Western front, barely escaping death on numerous occasions, and earning several medals. When the war ended, he was recovering from a gas attack in a military hospital. But his injury did not unnerve him nearly as much as did the news of the German defeat, which caused him seriously to think about its reasons. Two things impressed him the most about Germany's war experience: the defeatism on the home front and the effectiveness of Allied propaganda. His political career in the following years was informed in large measure by his reflections on these matters.

He actually entered politics while he was still in the army, when he was given the assignment to investigate a local group in Munich, called the German Workers' Party. After speaking out at a few meetings, Hitler impressed the leadership sufficiently to inspire them to persuade the intense and articulate corporal out of the army and into their organization as one of the officers. Hitler did so, and instantly became the leading personality of the party; indeed, he soon demonstrated that there was no room for anyone else but him at the top. And after the party was renamed the National Socialist German Workers Party in 1920, its rise to prominence in German politics was linked directly to the rise and development of Adolf Hitler. In short, he founded the Nazi Party.

In was in every respect a political organization that reflected the priorities and energies of its founder. A party newspaper was formed; much more importantly, so was a private army, the Sturmabteilung, or the SA. It consisted of large numbers of young men and war veterans, who had time on their hands and bitterness in their hearts. The SA could always be counted on to provide a show of strength at party rallies, and to intimidate the opposition. But other aspects of the party's internal structure were probably even more important. All manner of new associations in the party were developed for nearly every politically relevant group—young people, professionals, workers, along with a variety of other occupational categories. Hitler placed great emphasis upon expanding Party membership, while at the same time insisting upon total and complete control over all party activities—no dissent from the Führer's will was allowed, and no challenge to his authority was tolerated. He even set up a mock government. Basically, Hitler created a nonstate entity under his direct control that practiced what the Nazis intended to do after assuming power, when that time would come.

But what exactly did the Nazis intend to do? This too was outlined by Hitler with stunning force and clarity, in a book that he wrote while in prison, called *Mein Kampf* ("*My Struggle*"). Seen against the background of traditional German political and racial concepts, much of it actually contained very little that was new. In fact, as Werner Maser has pointed out, throughout his life Hitler's "face was turned to the nineteenth century," a point that is evident in everything the Führer said.[23] When he declared in *Mein Kampf* that "all great cultures of the past perished only because the original creative race died out from blood poisoning," he echoed the gloomy conclusions of Arthur de Gobineau, one of the most notorious nineteenth-century racists.[24] When he insisted that "everything we admire on this earth today . . . is only the creative product of a few peoples and originally perhaps of one race," he restated the comments of Houston Stewart Chamberlain, himself a master compiler of Volkish thought.[25] To the body of conclusions about Jews and Aryans that had been stated before him, Hitler added only one, and that concerned Marxism. He considered the Marxists in Europe and the Bolsheviks in Russia as simply the most recent contrivance of the Jews to despoil civilization and conquer the world. The Marxists' contention about society's being divided along class lines was anathema to him, an insidious plot to divide the German people and to destroy the common soul that united them all.

In fact, Hitler was against any division in German society that contributed to social conflict. He had contempt for those members of the property-owning classes who were indifferent to the plight of their workers, forcing them to form organizations like unions to oppose them. He delivered scathing rebukes to German politicians whose endless and meaningless debates perpetuated a party system that functioned only to weaken the country. In place of political parties, legislatures, and democratic processes generally, he called for "Germanic democracy," in which "the leader is elected, but then enjoys unconditional authority."[26] This would also eliminate the "weaklings," "fools," and "incompetents" who swelled the ranks of political parties. The Nazis he did not consider to be a political party at all; rather, they constituted a movement guided by a philosophy that allowed no compromise, no division, and no internal conflict. Their task was to work for "the victory of a revolutionary new order on this earth,"[27] one that embodies "the will to a new creation of man."[28]

It was this totalistic, messianic flair of Nazism that was most directly the result of Hitler's founding, and that gave the German state under his leadership its aggressive dynamism. For centuries Germans had been accustomed to all the traditional functions of the state to take care of its citizenry. But Hitler added to these functions the conclusions of Volkish ideology, which insisted that a race must either expand or die. And he made it emphatically clear that the state must be used as a tool of the party to advance the cause of the higher races by conquering and, in some cases, liquidating, the lower races. Further, in his conception "Germanic democracy" meant that all the virtues of the master race devolved upon one person, the leader, whose task it was to bring all this about. In short, this powerful and deadly combination of ideas about the state, its leader, and the mission of the German race is what constituted Nazism, and it was this combination that was founded by Adolf Hitler. His own words probably expressed it the best:

> What we must fight for is to safeguard the existence and reproduction of our race and our people, the sustenance of our children and the purity of our blood, the freedom and independence of the fatherland, so that our people may mature for the fulfillment of the mission allotted it by the creator of the universe.[29]

Hitler's Personality

To these convictions, Hitler added the overwhelming force of his personality, which in fact gave Nazism its relentless fervor and devastating drive. But what drove Hitler? This question has fascinated his biographers, and the scholarship on the matter has tended to converge upon a single conclusion. For instance, in his study of the origins of World War II, A. J. P. Taylor concluded about Hitler that "the driving force in him was a terrifying literalism."[30] Allan Bullock dismissed the originality of Hitler's ideas, but emphasized the "terrifyingly literal way" that he carried them out.[31] Ernst Nolte's assessment is perhaps the most severe: "The dominant trait in Hitler's personality," he stated bluntly, "was infantilism . . . This man never emerged from his boyhood."[32] Infantilism, literalism, boyishness—these are the traits of a person who never grew up, who never became an adult.

In short, the key to understanding Hitler's frequently bizarre behavior is his fundamental, incorrigible immaturity. This is the source of his "terrifying literalism." When, for example, he overheard some casual, intemperate remark in a beer hall to the effect that "the Jews stabbed us in the back in the war, and someday we ought to kill them all"—he took it with horrifying seriousness. This is also the reason why the ridiculous flights of the imagination that characterized Volkish literature had such enormous appeal to his childlike mind. Thus, the image of some pompous Teutonic hero who slays all of his enemies and then dies in a blaze of thunderous glory amidst the crack of lightning bolts on a mountainous ledge possessed a degree of reality to Hitler that it never could have attained for a normal, mature person. In short, Hitler never grew up.

Most of all, of course, Hitler took himself too seriously. When there was absorbing material like this, the Volkish writers had reached the conclusion that all the virtues of the Volk could be embodied in a single person, a single leader. This person then is charged with the messianic task of leading the Volk to the realization of its destiny, which it must, by virtue of its inherent superiority, follow.[33] Hitler was a man who had visions and heard voices throughout his life, telling him how special he was and what he should do. Thus, who else but he could be appointed by God to lead his Volk on its glorious mission?

None of these childhood fantasies would have mattered, of course, if he had simply stayed out of politics and dabbled in the arts, which is what he originally wanted to do. But politics acquired a special meaning to Hitler, and he brought to it his particular and very considerable talents. The most obvious one was his ability to speak in public, a talent that ranks him as probably the most effective orator—or demagogue, if you prefer—of the twentieth century. Clearly, his effect on audiences was nothing short of extraordinary. "Hitler responds to the vibration of the human heart with the delicacy of a seismograph . . ." one observer noted, "enabling him, with a certainty with which no conscious gift could endow him, to act as loudspeaker proclaiming the most secret desires, the least permissible instincts, the sufferings, and personal revolts of a whole nation."[34]

How was he able to do this? The answer is that Germany and Hitler seemed to match each other perfectly, in the sense that Germany was Hitler writ large and Hitler was a microcosm of Germany. His words, his life story, his various experiences, his helpless rage—all seemed to many to be a nearly perfect expression in individual terms of what had happened to the nation at large. Everything that Germany as a nation went through between 1918 and 1933 Hitler had already experienced as an individual: defeat, humiliation, and aimless disorder (Hitler in Vienna); followed by a period of relative stability and normality (Hitler in the army during World War I, perhaps the only place where he really felt at home); then severe depression, loss of self-esteem, degrading impotence, and disorientation (Hitler in the hospital at the end of the war). Joachim Fest summarizes this point beautifully concluding that, "were it not for this congruence between the personal and the social-pathological situation, Hitler could never have wielded such hypnotic power over his fellow citizens."[35] In short, only Hitler was able to proclaim, as he frequently did, with stunning force and accuracy, "I am Germany!"

Domestic Policy

Hitler came to power through constitutional means by being appointed chancellor in January 1933 by President von Hindenberg. Actually, the venerable octogenarian and war hero could hardly stomach the former army corporal, and agreed to appoint him only after being convinced that there was really no other choice. The country continued to suffer from an economic depression that had generated years of political and social chaos, and the Nazis seemed to be the only group capable of restoring order. Besides, von Hindenberg was finally persuaded by his associates that the hard responsibilities of governing would temper Hitler's volatile personality, mature him, and cause him to moderate his views. Unfortunately, he was among the first of a long line of European statesmen who completely misjudged the nature of man with whom they were dealing.

Hitler was not the sort of person who conformed to the demands of the situation; quite the contrary, he did whatever he could to change the situation to conform to his demands. In the years immediately after assuming power, this meant concentrating his energies upon founding something completely new, the Third Reich—under his sole and undisputed command.

Hitler moved quickly. In about two years he managed to consolidate his power as undisputed leader of all Germans, and to engage systematically in transforming the country into a totalitarian state. During that time the Reichstag had conferred sweeping dictatorial powers upon him, the remaining internal opposition in the party had been expunged, and von Hindenberg, the last remnant of the old order, was safely in his grave. The remaining years prior to the war were spent building the social and political forms of totalitarianism. "We must develop organizations in which an individual's entire life can take place," he declared in 1933. "There are no longer any free realms in which the individual belongs to himself . . ."[36] Hitler accomplished these goals with enormous success. By 1939 every German felt in personal terms the impact of Hitler's rule.

Indeed, everything in the "New Germany" bore the stamp of its founder. Hitler had enormous intellectual breadth, and everything in Germany reflected this in various ways. His concern for the restoration of Volkish pastoral delights was reflected in national beautification campaigns in factories, homes, and youth clubs; his artistic endeavors found expression in all sorts of new buildings and monuments; his passion for building national strength and unity emerged in enormous public-works projects that employed millions; working conditions generally improved, many class barriers broke down, and Germans everywhere quickly took new pride in their country and especially in their Führer. They also benefited from Hitler's aesthetic interests, which were applied to things as diverse as pollution control and the design of a new "people's car" that he insisted should look like a beetle (for aerodynamic reasons), get forty miles to the gallon, and be affordable for every German. Hitler further insisted that every German should participate in the pageantry of the Third Reich, and for that reason ordered enormous celebrations and state festivities. Probably the most impressive of these occured at Nuremberg in 1934—the Nuremberg Rallies—which was captured brilliantly by Leni Riefenstahl on film, and entitled, *Triumph of the Will*. It literally has to be seen to be believed.[37]

Events like this revealed Nazi Germany to be uniquely the product of its founder. In fact, in many respects it is fair to say that the Third Reich was not fundamentally a political, social, or even military phenomenon at all, although it is in these terms that it is most often remembered and written about. Rather, Hitler's Germany was essentially an *aesthetic* production with political, social, and military implications. Its vast, breathless pomposity, its gargantuan, mind-boggling displays of national glory, its thunderous, raging arrogance—all these things in various ways reflected the personality of Hitler, especially the characteristics he acquired during his formative years in Vienna. During his stay there, Hitler immersed himself in the music of Richard Wagner, a Volkish thinker in his own right who frequently expressed his commitments in his music. Joachim Fest suggests that Wagner became a role model for Hitler, and in some respects lived on through Hitler's leadership in Germany.[38] This can especially be seen in his speeches, which were hardly ordinary affairs by any standard. His vigorous body language— the grand sweeps of his arms, his dramatic turns back and forth—bring to mind a conductor flamboyantly orchestrating, from the depths of his soul, the surging power and majesty of Wagner's *Ride of the Valkyries*. It was a role the Führer cherished.

There were other things he cherished too, of course, which he was now in a position to get. One was the total commitment of the armed forces, whose officers were required to give an oath of loyalty personally to him. Another was the adulation of all the citizens of the Reich, which, thanks to his minister of propaganda, he regularly received everywhere he went. He also was in the position finally to carry out his unspeakable plans of persecution of the Jews, which began almost immediately upon his assumption of power. At first Jews were simply harassed, though often viciously, but by the decade's end those who couldn't escape to other countries were being herded into concentration camps. This was just a preview, of course. Far worse was to come when Hitler turned his aggressions outward to Germany's neighbors in a program of conquest that would give the Jews no place to run for refuge.

Hitler outlined his intentions to a group of top military leaders in a private conference held in November of 1937. He declared the necessity of acquiring "living space" for Germany, and showed to them the probable routes of expansion. To their horror they realized that their Führer actually did mean all those things that he had been talking about over the years. The minutes of this meeting were preserved by one of those present, a certain Colonel Hossbach, and became known as the "Hossbach Memoranda." Their contents revealed that the German leader planned to solve Germany's "living space" problem within the next five or six years, while he was still in his prime. In fact, the attempted solution was to begin less than two years from that point.[39]

By the time it began, Hitler's status as the principal figure in Nazi hagiology had been firmly established. All of Germany had been forced to accept the Nazi meaning of political existence, with its emphasis upon safeguarding the racial purity of the "master race," and the grand mission allotted to it. Most of Hitler's actions to this point had involved efforts to build up the Reich internally. But the most important justification for political action by Nazi ideology concerned foreign policy, and would lead Hitler to guide the Third Reich on a quest for domination that ultimately would end with its total destruction.

Hitler's Prewar Foreign Policy

Few of Hitler's long-range designs for expansion were taken seriously by foreign statesmen when he came to power. Those few who had read *Mein Kampf* or had listened to some of his more aggressive speeches tended to regard both as rhetorical exaggerations. The dead seriousness of his intentions was not clear until the spring of 1939, by which time it was too late to stop Germany without a full-scale war. But prior to that point, many in the West felt that the Führer's demands actually were not terribly unreasonable, even if he was, on occasion. Indeed, any German leader would have sought the same things. Hitler wanted to free Germany from the restrictions of the Treaty of Versailles; he desired further to build up the German army to a respectable although not necessarily monstrous level, and to change Eastern European national boundaries. None of these things was impossible to achieve. Western statesmen showed by their actions—or inactions—that the Versailles Treaty was (re)negotiable, that the German army could not be kept to its miniscule size (for Germany) indefinitely, and that they were not really interested in the fate of Eastern Europe. In short, many in the West were in sympathy with, or at least not opposed to, the Führer's program.[40]

Still, it is true that the French were generally more nervous about the Germans than Great Britain was, and for good reasons. France had wrested two provinces, Alsace and Lorraine, from Germany at the end of the war; Hitler was surely angry about that. Certainly he made some snarling, hateful comments about France, in *Mein Kampf* and elsewhere. But the Führer made such comments about almost everybody who disagreed with him, so the French had little reason to feel singled out. Moreover, he was not, in fact, much interested in those two provinces, any more than he was interested in damaging or even challenging the British Empire. Quite the contrary; he admired it. He was not, in short, terribly interested in the West. Basically all he wanted from France and Great Britain was to be left alone so that Germany could have a free hand in the East, which was the primary, if not the sole, objective of his foreign policy. And for a time, it appeared that the two Western democracies would give him that free hand. The fact that they did not in the end constitutes one of the grand ironies of World War II, in that it came about as a result of a dispute over an area that neither France nor Great Britain was especially interested in or in the least able to defend.

Before the actual outbreak of war, of course, Western leaders tried their hardest to put the least disturbing interpretation upon Hitler's foreign-policy moves. The harshest thing the governments of France and Great Britain did was to register official protests, as they did when Hitler reinstituted military conscription in March 1933, and when he ordered troops into the demilitarized Rhineland in the following year. However, they could always comfort themselves by pointing to the nonaggression pact that Germany had signed with Poland, or even to the naval agreement Hitler had concluded with the British. More disturbing, of course, was the movement of German troops into Austria, in an event that politically united those two countries, called "Anschluss." But it could still be pointed out that Hitler was just moving into his own backyard, trying to put all the Germans together in one state. After all, wasn't that what the "self-determination" principle was all about—allowing the various nations of Europe to be ruled by their own states? And Hitler shrewdly pointed out that he hadn't invented that idea; a Western statesman had—President Wilson of the United States. Still, all of these things were achieved without firing a shot, and Hitler's ability to win bloodless victories seemed unstoppable.

This conclusion was reinforced in the fall of 1938, when Hitler made what he vowed was his last territorial claim in Europe. It involved joining to the Fatherland the so-called Sudetenland Germans, who lived in a territory that surrounded the western half of Czechoslovakia. This was also an area that contained the best part of the excellent Czech defenses, and without question any attempt to take the area by force would have run into formidable opposition. Hitler knew this, of course, and tried to bluff, threaten, and intimidate the Western democracies into giving him by diplomatic means what surely would have been difficult to achieve by military ones, at least in 1938. Although the Czechs stood firm, the Western leaders did not. After some nerve-wracking exchanges of proposals between Berlin and London, Prime Minister Chamberlain of Great Britain agreed to come to Munich with the representatives of France and Italy to discuss the dismemberment of Czechoslovakia. The agreement that resulted has since been regarded as synonymous with craven appeasement. It was not, however, looked upon that way at the time. The four powers came to Munich basically in agreement with the validity of the Führer's claims, and left feeling that justice had been done.

It was not, of course. Indeed, considering the resistance that Czechoslovakia would have offered, the Munich Agreement must be considered as one of the greatest military triumphs ever achieved by diplomatic means. But it was also the last one that Hitler would enjoy against the Western powers. When he tried the same tactics in 1939 against Poland, he was faced with opposition from Britain and France that simply could not be bargained away. Of course, by that time German troops had already occupied what was left of the Czech state, in clear violation of their agreement, and even Chamberlain realized that he had been tricked. The Poles were understandably nervous as well, and stoutly resisted Hitler's overtures to make a deal with them for the Reich's "lost territories" under Polish rule. Instead they made a deal with Prime Minister Chamberlain, whose offer of a British declaration of Polish territorial integrity was accepted by the Polish minister in less time "than was needed to flip the ash from a cigarette."[41] Hitler was outraged by this, and quickly ordered preparations for the invasion of Poland, under the code name Case White. The attack was scheduled for some time after September 1.

One of the most curious elements of this series of events centered upon the Western governments' approach to the Soviet Union. Like those of Czechoslovakia at Munich, the Soviets' interests were simply ignored, in spite of the fact that they had almost as much to lose as the hapless Czechs. Certainly they would be valuable as an ally against the Germans, but the Western diplomats could not quite bring themselves to discuss any agreement with Stalin, with all the commitments, probable concessions, and ideological stresses that entailed. On the other hand, Stalin was of a much more practial bent, especially as he had to deal with the Germans whether or not the French and British liked it. And his ideological opposition to Hitler was not as strong as his withering contempt for the spineless and vacillating democracies. The result of his pragmatism and Western temporizing was the Nazi-Soviet Pact, signed on August 23, 1939. The British were shocked by this, and followed it up with a guarantee of assistance to the Poles, should they be attacked. These were the last actions taken by the major powers before the final curtain was raised on the Second World War.

The War Years

The war that began in September 1939 was the result of Hitler's determination to act upon the principles of his policy in the East that had been spelled out fifteen years earlier in *Mein Kampf*. In short, he "founded" this war, even though, when it came, he really did not want it. In fact, Hitler ended up with two wars he did not really want, or, rather, wished to avoid if he could: the invasion of Poland, which triggered the second one, war with the Western democracies. The fact that in the short run he won these conflicts in a series of sharp, decisive engagements was temporarily exhilarating, but still detracted from his main objective, which was a war of annihilation in the East. He never seriously wavered from this goal.

Thus his acid denunciations of the British during these years really betrayed a bitter disappointment that they would not somehow come to terms with him so he could pursue that project. He never gave up hopes about reaching an agreement with them. In fact, in the spring and summer of 1940, when the German war machine was unleashed against Denmark, Norway, and Western Europe, Hitler still attempted to influence the British to leave the continent to him and keep their empire overseas. His orders to halt the advance of the panzers before Dunkirk, which allowed the British to escape from France in one of the most dramatic withdrawals in military history, has been interpreted by some as a final attempt on his part to mollify England into making peace, once France was crushed. Hitler was wrong; the British kept on fighting anyway.

But the Führer would not be put off. Even though the British were hopelessly outclassed militarily by the Third Reich, Hitler reasoned that they still might see the light and come to terms with him after the destruction of the Soviet Union. This gave him an additional reason to attack the Russians, one that he could also use against the arguments of his generals, who were usually doubtful about his military excursions. Of course, there was never any doubt at all in Hitler's mind about this invasion. He had pronounced a death sentence upon the Soviet Union years before; now it was simply a matter of determining when to carry it out. June 22, 1941, was that time. By that point German armies had overrun nearly everything worth conquering in Northern and Western Europe, Rommel was making the British look like fools in North Africa, and German submarines were ravaging the seas of the North Atlantic. The United States was an ocean away, and Great Britain was neutralized. Only Russia remained.

The Soviet Union was the perfect enemy; indeed, a more perfect enemy for Hitler and the Nazis could not be conceived. The Nazis hated Jews, Bolsheviks, and Slavs; they wanted living space. What better enemy could be found than a nation of Slavs ruled by Bolsheviks, who espoused a philosophy invented by a Jew (Karl Marx)? Moreover, they lived in a land wanted by the Nazis, much of which had been won by Germany in World War I and taken from it by the terms of the Versailles Treaty. Now Hitler wanted it back. He envisioned a "New Order" for it, one that entailed death for about three-quarters of its inhabitants and slavery for those who remained. The whole area east of Germany was looked upon as though it were a clean slate, possessing no history, no culture, and no people—just hordes of "subhuman" Slavs whom the Nazis were convinced were too stupid to govern themselves. They would be taught only enough to enable them to obey their German masters and to supply the greater Reich with what it needed. Their lands would be populated by Germans, who would build vast cities, connected by trains going two hundred miles per hour. Such were the plans Hitler had for the Nazis' perfect enemy.[42]

Much of this policy was actually carried out. The Germans captured an enormous amount of territory—enough to equal approximately the area of the United States east of the Mississippi. In it they perpetrated barbarisms of unspeakable brutality, in a sort of "double war" the Third Reich conducted in the East—one against enemy soldiers, and the other against enemy civilians. Among the latter, especially singled out were Jews, who were rounded up by special formations of the SS (Schutzstaffel) and sent to the death camps throughout Eastern Europe, including Auschwitz. But hundreds of thousands of others were systematically murdered as well, and the effect was quickly to transform the image of the German soldier in the Soviet Union from that of a liberator to that of an enemy who had to be destroyed at all costs. Actually, Hitler was his own worst enemy, since his population policies, which propelled him to attack the Soviets in the first place, ultimately led to the defeat of his armies in the East.

In fact, this was generally the case in the Second World War. It is perhaps only a slight exaggeration to suggest that Adolf Hitler was the sole "founder" of the war; but certainly it was true that he played the principal role in determining the main directions it took from 1939 to 1945. Hitler's attentions and concerns ranged from the heights of global strategic doctrine to the minutiae of developing specific weapons systems. From beginning to end he simply dominated events more than any other single figure in that long conflict. Even his best generals were reduced to a state of stunned obeisance when the Führer went into one of his characteristic rages. General Alfred Jodl, Chief of Wehrmacht Operations Staff, remarked shortly before his execution at Nuremberg: "His knowledge and intellect, his rhetoric and willpower triumphed in the end in every spiritual conflict over everyone."[43] Hitler dominated everything and everyone. World War II is simply unthinkable without him.

This was true in defeat as well as in victory. As Hitler's mental acuities deteriorated with his health after early 1942, especially after the first serious setbacks on the Russian front, so did the military effectiveness of the armies under his command. Although he did show some occasional flashes of brillance after that time, by the end of 1944 he was a physical and emotional wreck. His left hand trembled; his face became puffy and flaccid. He had insomnia, and forced those in his entourage to endure his nightlong sleeplessness. He talked incessantly and in a scatterbrained fashion on a variety of subjects, ranging from geographical and military history to assessments of assorted artists. The medication prescribed for him by his doctor included treatments to calm his nerves, settle his stomach, relieve his anxiety, and generally enable him to function.[44] But as Allied armies closed in on the Reich, nothing seemed to help. Hitler's voice was feeble, his face ashen, his posture stooped and weary; he dragged his body along and could not walk for any distance without frequent rests. His limbs shook; saliva dribbled from the corners of his mouth. By the war's end Adolf Hitler was a broken man.

And as he crumbled, so did the German army. There is no question that the irrational decisions he made during the second half of the war hastened its end, and very likely they determined its ultimate outcome. Hitler temporized, equivocated, sent the wrong troops to the wrong places, generated administrative confusion of all sorts, and when the military situation became perilous because of these things, he raged against his generals for failing him, calling them cowards, idiots, and traitors. He put off mobilization for total war until after the events of 1943—by which point it was probably too late. He refused to accept gloomy assessments of the increasingly disastrous situation that was developing on the Russian front after the spring of 1943. And for all his technical acumen, he did not recognize the importance of atomic research or the jet fighter—when Germany was on the defensive, he originally wanted to mass-produce a jet *bomber,* of all things—until it was too late. In fact, his extraordinary grasp of weapons capabilities also slipped very badly as the war went on, or was misdirected in futile, last-ditch efforts, as represented by the "vengeance weapons," the V-1 and V-2. From the big things to the little things, the Führer increasingly lost touch with reality.[45]

This was especially the case with strategic matters. Hitler made operational errors in the deployment of troops and the direction of offensives and counteroffensives that had a staggering impact on the course of events during the war—in North Africa, in the Soviet Union, and in France in 1944. Observers who point to the materiel and manpower inferiority of the Germans, particularly in light of the enormous output of the Americans and Russians, often conclude that victory for the allies was inevitable. This opinion, easily made in light of the final outcome, assumes that sheer numbers in everything conceivably related to war is sufficient to assure victory. But this is true only up to a point. The Germans did not win by sheer force of numbers, except, of course, in overrunning the dozen or so minor countries they invaded. But in the major campaigns of the war against first-class military opponents, the German war machine usually attacked when the overall numerical relationship between its forces and those of its opponent was approximately one to one.[46] In fact, sometimes it was even less favorable to them, especially in Russia. Certainly the Germans never lost at that ratio. On the other hand, it took a military superiority of five, six, or seven to one on the part of the Allies over Germany to achieve final victory.

Even this might not have been sufficient if Hitler had used the forces at his disposal with greater skill and had made a more realistic appraisal of Germany's strategic situation. This is not to say that Germany could have won the war if someone else had been guiding the fortunes of the Reich after, say, the early part of 1942. But it is entirely possible that Germany, in command, as it was, of the materiel and human resources of Europe, could have maintained a position where it could not have been beaten—at least not in the decisive manner that it was by the spring of 1945. Fortunately for the Allies, Hitler stayed at the helm for the duration of the conflict. And the enormous materiel superiority of the United States and the Soviet Union was aided by the precipitous decline in the quality of his leadership. That is, the Grand Coalition was aided in its conquest of Nazi Germany by the decline of its founder, Adolf Hitler.

As the allied armies closed in on Germany in the last months of the war, Hitler directed his pathological hatred against the entire German people. He declared that if Germany did not meet the ultimate test of victory over its enemies, then it did not deserve to live. He issued orders to destroy everything in the path of the advancing armies—buildings, water facilities, sewage-treatment plants, electrical-power plants, even entire cities—nothing was to be left. The means of civilized life were to be utterly destroyed in a final orgy of national suicide. Fortunately, very little of this was actually carried out, at least not on Hitler's orders. His hatred of everything found its instrument in the Allied Forces, which by that point had destroyed much of Germany by airpower, and were in the process of mopping up the remaining opposition as they swept through the Reich. Hitler's Germany was coming to an end.

Before its demise Hitler managed to marry his longtime fiancée, Eva Braun, in a ceremony that took place on April 29, 1945, in his Berlin bunker. He expressed some satisfaction that he had exterminated as many Jews as he had, and declared that he had never really wanted war; it had been forced upon him, "provoked exclusively by those international statesmen who either were of Jewish origin or worked for Jewish interests."[47] The mad fury of his anti-Semitism never wavered. In his testament, composed on the day after his marriage, he stated, "Above all, I charge the leaders of the nation and those under them to scrupulous observance of the laws of race and to merciless opposition to the universal poisoner of all peoples, international Jewry."[48] With dramatic, theatrical finality he declared the end of National Socialism, and took his own life on April 30, 1945. The death of Adolf Hitler signaled the end of the regime founded by him. All that remained of the Third Reich was ashes and smoke and the spilled blood of its thirty to forty million victims.

THE IMPACT OF HITLER

The impact of Adolf Hitler was enormous, especially when considered in light of the consequences of the war he unleashed upon the world. Among these include the lessened influence of European nations upon the course of events everywhere in the world, including on the European continent. No longer was Europe the focus of world problems; attention was shifted elsewhere, to the nations of the Third World, which were created from the remains of the colonial empires that were dissolved within a decade of the war's end. Even events in Europe were no longer determined by the traditionally "Great Powers" of that region—England, France, Germany, Italy, and, in earlier times, Spain.

For the first time in its history, the fate of Europe was decided by states outside or on the periphery of the European continent; namely, the United States and the Soviet Union. In fact, each had grown so powerfully as a result of the war that to call them Great Powers did not seem appropriate anymore; they were called "superpowers." The antagonism between the two resulted in Europe's being split into two rival ideological and military camps. And this bifurcation of Europe went through the heart of Germany; its divided capital symbolized dramatically the hostility between East and West. All this was the result of World War II.

The "German problem"—What do we do with Germany?—had been solved, although at great cost and with ironic overtones. Instead of the Soviet Union's being split up and made into German vassal states, very nearly the opposite had occurred: Germany was split up, and portions of its remains became satellites of the Soviet Union. And now the world was faced with another problem, the "Russian problem," or, "What do we do with Russia?" The country is too big and powerful and bursting with energy to be ignored—like Hitler's Reich of years before— and demands international attention and respect due to its status as a superpower. The fortunes of Germany and Russia have been powerfully linked together in the twentieth century. It may be that the solution to the "Russian problem"—if there is one—will somehow involve Germany in the future as well.

If it does, it will involve a Germany rather different from the one created by Adolf Hitler and destroyed in World War II. Although a portion of the old Reich, East Germany, in numerous ways resembles Hitler's Germany, the Western part has developed over the years into a viable democratic polity. Of course, this did not happen immediately. In the years after the war Germans withdrew from politics into their own private worlds, and concentrated upon the immediate and urgent tasks of personal survival. Even when this was no longer a problem, by the mid-fifties, many Germans still had the basic political orientations of their earlier years as citizens of Nazi Germany. For instance, when questioned in 1956 as to whether Hitler would have been considered one of Germany's greatest statesmen if it had not been for the war he lost, almost half of the population in the Federal Republic of Germany answered yes. In fact, in 1951 fully a third of the adult population favored restoration of the Hohenzollern dynasty, which had ruled Germany until its collapse in World War I! Clearly, if Germany were to develop into a modern, parliamentary democracy, it had a long way to go.[49]

But this distance has been traveled, and democratic values have taken root in the Federal Republic, particularly as the horrors of the

Nazi past fade into distant memories. By the 1970s, Germans of the Federal Republic had accepted the basic legitimacy of their government by overwhelming numbers. Fifty-six percent of the population flatly rejects Hitler as "one of Germany's greatest statesmen"; a greater percentage would do "everything possible" to prevent the rise of another Nazi party. Furthermore, totalitarian values have been slowly expunged from the current political system as the Federal Republic has gained acceptance and prestige. Instead of embracing political unity as an ultimate value and rejecting political parties, Germans today overwhelmingly believe that "the common good can only be achieved through open conflicts between differing interests and their resolution by mutually acceptable compromises."[50] In short, Germans today accept the government in Bonn, feel that it essentially represents their interests, and support political and social pluralism. After three regimes and two horrible world wars in the one hundred years since unification, Germany has finally adjusted to the modern world and developed into a stable, democratic state.

In an indirect way, this also was the result of Hitler. Hitler brought to a furious culmination centuries of German political and philosophical development, and by his defeat in the Second World War contributed heavily to the discrediting of ideas and practices that provided fertile soil for Nazi ideas. Few people in Germany today seriously entertain extremist notions deriving from the statist, Volkish, and racist legacies that the Nazis found so conductive to their rule. In short, Nazism as an ideology did not die immediately with Hitler's death. But the Allied occupation in the West, the German "economic miracle" of the fifties, which transformed the country again into the leading economic force on the continent (after the USSR), the success of the Bonn government, and the simple passage of time have worked collectively to insure its ultimate demise in German affairs. Thus, it is reasonable to conclude that the type of ideological leadership provided by Adolf Hitler, probably the twentieth century's most influential founder, will not come again to plague the affairs of Germany or the world.

ENDNOTES

[1]Quoted by John Toland, *Adolf Hitler* (New York: Ballantine Books, 1976), p. 14.
[2]Ibid., p. 21.
[3]Ibid., p. 73.
[4]Ibid., p. 682.
[5]Ibid., p. 200.
[6]A. J. P. Taylor, *The Origins of the Second World War* (New York: Basic Books, 1972), p. 144.

[7]Walter C. Langer, *The Mind of Adolf Hitler* (New York: Basic Books, 1972), p. 144.

[8]Quoted in Toland, p. 813.

[9]For a good account of this early episode in Hitler's career, which also includes information on his military experience, see Richard Hanser, *Putsch!* (New York: Pyramid Books, 1970).

[10]Quoted in Toland, p. 282.

[11]One of the best works that deals with the philosophical and historical roots of Nazism was completed during the Second World War by William M. McGovern, *From Luther to Hitler* (Boston: Houghton Mifflin Company, 1941). Much of the following account is taken from this clearly written and interesting account.

[12]Quoted in Ibid., p. 150.

[13]*Hegel's Philosophy of Right*, trans. T. M. Knox (New York: Oxford University Press, 1967), p. 279.

[14]Quoted in McGovern, *Luther to Hitler*, p. 377.

[15]For a discussion of these views see Barbara Tuchman, *The Guns of August* (New York: Bantam Books, 1962), pp. 25–6.

[16]This phrase is of course Tuchman's.

[17]Quoted in A. J. P. Taylor, *Bismarck: The Man and the Statesman* (New York: Vintage Books, 1955), p. 115.

[18]Probably the definitive work on the development of Volkish thought is George L. Mosse, *The Crisis of German Ideology* (New York: Grosset & Dunlap, 1964). I am heavily indebted to this excellent and detailed account.

[19]Among the biographies of Hitler that treat his intellectual background, the account in Werner Maser, *Hitler: Legend, Myth, and Reality* (New York: Harper & Row, 1971), Chapter 5, is especially informative. Maser's reputation as a Hitler scholar was recently enhanced by his early and unambiguous denial of the authenticity of the so-called *Hitler Diaries* that appeared in the spring of 1983. He declared immediately that they were fakes.

[20]An excellent discussion of these matters may also be found in James Rhodes, *The Hitler Movement: A Modern Millenarian Revolution* (Stanford, Calif.: Hoover Institution Press, 1980). See also the account in John Hallowell, *Main Currents in Modern Political Thought* (New York: Holt, Rinehart & Winston, 1950), pp. 581–86.

[21]Karl Bracher, *The German Dictatorship* (New York: Praeger Publishers, 1970), p. 490.

[22]Among the accounts of Hitler's youth, the one contained in Toland, *Adolf Hitler*, chapters 1–3, is especially complete. Toland makes numerous references to the remembrances of Alois Hitler, Jr., as well as to those of Gustav Kubizek, Hitler's boyhood friend for a short time in Vienna.

[23]Maser, *Hitler: Legend, Myth, and Reality*, p. 130.

[24]Adolf Hitler, *Mein Kampf*, trans. Ralph Manheim (Boston: Houghton Mifflin Co., 1971), p. 21.

[25]Ibid., p. 288.

[26]Ibid., p. 344.

[27]Ibid., p. 533.

[28]Quoted by Joachim Fest, *Hitler* (New York: Vintage Books, 1975), p. 214.

[29]Hitler, *Mein Kampf*, p. 214.

[30]A. J. P. Taylor, *Origins*, p. 72.

[31]Allan Bullock, *Hitler: A Study in Tyranny*, abr. ed. (New York: Harper & Row), p. 368.

[32]Ernst Nolte, *Three Faces of Fascism*, trans. Leila Venewitz (New York: New American Library, 1965), p. 368.

[33]For a discussion of the concept of the Volkish hero, see especially the excellent survey by George Mosse, *German Ideology*, pp. 204 *passim*.

[34]This quote comes from one of Langer's informants, *Mind of Hitler*, p. 54.

[35]Fest, *Hitler*, p. 149.

[36]Quoted in Ibid., p. 418.

[37]See the treatments in Bracher, *German Dictatorship*, pp. 229–87, 330–400; Toland, *Adolf Hitler*, pp. 491–98, 549–62; and Maser, *Hitler: Legend, Myth, and Reality*, pp. 128 passim.

[38]Fest, *Hitler*, pp. 47–53.

[39]For accounts of the Hossbach Memoranda, see Ibid., pp. 539–42; Taylor, *Origins*, pp. 277–93; and Bracher, *German Dictatorship*, pp. 307–10.

[40]An especially intriguing account of the reaction to Hitler's foreign policy demands is contained in Taylor, *Origins*, pp. 72–87

[41]Quoted in Fest, *Hitler*, p. 578.

[42]Ibid., pp. 678–94; See also Peter Calvocoressi and Guy Wint, *Total War* (New York: Penguin Books, 1972), pp. 211–42.

[43]Quoted in Maser, *Hitler: Legend, Myth, and Reality*, p. 122.

[44]Fest, *Hitler*, p. 727; and especially, Maser, Ibid., pp. 209–33, on Hitler's deteriorating physical condition throughout the war years.

[45]On Hitler's prowess as a military leader, a favorite topic among his biographers and military historians, see Maser, *Hitler: Legend, Myth, and Reality*, pp. 267–321, which is especially informative; Fest, *Hitler*, pp. 605–66; Bullock, *Study in Tyranny*, pp. 321–485; and B. H. Liddell Hart, *Strategy* (New York: New American Library, 1974), pp. 207–319.

[46]There are exceptions. In overrunning France and the Low Countries, German armies were numerically equal to those of its opponents in all but one category—aircraft. The Germans were vastly superior in military tactics until the Allies were able to match them by 1943.

[47]Quoted in Toland, *Adolf Hitler*, p. 1211.

[48]Quoted in Bullock, *Study in Tyranny*, p. 479.

[49]These data come from David P. Conradt, *The German Polity*, 2nd ed. (New York: Longman, 1982), p. 54. See his discussion of the political orientations of West Germans, pp. 48–85. See also Lewis J. Edinger, *Politics in West Germany*, 2nd ed. (Boston: Little, Brown, 1977), pp. 74–118.

[50]These figures come from Conradt, *Germany Polity*, p. 57.

RUHOLLAH KHOMEINI

Fundamentalist Practitioner and Founder of the Islamic Republic of Iran

10

Several centuries may pass before a man with his [Khomeini's] superior qualities and characteristics and [similar] conditions of time and place, arise again. (An Iranian cleric)[1]

The message from Iran . . . is in my opinion the single most impressive political ideology which has been proposed in the twentieth century since the Bolshevik Revolution. *Dr. Marvin Zonis,* Middle East expert[2]

We look to the Iranian revolution, in my opinion, as the third great revolution in history. First there was the French, then the Russian, and now the Islamic revolution, which is changing many things in the world. It has renewed the way for Mohammed. *Nabih Berri,* leader of the Amal Party, a Shi'a group in Lebanon[3]

All of Islam is politics. *Ayatollah Ruhollah Khomeini*[4]

INTRODUCTION

On January 31, 1979, a bearded, septuagenarian Muslim leader took power in a country that the United States had always considered vital to its interests in the Middle East. Amidst the tumultuous enthusiasm of a crowd numbered in the hundreds of thousands, the Ayatollah Ruhollah Khomeini thanked all those who had supported him over his long years in exile, and promised to establish a truly Islamic government and to exact vengeance from all his foes.[5] Two months later he proclaimed the birth of the Islamic Republic of Iran, a country that he promised would be led by a "Government of God," one that, "fearing neither East nor West" would cultivate an "independent outlook" and "purge all remnants of the tyrannical regime" that had just fallen.[6] True to his word, Khomeini moved swiftly in approving the execution of thousands of persons associated with the shah of Iran, and sent many more thousands to jail, while those fanatically committed to him carried out a thorough Islamization of the country. Thus, a state that had only shortly before been declared as a "bastion of stability" in the region by an American president now became the prime exporter of revolutionary violence under the banner of Islam—throughout the Middle East and beyond as well.

The following years witnessed events that Westerners, Americans especially, viewed with equal parts of astonishment and shock. An endless litany of searing denunciations of the United States filled the airwaves: "Death to America!" "Death to the Great Satan!" "Death to Carter!" (and, later, Reagan). The insults were complemented by one of the most exasperating experiences the United States had ever gone through—the taking and holding of American diplomats as hostages in Tehran for over a year, by a group of "students" claiming to follow the Imam's (Khomeini's) line. Although the hostages were eventually released, the danger to Americans in the Middle East has remained: hostage-taking continues, American embassies have been bombed, airplanes containing American passengers have been hijacked, and American soldiers have been killed—all by those committed to wage a *jihad* (holy war), inspired by the Ayatollah Khomeini. Without question, the Islamic revolution unleashed by Khomeini is one of the most significant political events of the twentieth century.

But this is just as he wanted it to be, and just as he had always insisted: revolutionary Islam is foremost a *political* phenomenon, one that elevates to positions of political power individuals committed to the teachings of Islam. And Khomeini is clearly the most important and certainly the most influential practitioner of revolutionary Islam in the modern era. More specifically, he represents a form of Islamic fundamentalism that traces its roots to events that occurred over thirteen hundred years ago. In fact, Khomeini's ideas and actions as a practitioner of Islamic fundamentalism cannot be understood without reference to the history and development of Islam. For this reason, it will be necessary to devote somewhat more attention to background material than we would otherwise. This will lead us to discussions of the basic teachings of Muhammad and the course of Islamic history that bears directly upon the development of Khomeini's thought and the recent events in Iran. We shall then deal with the Ayatollah's actions as leader of the Islamic Republic of Iran, in terms of domestic and foreign policy. We shall finish with some conjectures about the future of the Islamic revolution for the Middle East, as well as for global relations on the whole.

THE ISLAMIC HERITAGE

Fundamentals of Islam

Probably one of the most striking aspects of Islam to a person from the Western world is the totality of its requirements for believers.[7] There is no aspect of an individual's life that is not covered by Islam; every action, every thought, no matter how minor, has religious significance, from the time of a person's conception in the mother's womb to one's final end in heaven or hell. Thus there are very detailed rules governing sexual intercourse, birth, child-raising, death, and burial. Muslims are expected to follow sacred laws outlining the correct procedures for eating, sleeping, waking, dressing and undressing, talking and remaining silent, defecating, bathing, and cleaning one's teeth. Naturally, rules for worship are outlined with meticulous care, and interpersonal relationships are especially important. Ways to behave toward family members, friends, acquaintances, those in authority and those who are not, enemies, nonbelievers and atheists, monotheists (such as Jews and Christians), as well as fellow Muslims, are all dealt with by the *Shari'a*, the Sacred Law of Islam.[8] It is no wonder, then, that politics has religious significance for Muslims as well. In fact, given the extraordinary scope and detail of Islamic thought, some observers have equated the Muslim way of life with modern totalitarian practices.

Although there is some resemblance, the focus of commitment is completely different. Totalitarianism is a political phenomenon; everything is subordinated to politics. Islam, on the other hand, is based upon total and unquestioning submission to God. Indeed, Islam means "submission," and a Muslim is "one who submits." Muslims believe that God has revealed Himself actively throughout history, and they trace their religious lineage to the Biblical prophets who conveyed God's messages to His people. Moses and Jesus are usually singled out, but Muhammad is the most recent of the prophets, and is regarded as the last and most significant one. This conviction is embodied in the Muslim Declaration of Faith, the *Shahada,* which declares: "There is no God but Allah, and Muhammad is His prophet." This is also the first of the Five Pillars of Islam. The other four include prayer (at least five times a day, according to procedures carefully prescribed), the giving of alms for the care of members of the community of Muslims (the *umma*), fasting during the month of Ramadan (a lunar month that comes at different times of the year), and, finally, the *Hajj,* or pilgrimage to Mecca, the birthplace of Muhammad and Holy City of Islam. These beliefs form the core of every Muslim's personal faith, regardless of race or nationality.[9]

Ultimately, Islam's central tenets are derived from the Qur'an, the Muslim holy book, which consists of a set of chapters called *suras.* Qur'an literally means "recitation," which Muslims believe came directly from God, through the Angel Gabriel, who appeared in a series of visions to Muhammad. The Qur'an is thus regarded quite literally as the Word of God, faithfully transmitted by Muhammad, His prophet, for all the peoples of the earth. Its contents are rich and varied, ranging from instructions about family life and the worship of Allah, to each Muslim's duty to extend the boundaries of *Dar al-Islam* ("House of Islam"— territory ruled by Islam). All English commentators versed in Arabic remark on its poetic beauty and insist that it is not a work that can be translated into other languages without losing a great deal. Even non-Arabic Muslims memorize *suras* from the holy book in the original tongue. However, this is less necessary for the *Hadith* ("Reports"), which, as opposed to the Qur'an, consist of the Prophet's sayings about various matters and are considered as divinely inspired, but not literally as the Word of God. In fact, as we shall see, several of Muhammad's followers generated a large corpus of *Hadith,* and this became especially important for the development of Shi'a Islam, the second most significant branch of the faith, which became predominant in Iran.

About 90 percent of the Muslims in the world are committed to Sunni Islam (from *Sunna,* "beaten path," or tradition associated with Muhammad and his companions). The Sunni-Shi'a split occurred within the first century of Islam's existence, and has had important political consequences for Muslims ever since. In order to understand these, it is necessary to deal briefly with the life of Muhammad and the spread of Islam in the centuries after his death. It was during that period that Muslims developed their characteristic reactions to the exercise of political power. In fact, although it may seem incredible to non-Muslims, Ayatollah Khomeini's beliefs and actions as head of the Islamic state of

Iran can hardly be understood without reference to the events that occurred within a scant generation of the Prophet's death.

Muhammad and His Legacy

The Arabia of Muhammad's day was characterized by a number of social conditions and ethical practices against which he reacted strongly. Unlike the more mature, urban civilizations of the North, Arabian lands still contained many nomadic groups, whose main commitments were based upon kinship and tribal loyalties. Although these Bedouin groups that inhabited the peninsula stressed many laudable virtues, such as generosity and honor, the ferocity of many other practices based upon the intense loyalty to local and blood relations made it difficult for them to adjust to more urbane, cosmopolitan values. This was even true for the groups that did inhabit the cities, such as the ruling Quraysh tribe, which dominated affairs in Mecca, Muhammad's place of birth. Mecca was an important city located in the *Hijaz,* a region in western Arabia through which several important trade routes were located. Although removed from the nomadic existence of their Bedouin forebears, the Quraysh ethic still stressed tribal commitments as primary, and Quraysh leaders were able to maintain their position largely through military strength. What was needed was a religious and social ethic that transcended group differences, stressed spiritual unity of all peoples above the fierce antagonism and destructive blood feuds that often ravaged Arabian lands, and curbed the frequently rapacious behavior of the ruling tribe toward other members of Meccan society. All this and more was supplied by Muhammad.

He received his first vision when he was forty years old, while in a cave located in a mountain outside Mecca, where he frequently went to reflect on matters that troubled him. That was in A.D. 610. Other visions followed at irregular intervals, and they were always very intense experiences, sometimes accompanied by pain, occasionally by seizures, frequently by episodes of emotional ecstasy, and always by proclamations ("recitations") of what God had transmitted to him from a book "preserved in Heaven." Clearly, Muhammad was familiar with the Jewish and Christian traditions, and much of what he said has a familiar ring to those acquainted with the Judeo-Christian heritage: There is only one God, Allah, Who is infinite, transcendent, omnipotent, compassionate and merciful, loving toward those who serve Him, but terrible toward those who reject Him. All people are equal before God, and He requires justice and righteousness in all their actions. Earthly goods count for nothing in the Day of Judgment; mankind has a higher end in Heaven, before which social standing and wealth in this world have no meaning. Forsake pride, greed, and other gods—there is no God but Allah. Submit to His will in your every thought, word, and deed, always. In short, Muhammad's teachings seemed to be an antidote for all the evils he saw around him. No one committed to them could ever be the same again.

This was also precisely the conclusion of the ruling members of the Quraysh tribe in Mecca, who reacted to Muhammad's thought with suspicion and, later, violence. Clearly, much of what he said undercut their authority; what would happen if people took seriously, for instance, his injunctions against inequality, greed, the grasping for material wealth, worshiping several gods—all of which benefited them greatly? There was also an element of snobbishness in the Quaraysh response. Although he was a respected businessman with an excellent reputation—he was known as al-Amin, "the trustworthy"—Muhammad had come from relatively modest circumstances, and his worthy though unspectacular accomplishments hardly seemed to justify his assuming the mantle of prophethood. Accordingly, the Quaraysh denounced him as a fraud, persecuted the growing number of his Muslim followers in the city, and succeeded in driving Muhammad out of Mecca by A.D. 622.

The Meccans were aided greatly in their efforts by a group of Muslims from the city of Yathrib, about two hundred miles to the north of Mecca, who asked that Muhammad relocate to their city. Their strife-ridden town had been subject to terrible conflicts among the tribes, and Muhammad seemed to them to be the only person capable of bringing peace and order. Muhammad's acceptance of this call became the most significant event in Islamic history, and the time of his emigration (*Hijrah*), in 622, became the first year of the Muslim calendar. Thereafter, the city of Yathrib was known as *Madinat al-Nabi*, "the City of the Prophet"—better known simply as Medina. For the first time in his ministry, Muhammad was able to put into practice the tenets of the new faith without persecution or any significant opposition.

Thus, Medina became a religious laboratory for Islam, and Muhammad went about his tasks with great energy. He continued to receive revelations in Medina, which, together with his earlier visions, were embodied in what became the Qur'an. Mostly these Medinan "recitations" had to do with the practicalities of regulating social, political, and economic relationships—family matters, inheritances, treatment of women, slaves, members of other tribes and religions, collecting of alms for the poor, and so forth—and lacked the earlier, more spiritual and apocalyptic character of Muhammad's Meccan experiences. Most importantly, however, Muhammad found himself in the position of being both the religious *and* political leader of the *umma*. The Christian conception of separation of church and state had no meaning in early Islamic practices. Indeed, since the only purpose of human existence was to worship God and prepare oneself for the greater glory of the life after death, it made no sense to separate the functions or even assume they could be separated. In short, the first ruler of *Dar al-Islam* was the Prophet himself, and he assumed both religious and political leadership of the community of Muslims.

After consolidating his position in Medina, Muhammad turned his attention again to his city of origin, with the goal of subduing the stubborn Meccans and bringing the city under Muslim rule. After a series of military engagements, some of which were won by Muhammad's forces against armies that greatly outnumbered them, this task was accomplished by 630. Mecca's submission to Islam greatly impressed the pagan tribes of the area, and Muhammad had the satisfaction of seeing most of them in the Arabian peninsula convert to the Muslim faith during his lifetime. In fact, there is no question that a principle reason for the spectacular spread of Islam among the Arab tribes centered upon the success of Muslim armies against all their enemies. After all, nothing succeeds like success; a faith that produces unremitting victories over its opponents *must* have God on its side.

Certainly this seemed the case during the century following Muhammad's death, in 632. Under the first four caliphs, until 661 (*Khalifah*—"successor to the Prophet"), Islam conquered all the lands of the Middle East up to the borders of India in the east and Tripoli in the west. During the ensuing century the rest of Northwest Africa and Spain were added to *Dar al-Islam,* and Muslim advances pressed farther into India and central Asia. The following centuries would find Muslims dominating such faraway places (from Arabia) as Indonesia and parts of China; closer to home, Muslim conquests under the Ottoman Turks in the sixteenth and seventeenth centuries nearly engulfed all Christian Europe. In short, the truth of Islam seemed to be embodied in its successes. Indeed, it is only very recently that European encroachments into traditional Islamic lands have forced many Muslims to reevaluate those aspects of their faith and Islamic history that assumed the natural superiority of Islam over all non-Islamic ways of life.

But in 632, all that lay in the future, of course, and the shock of the Prophet's death forced his followers to deal with the painful question of who should take his place. The resolution of this question had far-reaching consequences for the development of Islamic political theory and what became traditional Muslim ways of dealing with political authority. The Sunni-Shi'a split in fact was not occasioned by a dispute over some doctrinal matter—something that happened with depressing frequency in the Christian world—but rather over who should be considered as the legitimate successor to Muhammad, and what his role should be in the world ruled by Islam. The distinctive answers given to these questions by Shi'a Muslims ultimately turned it into a militant political force in the twentieth century.

The Sunni-Shi'a Split

Shi'a means "following," and refers to those who sided with the fourth caliph of Islam, Ali, Muhammad's cousin and son-in-law by his daughter, Fatima.[10] According to Shi'a accounts, Ali initially had been passed over as the successor in favor of Muhammad's uncle, Abu Bakr, a trusted companion of the Prophet, whose tenure lasted only two years.[11] He nonetheless succeeded in putting the rest of the Arabian peninsula firmly within the fold of Islam. The conquests of his successor, Umar, a man designated by Abu Bakr to follow him, were even more impressive. His ten-year reign resulted in the creation of a vast Islamic empire that for the first time brought large numbers of non-Arabic peoples into *Dar al-Islam*. Umar was succeeded by Uthman, who continued the Islamic *jihad* ("struggle"; against infidels its most usual rendering is "holy, or righteous, war"), but also generated considerable opposition, which resulted in his assassination in Medina in 656. Ali was finally selected as the fourth caliph, and his reign lasted only five years. But it was during his leadership that Muslims experienced their first serious civil war.

The issue turned on Ali's failure to cope successfully with the animosities generated by the death of Uthman. The most serious one involved Mu'awiya, the governor of Syria and nephew of Uthman, who revolted against Ali and refused to acknowledge him as caliph. In a surprising turnabout, Ali's refusal to deal firmly with Mu'awiya's insubordination led some of his own followers to revolt against him. These dissidents were known as the *Kharijites*, an Arabic term implying separation or revolt, and they succeeded in killing Ali and a good many of his followers in 661. After that point the caliphate passed on to the family of Umayyad, where it remained for ninety years, and in the following centuries developed politically in increasingly secular directions. But the *Shi'at Ali*, or partisans of Ali, rejected this development and insisted that only the legitimate heirs of the Prophet had the right to rule the *umma*. Thus, the struggle continued through the line of succession of Ali's sons and their descendants. Together they are known as the Twelve Imams (*Imam*—"spiritual leader"), and have remained at the core of Shi'a beliefs about the Muslim approach to political and spiritual leadership.

The first Imam was, of course, Ali himself, for whom Shi'ite Muslims reserve a special affection. The second Imam was Hasan, a son of Ali, but his status was eclipsed by that of his brother, Husayn. Imam Husayn was a tragic figure who was murdered along with his friends and most of his family by Mu'awiya's son at the Battle of Karbala in 680. Together this group, the "Kin of the Prophet," occupy a special place in Shi'ite hagiography, and, as Edward Mortimer has pointed out, "are a Holy Family in almost the Christian sense of the phrase."[12] Husayn's death, or "martyrdom," is especially important, and is commemorated annually in passion plays rivaling those centered upon the crucifixion of Jesus Christ. The tombs of Ali and Husayn are located in Iraq and considered holy places by Shi'a Muslims, nearly as important as Mecca. The remaining Imams contributed greatly to the legacies of tragedy and opposition bequeathed by Ali's family by themselves suffering unfortunate deaths, usually by being murdered. However, the twelfth and last Imam, who was born in A.D. 869, is said not to have died at all, but is believed to remain present in this world in an invisible state, to return again someday to assume his rightful role as ruler of all Islam. As he announced that there would be no others to follow him, the Imamate ends with him, and all faithful Muslims must expect his return.

These beliefs, known as Twelver Shi'ism, eventually took root in and dominated the religious culture of Iran. Shi'ite ideas had at least two significant political consequences for the course of events in modern Iran. First, Shi'ites remained convinced that all political authority, until the return of the hidden Imam, is fundamentally illegitimate.[13] That is, Shi'a Muslims grudgingly accept non-Muslim or Sunni Muslim rulers out of necessity, not commitment. In fact, when the principle division between ruler and subjects centered upon the Sunni-Shi'a split, the latter, who were usually in a minority, had the habit of practicing *taqiya* ("dissimulation, concealment"), which meant that they did not indicate their true beliefs, and obeyed the existing rulers only because they had no choice. This practice remains in effect today, and it is sometimes difficult to get a Shi'a Muslim to state his true beliefs if he feels the circumstances are threatening.

Second, and more importantly, the position of the *ulama* ("religious scholars and leaders") in Shi'a Islam has taken on special significance, more so than in Sunni Islam. Shi'ites believe that until the return of the hidden Imam, Muslims have a special responsibility to their religious leaders, those learned in the Qur'an, the traditions and sayings of the Prophet, and the Imams for their guidance. This view is best expressed by Mahmood Shehabi, himself a Shi'a Muslim. Referring to the scholars of Islamic jurisprudence and religious studies as "public deputies," he asserts that they are "like an Imam, and following them is comparable to following an Imam." He concludes by saying:

> Since Shi'a depends upon the one who is the most learned and accepts him as the public deputy, in every epoch the person who is the most learned and most pious is regarded as the public deputy, and the people follow his ideas and his decisions concerning religious affairs.[14]

Clearly, the authority wielded by Khomeini in Iran today can be explained in large part by the long tradition of Shi'a reverence for outstanding religious leaders.

More than that, this philosophy of "Mahdism" (*Madi* means "divinely guided, or awaited, leader"), as Hamid Enayat points out, has had profound implications for the Shi'a view of history, compared to the Sunni approach: "The Shi'is agree with the Sunnis that Muslim history since the era of the four Rightly-Guided Caliphs [the first four caliphs] . . . has been for the most part a tale of woe. But whereas for the Sunnis the course of history since then has been a movement *away* from the ideal state, for the Shi'is it is a movement *toward* it."[15] In short, Shi'ites have reason to be hopeful about a time when the reunification of political and religious authority will lead all Muslims to new heights of glory and esteem. But the question remains: why have both Sunnis and Shi'ites believed that history has been "for the most part a tale of woe" since the death of Ali, especially from the standpoint of Islamic politics? The answer to this question lies in the events that occurred during Islam's "Golden Age," after Muhammad's death, and concerns how Muslims learned to cope with political power under circumstances very different from those when the four "Rightly-Guided Caliphs" ruled *Dar al-Islam*.

MUSLIM APPROACHES TO POLITICAL POWER

Muslim reactions to the exercise of political power have been shaped by three significant factors. The first is the secularization of public authority that began early in the history of the faith, and intensified especially as the Muslim world expanded and the various political divisions of *Dar al-Islam* waged war against one another. This was an extremely disturbing development for believers, and by the tenth century most Muslims concluded that any government that provided peace and order was acceptable, so long as it did not seriously encroach upon the practice of their religious beliefs. However, the failure to end the often devastating wars among Muslims seriously disturbed those committed to the *umma*, and the goal of Islamic unity has remained important throughout Muslim history, to this day.

The secularization of Islamic political power was aided also by the simple fact that the Arabs, who were never very numerous, found it necessary to recruit many *kafirs* ("non-Muslims") for government positions. And they were in the anomalous position of attempting to apply the Sacred Law to adjudicate disputes and generally administer Muslim lands. But both Muslims and *kafirs* found the *Shari'a* an impossible code for ordinary governance. Its rules of procedure were cumbersome to the point of being ludicrous. For example, an unmarried girl having a baby does not constitute proof of fornication; the act of conception itself must have a witness. In addition, many of its stipulations were simply impractical, such as the banning of interest on loans. Accordingly, judicial authorities usually tried to get around the *Shari'a* by applying other legal standards stressing equity, relevant legal precedents, or political mandates of the local ruler. The impact of these practices over the years was significant for the development of Islam. Most believers came to expect something less than full implementation of the *Shari'a* in public affairs, and this was the second major influence upon Muslim attitudes toward political power. The Sacred Law was looked upon as a noble set of ideals in accordance with which people should strive to act, even if this actually proved practically impossible.[16]

The result of these lowered expectations—the search for a middle ground that balanced *Shari'a* ideals with practical necessities—was what Daniel Pipes calls the "Medieval Synthesis."[17] Acceptance of the Medieval Synthesis also defines the *traditionalist* approach of Muslims to political power. It is important to note, however, that traditionalism is defined in terms of the extent to which the rulers apply the *Shari'a*, and not so much in terms of the rulers themselves, or even the form of government in question. This point often seems to be misunderstood, probably because of the influence of the recent events in Iran upon Western audiences. The rulers of Muslim states are relevant principally in terms of how deftly (or incompetently) they handle those aspects of the *Shari'a* of most concern to their subjects (chiefly the *ulama*)—the veiling of women, for instance, or administering the educational system, or regulating worship. By contrast, *fundamentalists* insist upon a more complete implementation of the *Shari'a* than traditionalists, but do not necessarily agree upon the type of government that should be in charge. Again, in his discussion of Islamic fundamentalism, Daniel Pipes remarks that "Islam buttresses hereditary monarchies in Morocco and Saudi Arabia, theocracy under Khomeini in Iran, and military rule under Zia-ul-Haq in Pakistan."[18] As we shall see, all observers note that what makes Khomeini different is that he is a *Shi'a fundamentalist*, who insists that an Islamic state must be run by the *fuqaha*, those "learned in the principles and ordinances of Islamic law, or more generally, in all aspects of the faith."[19] It is this type of Islamic fundamentalism that has generated the most turmoil and controversy in the Middle East today.

Fundamentalist movements have been around since the formative years of Islam, but more recent Muslim reactions have been in response to Western domination, the third major influence upon Muslim approaches to political power.[20] The conquest and subsequent domination by Western governments of the Islamic world has had a deeply unnerving impact upon the *umma*. Beginning in the eighteenth century, for the first time *Dar al-Islam* was confronted with a civilization that dwarfed it in technological sophistication, apparent cultural appeal, and raw military power. Efforts to cope with this astonishing development led to two other responses, *reformism* and *secularism*.[21] The first refers to efforts on the part of scholars to change, reinterpret, or simply discard those aspects of the *Shari'a* that conflict most sharply with Western values. The effort is then to graft as many Western, liberal values and institutions— such as universal suffrage and parliamentary democracy—upon Islamic culture as possible. Secularism takes this process a step further, by eliminating any trace of Islamic influence on public life, and consigning religious faith purely to the realm of private beliefs. Although both are repugnant to fundamentalists, secularism in particular has been viewed as a threat to the very existence of Islamic civilization.

In fact, the main instigation for Khomeini's entry into politics was what he and the Iranian *ulama* regarded as the vicious and determined efforts of the Pahlavi shahs to eradicate Islam from Iran and create a completely secular, modern state. Indeed, throughout most of his life Khomeini spoke and acted as a traditionalist with regard to the actions of the Pahlavi governments. But the policies of Muhammad Reza Pahlavi, more familiarly known to Americans as the (last) shah of Iran, radicalized the Iranian *ulama*, set Khomeini on a path of Shi'a fundamentalism, and ultimately catapulted him to the position of national and international prominence that he enjoys today. Since Khomeini's biography is inextricably bound up with the course of twentieth-century Iranian history, we shall consider the two together.

THE RISE OF KHOMEINI

Khomeini and the Pahlavi Dynasty

The life of Ruhollah Khomeini can be divided into three parts. The first begins with his birth, in 1902, continues through his adult life as one of the leading members of the *ulama* in Qom, an important center of Islamic studies in Iran, and ends with his first serious political involvement, in 1961. The second covers the period between 1961 and his assumption of leadership of Iran, in 1979. The third deals with his role as head of the Islamic Republic of Iran and continues to the present.[22]

During this time Khomeini saw Iran develop politically from a semicolonial appendage to the British and Russian empires, buffeted by the vagaries of European power politics, to a modern regime complete with the trappings of Western-style industries and military establishment, and finally to a religious theocracy in which he played the major role. The development of Khomeini's thought cannot be understood apart from modern Iranian politics.

Khomeini was a religious instructor at Qom when the events surrounding the modernization programs of Reza Khan, who took office in 1921 and was crowned shah in 1925, began to sweep over Iran. Emulating the far-reaching programs of Kemal Ataturk in Turkey, Reza Shah attempted to transform Iran into a modern, secular state by drastically curtailing the functions of the *ulama,* with the ultimate aim of permanently ending their role in Iranian society. Accordingly, he pushed through a radical secularization of Iranian law, required judges to have degrees from the newly established (and secular) Tehran University, and ended many other clerical prerogatives, even in the crucially important area of religious education. Clerics were harrassed in a multitude of other ways as well; religious dress was regulated, various details of worship were prescribed, and the annual holding of passion plays based upon Imam Husayn's death were banned. The Shah was not above violence either; on numerous occasions religious leaders and believers were imprisoned, tortured, and sometimes shot. Fortunately for the Muslim population of Iran, these oppressive policies were cut short by Reza Shah's abdication in 1941.

Three years later Khomeini published a book entitled, *Kashf-ol-Asrar* (*"The Discovery of Secrets"*), in which he outlined the depredations of the shah's regime and how grossly it had violated the *Shari'a,* and he went on to affirm the proper role of the *ulama* in social and political affairs. More specifically, Khomeini asserted that only God is sovereign and the only legitimate government is "the government of God." He also reiterated the orthodox Shi'a doctrine about the authority of the *fuqaha* in the place of the Hidden Imam, but did not conclude that religious leaders should actually run the state, a decision he arrived at some twenty-five years later. Rather, he believed that the government should be run with the *supervision* of the clerics.[23] This position is not strikingly different from one that would be made by a Muslim traditionalist interested in safeguarding the place of the *ulama* in public affairs.

But Khomeini was driven to a more radical position by the policies of Reza Shah's successor, Muhammad Reza Shah. The new shah's attempts to transform Iran into a modern industrial and military power began the activist, political phase of Khomeini's life. Certainly, much of the Islamic fundamentalism that he was to articulate in the years ahead can be explained by reference to the factors cited earlier—the Shiʻa view of political authority and the secular, Westernizing policies of Reza Shah. But there was another influence that was peculiar to the time and circumstances; namely, the impact of the two-decades hiatus between the departure of Reza Shah in 1941 and the continuation of his policies by his son in 1961. During that time Iran was too involved in world events for any ruler to try to remold Iranian society. In the meantime, many of the *ulama's* functions in Iranian life had been restored, and the traditional place of Islam in public life seemed to be secure. Thus, when Muhammad Reza Shah began his "White Revolu-tion" in the early sixties, which included government measures similiar to those of Reza Shah, Iranian clerics understandably reacted with fear and suspicion. To them the new shah was just another version of Reza Khan again, up to his old and very dangerous tricks. However, this time they could not hope to be saved by the accidental confluence of events abroad; indeed, the shah was supported in his "reform" policies by the most powerful country in the world, the United States. Thus, the *ulama* had to take matters into its own hands. And Khomeini was at the forefront.

The policies pursued by the government before and after the actual announcement of the White Revolution in January 1963 had the cumulative effect of undercutting practically all of the gains made by the *ulama* since the abdication of Reza Shah. The Local Councils Law of 1962, for instance, gave women the right to vote, repealed requirements for officeholders to be Muslims, and extended religious tolerance to groups that many Shiʻites felt to be apostates. A literacy corps was established that year also, which sent teachers conscripted by the government into rural areas, a practice that threatened to end the educational functions of the *mullahs* ("local clerics") to impart the Islamic faith among the young. Land reform threatened the financial indepen-dence of all the religious establishments by denying them control over their sources of revenue. And the shah's close links with the United States and its tolerance of Israel was seen as an affront to Muslims everywhere. Probably the most insulting measure came with the Status of Forces Law of 1964, which removed resident Americans from the jurisdiction of Iranian courts—a policy that revived bitter memories of the humiliations suffered by Iran at the hands of the British and Russians during the previous century. In fact, the entire program of the shah was seen by the *ulama*, Khomeini especially, as the product of the evil designs of imperialistic foreigners, especially the United States and Israel.

The *ulama's* reaction was immediate and vehement. Protests were organized against the government, especially in seminaries and religious schools, and clerics all over country preached vehemently against the shah's new policies. Khomeini's position was the most extreme, and he was quickly developing into the central figure of the Islamic opposition to the government. In 1963 he declared that "love of the Shah means rapine, violation of the rights of Muslims and violation of the command-ments of Islam," and declared the shah an agent of Jewish interests.[24] Khomeini's strong antigovernment speeches resulted in his arrest that year, which led to further vigorous demonstrations and protests. These were savagely put down by the army, and Khomeini remained in jail for ten months. But the following year his vehement declaration against the Status of Forces Bill led to his expulsion from the country. He spent most of his time at the Shi'a shrine in Najaf, Iraq, and continued to voice his opposition to the shah in speeches, lectures, writings, and inter-views—all the while maintaining an extensive network of contacts inside Iran. But, as the Shah was to discover, to his ultimate doom, Khomeini outside Iran was just as dangerous to his rule as he was inside the country.

This was clearly demonstrated in 1978, when a series of new protests against the government finally succeeded in bringing about its downfall. A full discussion of the causes of the fall of the Pahlavi dynasty is beyond the scope of this inquiry, but at least two points can be made in the present context.[25] First, the government had so thoroughly alienated practically all sectors of Iranian society—in addition to the clergy—during the 1970s that by the end of the decade it had very few reserves of support left, in spite of possessing a large apparatus of repression. Thus, instead of quieting things down by intimidating the opposition, the brutal suppression of demonstrations during that year only made matters worse. Secondly, the role of the Shi'a clergy, operating on instructions from Khomeini, who was in Paris at the time, was crucial in maintaining revolutionary momentum; at no time would Khomeini tolerate any thought of compromise with the shah. He was determined to destroy the Pahlavi regime and create an Islamic republic in its place. And when he triumphantly returned to Tehran in January 1979, he finally was in the position to carry out his program of Shi'a Islamic fundamentalism.

The question, of course, was just what Khomeini had in mind when he insisted upon building the Islamic Republic of Iran. A great deal could be gleaned from his speeches and writings, but the most systematic outline of his proposals was contained in a document entitled, *Islamic Government*. This book consists of a series of lectures delivered to his students when he was in Najaf, Iraq in 1970. It remains the most complete exposition of his views, and our treatment of his Islamic fundamentalism will proceed largely on the basis of this work.

Khomeini's Shi'a Islamic Fundamentalism

Islamic Government is a treatise designed mainly to argue for the necessity of Islamic government ruled by jurists, or *fuqaha* (the plural of *faqih*), under the overall guidance of a single authority (*vilayat-i-faqih*—"the governance or guardianship of the jurist"), for the purpose of establishing a just Islamic social order as well as to struggle to reestablish the unity of the *umma*. Other themes are dealt with in conjunction with these ideas, such as the illegitimacy of monarchical government (or any non-Islamic government understood in the foregoing terms), a virulent antiimperialist, anti-Western stance—especially where the United States and Israel are concerned—and the reassertion of Islamic identity and pride. Khomeini is less interested in outlining the operating details of the government he has in mind; rather, the bulk of his emphasis is upon establishing the principles to guide the establishment of Islamic government, and justifying those principles with appropriate references to the Qur'an and documents from the formative years of Islam.

The Necessity for Islamic Government.   This is the foundation of Khomeini's analysis, and is justified by reference to the Qur'an and the early days of Islamic rule, but especially the words of Muhammad and some of the Shi'a Imams. There are various reasons for establishing Islamic government, but fundamental to them all is the principle of the *political* nature of Islam. Indeed, perhaps the most significant aspect of Khomeini's leadership in this century as a practitioner of Muslim fundamentalism has been to affirm the Islamic faith as a relevant modern *political* ideology, rather than something that can be confined to one's private belief system. This is an extremely interesting position from the perspective of those accustomed to understanding the development of Western political thought and institutions. Indeed, even the most strident denunciations of communist misbehavior do not seem to catch the attention of Western publics as much as Khomeini's frequently insulting comments about the West. Communism is, after all, still a *Western* ideology. But for the first time in modern history, at least since the domination of Muslim lands by Western states, the familiar Western political *-isms* are faced with a new competitor—Islamic fundamentalism. And there is no question that this new experience for Western thinkers and statesmen has made them distinctly uncomfortable and often bewildered.

Yet to Khomeini nothing is more clear than the political nature of Islam. In 1964 while in prison he claimed that "all Islam is politics,"[26] and in *Islamic Government* argued the case further by asserting frankly that a much greater proportion of the Qur'an is devoted to treating social and political matters than to affairs relating to worship.[27] Indeed, the view that religion can be separated from politics he dismisses as a piece of imperialist propaganda.[28] True Muslims, on the other hand, are acutely aware that the "Prophet . . . was also a *political* person" [emphasis added].[29] Again, Khomeini accuses imperialists of distorting the meaning of Islam for their own evil purposes, to prevent the faithful from "intervening in the affairs of society and struggling against treacherous governments and their anti-national and anti-Islamic policies."[30]

Khomeini goes on to justify Islamic government by insisting that there are several crucial functions that only a "Government of God" could carry out. First, there is the necessity of meeting the requirements of *Shari'a*. The sacred law of Islam is absolutely complete, and in a long paragraph, Khomeini explains some of the subjects covered: "All the needs of man have been met," he asserts. "His dealings with his neighbors, fellow citizens, and clan, as well as children and relatives; the concerns of private and marital life; regulations concerning war and peace and intercourse with other nations; penal and commercial law; and regulations pertaining to trade and agriculture," to mention just a few matters.[31] Khomeini is also concerned about duties that only an Islamic government could do well or for the right purposes, in his judgment, such as collecting of taxes required by Islamic law, and distributing wealth in a fashion that benefits all members of the *umma*.

Second, and perhaps even more important, given the record of Western governments' interference in Iranian affairs, Khomeini has insisted that reasserting the unity and defending the territory of the *umma* requires the establishment of a distinctly Islamic government.[32] Without question Khomeini is most bitter when he talks about the relations that Western governments have had with Iran and with Islamic countries in general. Speaking of the "agents of imperialism"—a category that includes the Western European countries, as well as the United States and its "puppets," represented by the State of Israel and the government of the shah—Khomeini remarks that "their plan is to keep us backward . . . so they can exploit our riches, our underground wealth, our lands, and our human resources."[33] Thus, the shah's despotic government is condemned for its crimes against Islam, despoiling Muslim lands, and exploiting the people. In words reminiscent of Thomas Jefferson, Khomeini concludes with a flourish by declaring that the destruction of all corrupt, non-Islamic governments is a "duty that all Muslims must fulfill, in order to achieve the triumphant political revolution of Islam."[34]

The question arises: just what sort of Islamic government should take the place of the non-Islamic states? In answering this question, Khomeini reveals the crucially important role that his Shi'a interpretation brings to the problem of Islamic politics. In fact, the greater part of *Islamic Government* is devoted to justifying the line of succession for political and religious authority from the Prophet through the Twelve Imams, and presently to the *fuqaha* and the *vilayat-i-faqih*. Khomeini was never a self-serving individual (at least before his ascension to power), but his present position as *faqih* in the Islamic Republic of Iran should come as no surprise to those familiar with the argument he put forth ten years before the revolution.

Rule by Islamic Jurists.   Like all Shi'ites, Khomeini feels that Islamic history took a tragic turn for the worse with the death of Ali at the hands of Mu'awiya and the subsequent establishment of the Umayyad dynasty. From that point to the present the caliphate took on the characteristics of a secular monarchy, which is non-Islamic, in Khomeini's view. It is on this basis that he condemns the government of the shah, which, in addition to being the lackey of foreign interests, is equated with the usurpation of power that took place within the first generation of the death of Muhammad. This is the crucial period of time for Khomeini's arguments about the religious foundation of political leadership, and its importance to current developments in Iran cannot be underestimated.[35] As we have seen, the Shi'a view is that the Prophet was enjoined by God to designate his successor, who was Ali (his full name is Ali ibn Abi Talib). Khomeini argues with reverence that Ali was a man of outstanding qualifications, one who fulfilled completely the two essential requirements for the ruler of *Dar al-Islam:* possessing knowledge of the law, and practicing justice ("excellence in belief and morals").[36] He was the first and last Imam whose leadership exemplified perfectly the proper expression of religious-political rule.

Khomeini's main point in presenting this analysis is to conclude that the proper line of succession for rule passes through the Twelve Imams to the *fuqaha.* Moreover, it is the duty of the *fuqaha* to take on the burdens of leadership regardless of their personal desires; they are the "trustees of the prophets." In fact, he is convinced that the present troubles that Muslims have experienced are the result of Muslim leaders generally failing to do their duty, which includes asserting the primacy of Islamic law, standing up to foreign invaders, and teaching the people and leading them in the ways of the Prophet. Indeed, it is a basic tenet of Islamic fundamentalism, and Khomeini's thought especially, that Muslims have suffered at the hands of foreigners not because of any failings of Islam—a typical secularist or reformist view—but rather because they have forsaken Islamic ways. To get Islam on the right track, however, may require more than submitting to a just *fuqaha.* Khomeini believes that a single outstanding leader could do wonders for reasserting the glory of *Dar al-Islam*. More than that, he believes that this point is self-evident.

The Governance of the Faqih (vilayat-i-faqih). Khomeini asserts in the first paragraph of *Islamic Government* that "anyone who has some general awareness of the beliefs and ordinances of Islam will unhesitatingly give his assent to the principle of the *faqih* as soon as he encounters it; he will recognize it as necessary and self-evident."[37] He does not, however, specifically appoint himself to the task; the Shi'a argument is that since the occultation (disappearance into hiding) of the Twelfth Imam, the function of leadership has devolved upon the *fuqaha* as a class, a point Khomeini stresses throughout the book. But Shi'a Islam had also stressed the importance of *particular* leaders, and Khomeini was clearly aware of his role in that regard by 1970. Referring to both Muhammad's and Ali's political functions, he states: "And what now, if one of us becomes the foremost *faqih* of the age and is able to enforce his [Ali's] authority? In these matters, can there be any difference in the authority of the Most Noble Messenger [Muhammad], that of Ali, and that of the *faqih*?"[38] In fact, the thrust of his argument is that there is no difference.

Indeed, a major strength of Shi'a fundamentalism compared to its Sunni competitors derives from the line of authority that Shi'a leaders can claim, from Allah, through Muhammad and the Twelve Imams, to the *fuqaha*, and finally to a single outstanding leader, the *faqih*. To a non-Muslim, of course, it may seem that Khomeini's argument rests upon a strained interpretation of an extraordinarily narrow band of history. However, this Mahdist emphasis is reinforced by the generally patriarchal tradition of Iranian society (and the Middle East generally), lending additional authority to the leadership of the senior male figure. In fact, to anyone uneducated in the intricacies of interpreting the *Shari'a*, Khomeini's arguments in *Islamic Government* are rather persuasive. However, many commentators have concluded about his Shi'a fundamentalism that Khomeini has stretched things quite a bit in the sweeping claims he makes for the political authority of the *fuqaha* and the *faqih*, noting that much of his creative exegesis demands more than the historical or documentary evidence will sustain.[39] Although the argument that the *fuqaha* should actually be the rulers of the state, as opposed to existing as a parallel institution to provide guidance for state actions, did not originate with him, certainly he became its most powerful and best-known advocate. In any case, Khomeini's arguments provided a powerful rationale for conducting the political affairs of some 832 million Muslims. In short, his Islamic fundamentalism is, as he insists, a foremost *political* ideology, one that makes claims as extensive as any ever made by those originating in the West.

Islamic Pride. This principle of Khomeini's thought is derived less from a reading of *Islamic Government* than it is from a general overview of his various writings, speeches, and interviews with him. Certainly Khomeini justifies his conclusions with frequently painstaking analyses of sacred texts and interpretations, but all the specific aspects of his views tend to converge on a single theme, and that is the necessity to reassert the pride, unity, and identity of Islamic civilization. Khomeini often exhorts as much as he condemns or commands: take pride in your heritage, he tells all Muslims; don't be beguiled by non-Islamic ways of thought or patterns of living, he admonishes intellectuals especially; in short, struggle to reestablish and maintain the unity, glory, and supremacy of Islamic civilization, he preaches to *Dar al-Islam.* In fact, there is perhaps no better way to summarize Khomeini's significance as a practitioner of Islamic fundamentalism than to suggest that he represents a resurgent temperament as much as he does a particular perspective on government and politics.

In summary, Khomeini argues that a truly Islamic government is necessary to implement Islamic law, protect the *umma* from foreign predators, reassert Muslim pride and the primacy of Islam over all competing loyalties, and, ultimately, to promote the Islamic revolution throughout all Muslim lands and even beyond. His emphasis upon the central importance of the *Shari'a* in the lives of all Muslims has secured his place as one of the outstanding fundamentalist practitioners in the history of *Dar-al-Islam.* And his proposals for constructing a truly Islamic constitution, which were acted upon very faithfully by the new Muslim rulers of Iran, have made him also one of the most significant founders of the twentieth century. Without question, the combination of Khomeini's roles as practitioner of Islamic fundamentalism and founder of the Islamic Republic of Iran has made him a potent force in Middle Eastern politics, and in global affairs as well.

KHOMEINI IN POWER

Creating Islamic Government

Khomeini faced several tasks upon his return to Tehran from exile in January 1979. The first was to establish organizations that would enable him to set the stage for the transition of power and the creation of a truly Islamic government. This task was accomplished soon after his arrival by the creation of the Revolutionary Council, an ad hoc group of advisers appointed by him to give advice on all matters relating to the governing of Iran after the shah's departure.

The second task was to ensure that the forces unleashed by the revolution continued to function, so that the country could be purged of all non-Islamic elements, especially those associated with the shah's regime. In this Khomeini was helped by the Revolutionary Committees, which had come into existence all over the country, and were instrumental in overthrowing the shah's government. Finally, a more permanent institutional apparatus had to be created, one that would safeguard and ensure the continuation of a totally Islamic society. To this end, the Islamic Republican Party (IRP) was instituted, and work soon began on developing a new constitution. In all these matters Khomeini insisted that the Islamic nature of the revolution be maintained. The result was that the organizations that came into being under his guidance increasingly were dominated by radical fundamentalists.

Clearly, the course of events in Iran during the first three years of Khomeini's domineering presence indicated that he meant exactly what he said about creating a truly Islamic republic. This came as a surprise to many, including those who were actually in charge of running the new government. Thus, Mehdi Bazargan, Khomeini's first prime minister, who was in office from February to November 1979, and Abol-Hasan Bani-Sadr, president from January 1980 to June 1981, both fell from power largely because they did not appreciate the depth of Khomeini's commitment to an Islamic government run by the *fuqaha* and responsible to the *faqih*. Both had also once enjoyed Khomeini's special attentions and believed that he was on their side. But each also felt that once the revolution had succeeded in removing the shah's government and ridding the country of its worst excesses, the prime order of business was to return to "normal" governance as soon as possible. This meant employing those most able to carry out government functions, after duly assuring the Shi'a clerics of their role, so that order could be restored and Iran's relations with other countries could return to normal. None of these things was to take place.[40]

The downfall of both of these politicians was attributable to similar causes, but of the two experiences, Bani-Sadr's rise to and fall from power was the more dramatic and instructive. As the first elected president under the new constitution in January 1980, Bani-Sadr attempted to assert his control over the instruments of government, to make the year one "for a restoration of order and security" after the stormy events of 1979, and simply to get on with the business of governance. But by the spring of the following year, with the war with Iraq going at full tilt amidst strident calls for his resignation, Bani-Sadr found himself bitterly denouncing practically every institution and practice associated with the Islamic constitution and Khomeini's fundamentalism.

One of the primary reasons for his exasperation was the lack of control that he as president of a constitutional government had over the plethora of revolutionary organizations that had come into existence in Iran during the heady days following the shah's departure. Although Khomeini was not in charge of all these groups in terms of directing their day-to-day activities, clearly he was their inspirational leader. Certainly he felt that their work was crucial in fulfilling one of his prime objectives, which was to purge Iranian society of all non-Islamic influences. In fact, the various revolutionary organizations functioned as a parallel government, arresting counterrevolutionaries, administering their trials, carrying out the sentences of execution or imprisonment, and, finally, in the case of the Revolutionary Guard, defending the borders like regular army units. Like Bazargan before him, Bani-Sadr continually tried to exercise some control over these groups, to modify their behavior, at the least, but ultimately to eliminate them and have their functions carried out by regular government bureaucracies. Khomeini, however, valued them more than he did the government or any government official, causing his first prime minister, Mehdi Bazargan, to lament that the government was little more than "a knife without a blade."[41] He was right; the blade was in the hands of fundamentalist revolutionaries. And they wielded it with a vengeance.

Of course, the main purpose of the Revolutionary Committees was to bring to justice those who had perpetrated the worst abuses while the shah was in power. But as the new regime consolidated its power, the activities of the committees became notorious, frustrating government officials at all levels and terrorizing much of the population. Acting like local police forces, the Revolutionary Committees arrested anyone associated with the shah's regime, especially former agents of the secret police and security apparatus (SAVAK), army officers, high-ranking government officials, and many who simply ran afoul of local sentiments. The Revolutionary Tribunals were created at Khomeini's bequest, and thus were more directly responsible to him and the Revolutionary Council, but they were no less radical in operation. Employing the most shoddy judicial procedures, the tribunals sentenced at least five hundred fifty persons to the firing squad in their first year, and were responsible for the imprisonment of thousands more.[42] Clearly, Khomeini's goal of eradicating non-Islamic elements in Iran was being surpassed by the Revolutionary Committees and the Tribunals.

Indeed, to ensure the continued functioning of the committees, which were really spontaneous groups with little central direction, Khomeini instituted a new organization to carry out essentially the same functions, the Pasdaran, or Revolutionary Guards. The Pasdaran was charged with being the "eyes and ears of the Islamic Revolution," and regarded as "a special task force of the Imam Khomeini to crush counter-revolutionary activities within the government or any political usurper against the Islamic Government."[43] Eventually it became part of the government under the new constitution, and was directed by a separate ministry of the Pasdaran. In effect, the Pasdaran has functioned as a separate military arm of the clerics, quelling opposition against the regime domestically, as well as providing manpower for Iran's infamous "human-wave" assaults in its war against Iraq. It quickly acquired a reputation for ferocity, terror, and general harassment of citizens as bad as that associated with the committees. It also confirmed all the worst suspicions of Khomeini's critics about the nature of his Islamic republic.

This development was particularly ironic, given the rosy picture of Iran under Islamic rule that Khomeini had painted earlier. For example, he ended *Islamic Government* with a ringing statement about how all Muslims would benefit from the justice, peace, and security guaranteed by a truly Islamic system of rule.[44] But the most impartial assessment makes it extremely difficult to believe that these goals have been attained. For instance, Amnesty International has estimated that at least four thousand people had been executed by the regime by the summer of 1982. Some estimates put the number of political prisoners at around forty thousand.[45] And the methods used to mete out punishments were often blatantly sadistic. For instance, Shaul Bakhash reports that in 1980 four people charged with sexual offenses were buried up to their chests and stoned to death. Public hangings and executions by firing squads took place on the streets of Tehran, in full view of the public.[46] Meanwhile, purges of civil servants resulted in the departure of thousands of qualified persons from their jobs in the government. Finally, when things threatened to get completely out of hand, Khomeini was persuaded to issue a restraining decree in December 1982, the effect of which was to curb the worst brutalities. But he still declared his support for the revolutionary organizations, "as long as the Islamic revolution bears aloft the banner of divine unity and preserves its Islamic character."[47]He did not, in short, retreat in principle.

Indeed, throughout this time Khomeini acted rather consistently on the principles that he had established in *Islamic Government*. Although it was actually at the insistence of the Revolutionary Council that the Islamic Republican Party was established, the IRP has consistently acted upon Khomeini's principle about the rule of the *fuqaha* in an Islamic society. In fact, one of the main functions of the IRP has been to provide clerical personnel for all levels of government. It has also acted like a classic totalitarian political party, by intimidating and finally expunging opposition to the regime, generating mass support for the policies of the

Islamic Republic, engaging in enormous campaigns to mobilize and indoctrinate the citizens, and generally ensuring that fundamentalist policies penetrate to all elements of the population. Indeed, it is hard to see how the regime could have attempted to carry out its policies of Islamization without the Islamic Republican Party. It remains a permanent and significant element of Iranian politics, thus fulfilling Khomeini's third major goal, which was to establish the revolution on a secure and lasting basis.

This goal was also achieved amply in the new constitution, which was approved by the late fall of 1979. It embodies the main principles of Khomeini's Islamic fundamentalism. First, it established Shi'ism as the official state religion,[48] and, in language that could have been lifted from *Islamic Government,* declared further that "all civil, penal, financial, economic, administrative, cultural, military, political and other laws and regulations must be based on Islamic criteria." (Article Four)[49] Second, it was a central concern of Khomeini's that the *fuqaha* actually hold the reins of power in the Islamic state, a stipulation met by the establishment of the Council of Guardians. This body consists of twelve members, who are charged with ensuring that legislation from the Majles, the Parliament, conforms with Islamic law. The Council, in fact, functions something like the American Supreme Court, except that six of its members must be Islamic jurists, and they have the veto power of an American president, which cannot be overridden. They are chosen by the *faqih,* who is at the heart of the Islamic constitution.

The position of *faqih* embodies the third major principle of Khomeini's thought, discussed earlier, and was accorded to Khomeini for life. Its powers are impressive, especially in filling the top governmental and administrative posts. In addition to selecting the jurists on the Council of Guardians, the *faqih* is empowered to appoint the chief officials of the judiciary and the military, including the head of the Revolutionary Guard. He may also approve candidates running for president and dismiss the holder of that office if declared incompetent by the Majles or the Supreme Court—the fate, incidentally, that befell Bani-Sadr. The powers and duties of the *faqih* were justified with absolute clarity by reference to a cardinal tenet of Shi'ism, stated in Article Five: "In the absence of the Hidden Imam, the administration of affairs and the leadership of the nation is vested in a just, pious, brave and thoughtful theologian."[50] Arrangements were also made to fill the position in case of vacancy, but it is unlikely that a person of Khomeini's stature or influence could be found for the job when he passes from the scene. As one cleric remarked when the constitution was being debated, a person like Khomeini only comes along every few centuries or so.[51]

This comment suggests another aspect of the Iranian revolution that gave it special significance for those who contributed heavily to the events of the first few years of Khomeini's rule. The revolution was a deeply religious event, one fraught with consequences for serious believers committed to the doctrine of the Hidden Imam. Of course, all modern revolutions have been characterized by individuals who were convinced that they were ushering in a new age, and the Iranian revolution was no exception. Hossein Bashiriyeh explains that "for the fundamentalists, the revolution was not a lonely moment in history but a link in the nexus of history to which Shiite consciousness gives meaning. . . . They believed that the revolution happening here below was heralding the Second Coming of the Mahdi."[52] Although this apocalyptic meaning did not apply to all Muslims, clearly it is at the symbolic level that the Iranian revolution has attained its greatest success. In more practical terms, however, it has produced continuing hardship for much of the population and the brutal suppression of many, in spite of the best efforts of the new Islamic government to achieve justice and provide security.

Domestic Policies of the Islamic Republic

Khomeini's domestic agenda contained two main parts. First, the Ayatollah wanted to deal with the widespread Westernization of Iranian culture that had occurred during the reign of the two shahs. Accordingly, Khomeini, the Revolutionary Council, and the IRP immediately made efforts to Islamize Iran again, and to rid the country of what IRP pamphlets called the "cultural imperialism" of the West. Second, once the political arrangements were in place and the "agents of foreign imperialism" safely dispatched, Khomeini wanted to restructure the Iranian economy in a fashion that more nearly reflected Islamic criteria. His ideas on the first priority were by far more clearly developed, and he generally had more success in carrying them out. On economic matters, however, he was on less sure ground, and his indecisiveness over the years cost Iran dearly in the efforts of the government to get the country back on its feet. He was not alone in being frustrated by economic policy, however; both the Majles and the IRP were seriously divided on how best to proceed on matters of industrial, trade, and land policy.

Khomeini energetically began work on his first goal. Early in 1980 he declared a "cultural revolution," with the aim of reinculcating Islamic values into every aspect of Iranian life. Thus, clothing, eating habits, recreation, education, building design, and even language came under the mandate of a newly established Headquarters of Culture. This organization was aided in its task by bands of generally lower-class, unemployed, and undereducated people, called *hezbollahis*—"partisans of the party of God." Notorious for their ferocious, club-wielding methods of persuasion, *hezbollahis* mobs were also distinguished by their chant, "Only one party—of Allah; only one leader, Ruhollah" (Khomeini's given name).[53] Their efforts to intimidate were successful; no one opposed to the party had a chance against those who cared little about procedural niceties in implementing party policy.

Thus Iran became "re-Islamized"—often at the point of a gun, and with surprising quickness. Indeed, by 1981, after just two years of Khomeini's rule, the country had become, in Edward Mortimer's phrase, "a fearsome and depressing place, apparently determined to live up to all the most negative Western stereotypes about Islam."[54] Punishments became brutal, as we have seen, but more than that, the entire country was required to follow the strictest regime of Shi'a asceticism. Any "un-Islamic" music has been banned, along with dancing; drinking, sexual misconduct, gambling, and any form of personal vice have been subject to the most stringent punishments. Women have been forced to adopt *Hijab,* a particularly austere Islamic dress code. The IRP has proclaimed that all forms of art must reflect themes of revolutionary Islam; television and radio have been subject to strong regulation, for the purpose of making them convey only Islamic materials, and nothing antagonistic to the revolution. Finally, in 1982 Khomeini mandated that the entire Iranian legal structure completely expunge all non-Islamic law and proceed only according to Muslim jurisprudence. All judicial positions had to be filled by the *fuqaha,* or by secular judges strongly versed in Islamic law.[55] As we have seen, the comprehensive nature of Islamic legal codes ensured the rather complete penetration of Khomeini's "cultural revolution" throughout Iranian society.

The "economic revolution," by contrast, was considerably less effective. It was Khomeini's intention to remold the Iranian economic system in a fashion that corresponded to what several noted Islamic scholars, Bani-Sadr among them, insisted was the "third way." That is, Islamic economics was regarded as different from capitalism, Marxism, or any other economic system. Its distinctive thrust toward the achievement of social justice according to Islamic criteria meant that fundamentalist leaders did not have to look abroad for policy or ideological guidelines. Islam was complete in every way, as Khomeini had been saying for many years, and it was only necessary for the government to act upon its basic tenets.

In practice, however, this meant pursuing policies that were hardly distinguishable from those that any hard-line socialist government has ever undertaken. It is only a slight exaggeration to say that the Islamic government of Iran nationalized practically everything in sight, and in short order found itself in charge of a vast internal network of economic enterprises. Very few organizations escaped coming under government control, and those that did, operated in an atmosphere of insecurity and fear. The regime was most interested in controlling the "commanding heights" of the economy—banking and financial organizations, insurance, and a long list of heavy industrial concerns, including autos, petrochemicals, cement, mining and manufacturing, heavy-metal fabrication, shipbuilding, construction, and trade. Laws were passed to replace existing managers with those appointed by state, and a new organization, the Foundation for the Disinherited, was created to handle especially those enterprises associated with the shah. Its scope was hardly limited to that, however; the Foundation soon took over enormous numbers of other businesses, in an "orgy of seizures" that was given special impetus by very supportive judges and enthusiastic revolutionary guards. In short, the upheavals in the streets of Iran's cities were well matched by the disruption generated from the application of "Islamic economics" to the national economy.

The ostensible aim of these activities, of course, was to carry out measures designed to implement Islamic justice. Without question there were other objectives as well, chief among which was a desire to exact vengeance against institutions and people associated with the old regime. For decades Khomeini and the fundamentalists had been operating under the assumption that Iran had been the lackey of foreign interests under the two shahs. Thus, when the new Islamic government instituted its nationalization programs, the claim was made that Iranians were only taking back what had always been rightfully theirs; after all, they had been exploited for years. The usual argument was that all the property seized by the government had been acquired dishonestly or was used solely for the benefit of "imperialist exploiters." But property acquired or used illegally was still property; and there are strong calls in the Islamic tradition to respect property rights. However, these were taken more seriously with respect to redistributing land in the urban and rural areas than they were when dealing with larger business concerns.

Certainly Khomeini was sincere in his desire to provide homes for the poor and to redistribute land in a manner more in accordance with Islamic notions of equity. In fact, the Islamic legal tradition contained far more material relating to land distribution than it did regarding modern forms of property, and this tended to make the land question a test of the regime's sincerity. That was unfortunate, because three years' worth of land nationalization in the cities and property seizures in the countryside produced nothing but chaos in both areas. Landlords, renters, land-hungry poor farmers, property owners bitter over the often unjustified takeovers of their land, and even clerics were frequently involved in pitched battles against one another, sometimes with great loss of life. Confusing or contradictory legislation from the Majles often put it at odds with the Council of Guardians, while clerics fervidly argued doctrinal issues involving the claims for social justice versus the sanctity of property rights. The Council finally overturned much of the legislation that had caused the mischief, but Khomeini still failed to provide any clear guidelines. Indeed, even the exasperated request of Hashemi-Rafsanjani, the Speaker of the Majles, to the Imam for an authoritative ruling on the land question only resulted in Khomeini's vague rejoinder that government institutions cooperate better with one another, and that Iran should be made a "model for the world."[56] This seemed only to demonstrate that Khomeini was better at inspiring revolution than in actually fulfilling the practical requirements of being the *faqih.*

However, there still was a revolution to lead, although it was occurring beyond Iran's borders. Khomeini's proclamations about dealing with "the Great Satan" (the United States), the "puppet state" of Israel, and spreading the Islamic revolution to other Muslim countries continued to inspire radicals at home and abroad. And the war with Iraq, which broke out in 1980, had the effect of lending special urgency to Khomeini's calls for uniting all Muslims under a single governance. In short, the foreign policy of the Islamic Republic of Iran under Khomeini was to export revolution abroad.

Foreign Policy of Revolutionary Iran

One of the most striking aspects of the Iranian revolution is how its success led fundamentalists throughout the Middle East to look to Khomeini for inspiration and guidance. There were excellent reasons for this. First, his victory marked the first time since the days of Egypt's Nasser that a Muslim country successfully defied a powerful Western state. In fact, Khomeini's victory was even more impressive, because he succeeded in humiliating the most powerful country in the world without actually having to pay the consequences. Indeed, Khomeini seemed victorious in all his confrontations with the United States; whereas Nasser, by contrast, actually never did win any of Egypt's wars with Israel. But under Khomeini (although he was not directly responsible for this), Iran held American hostages for over a year, witnessed a pitiful attempt on the part of the United States to rescue them in the summer of 1980, and was able to rejoice in the electoral defeat of the man responsible for it all, President Carter. Thus, however infuriating it was for Americans to watch on their television sets the confident sneer of Foreign Minister Qotbzadeh as he calmly stated that Iran was not afraid of the United States, for Muslims, America's apparent helplessness in the face of determined Muslim opposition was a source of inspiration to believers everywhere.

A second reason for fundamentalists to look to Khomeini for leadership was the simple fact that Iran became the self-proclaimed center of the Islamic revolution. Indeed, the preamble to the Iranian constitution declares it the duty of the Revolutionary Guard "to extend the sovereignty of God's law throughout the world."[57] And Khomeini himself celebrated the anniversary of the shah's overthrow by proclaiming, "We will export our revolution to the four corners of the world because our revolution is Islamic, and the struggle will continue until the cry of *La ilaha illa 'llah* ['There is no God but Allah'] and *Muhammad rasul-ullah* ['and Muhammad is His messenger'] prevails throughout the world."[58] He also wasted no time in asserting the leadership role of Iran for the fundamentalist movement, boasting proudly that its task was to unite all Muslims under a single government. Declaring further that Islam "is the champion of all oppressed people," Khomeini gave the faith a militant internationalism that has had an exhilarating effect upon Muslim radicals everywhere, particularly Shi'ites.[59] Naturally, however, non-Muslim states, but especially the traditionalist leaders of other Islamic countries in the Middle East, were understandably nervous.

Reestablishing the unity of the *umma*, of course, had always been one of Khomeini's principal goals. But once the more immediate tasks of ousting the shah and eradicating the American presence from Iran were accomplished, the vision of bringing all *Dar al-Islam* under one rulership, free of all foreign influence, seems to have captured his imagination to the point of becoming an obsession. This accounts for much of the unbridled ferocity of Iran's war with Iraq. Iraq actually started the war, of course, but its war goals were limited, and it expected a brief engagement followed by appropriate negotiations that would bring the conflict to a quick and timely end. But for Khomeini's Iran, the war has acquired the status of *jihad*.[60] Khomeini, still bitter over his expulsion from that country in 1978 by Saddam Hussein, Iraq's ruler, has declared him an infidel, with whom no peace could be made. He has called for Saddam's death and promised the overthrow of his Baathist regime and the instigation of "war-crimes trials" of Iraqi leaders after the assumed Iranian victory. Appalled by this prospect, the Hussein government naturally has had no choice but to continue to fight for its own existence, in a war that has claimed hundreds of thousands of lives and led both countries to the point of bankruptcy.

Iraq has not been the only country to suffer from Khomeini's implacable striving for Islamic unity, regardless of cost. The Islamic government of Iran has trained thousands of terrorists at its Taleghani Center in Tehran, for the purpose of exporting the Iranian revolution to other Arab countries.[61] Its principal targets have been the Arab Gulf states, Saudi Arabia, and Lebanon. Near the end of 1981 Bahrain arrested some seventy-three individuals on the grounds of attempting to overthrow the government. All were Shi'ites who had been trained in the methods of terrorism in Iran. Probably the height of Khomeini's attempt to invest Islam with political meaning came with his efforts to use the *hajj,* the annual Muslim pilgrimage to the holy city of Medina in Saudi Arabia, as a vehicle to express revolutionary Islamic ideals. In 1982 a group of militants shouting pro-Khomeini and anti-American slogans instigated some violent demonstrations that prompted the Saudi government to expel a number of Iranians from the country. Undaunted, the Iranian government established a committee to coordinate efforts in emphasizing the political nature of Islam. President Ali Khamene'i unabashedly called for all Muslims to turn their mosques into centers for political and military instruction, as well as for religious observance.[62] In short, Khomeini's efforts to export revolution have demonstrated powerfully all of his convictions about Islam—its political nature, the necessity for rule by the *fuqaha* and *faqih,* and the militant, violent assertion of Islamic, especially Shi'a, identity and pride.

Probably no country has demonstrated these things more tragically than Lebanon. Khomeini's adamant declaration that he considers that country to be simply "a part of Iran" has been backed up with the export of weapons, revolutionary fanatics, and the establishment of an infrastructure of terrorism.[63] It is beyond our scope to untangle the complexities of Lebanese politics, but, as Alvin H. Bernstein points out, "the connection between the directors in Teheran and the Lebanese Front groups that implement their terrorist operations abroad is anything but 'shadowy'—a current media buzz word. Iran supports and directs these terrorists and wields them as a weapon."[64] The "front groups" he is referring to include most prominently the Islamic Jihad, an umbrella organization that consists of several radical Shi'ite groups that have received their training, weapons, logistical support, and, most importantly, leadership from Iran. The Amal and the Islamic Amal also figure importantly in the regional violence, especially in hijacking airplanes and taking Americans hostage. There is also the Party of God, which some experts have suggested may have been responsible for the bombing of the U.S. Marine headquarters in October 1983.[65] The common aim of these groups has been to eradicate the American presence from the area and, in the long run, to eliminate the state of Israel. As we have seen, both goals have figured prominently in Khomeini's agenda. And the first one, at least, has largely been achieved.

Khomeini's desire to export the Islamic revolution on a global scale may not succeed because of lack of resources and, perhaps, his own imminent demise. But it will not fail because of lack of effort, and Western security experts are becoming increasingly concerned about the international implications of Khomeini's Iranian revolution. For instance, the Iranian government has made serious efforts to use Shi'a groups to spread sedition in Muslim countries rather remote from the Iranian base, such as Indonesia. Khomeini is clearly seen as the inspirational leader for radical Muslims throughout Africa as well, especially in countries still harboring resentments against their former colonial masters, the Western powers. And where Muslims are not present, Iran has forged links with non-Muslim, anti-American countries, such as Nicaragua. Also, there is increasing evidence that the Khomeini government is establishing links with terrorist organizations in Western Europe, possibly under the auspices of a "Shi'a International." Without question, as the ramifications of Khomeini's Islamic revolution continue to unfold, the dangers to those regarded as his enemies become greater.

Khomeini's principal enemy, of course, remains the United States, which is still referred to as the "Great Satan," and the state of Israel. Increasingly, however, the Soviet Union has been regarded as a danger to Islam, and now is regularly being denounced in the sort of vicious terms usually reserved for the United States. The reasons for this have to do with the considerable support the Soviets have provided to Iraq, and the dangers posed by the Soviet presence in Afghanistan—probably the only issue of significance on which Iran and the United States agree. In every other way, however, Khomeini and the Islamic revolution remain an exasperating problem for the United States. Few Americans have forgotten the humiliations suffered at the hands of the Khomeini government, and this has set clear boundaries of permissible action on the part of the makers of American foreign policy. Even with this in mind, however, the Reagan Administration has thus far shown little more competence in coping with the bizarre twists of Iranian politics than the Carter Administration. In fact, at this writing the scandal associated with the sale of arms to Iran threatens to disgrace yet another American president. Thus, as Khomeini, who is reportedly seriously ailing, reviews the accomplishments of Iranian foreign policy since the onset of the Islamic revolution, he may close his years with yet another victory over the "Great Satan," making his vengeance more complete than even he ever imagined.

THE FUTURE OF THE ISLAMIC REPUBLIC OF IRAN

The overriding question that must be faced by the leaders of Iran in the near future focuses upon what will happen to the Islamic Republic when Khomeini passes from the scene. Given the importance of Khomeini, the answers they provide to this question will be not only of regional significance to the Middle East, or of religious concern to Muslims, but also of global import to the great powers, especially the United States and the Soviet Union. There are serious divisions in the Islamic Republican Party over policy issues, and the country still contains restless and frequently rebellious minorities who have not fully accepted the new government, such as the Kurds and the Baluchis. The economy is in wretched condition, and the war continues to consume Iranian lives at a fearsome rate. Also, the regime has suffered at least one serious and violent challenge to its authority: in 1981, the IRP headquarters in Tehran was bombed, claiming the lives of several important government figures; and many bombings and assassinations occurred in other Iranian cities as well. The government's reaction was swift, savage, extensive, and bloody—at least five thousand people were killed, and the process was stopped only when Khomeini himself decided to rein in the retaliators with his decree of late December 1982. But clearly the divisions in Iran remain serious, its problems are weighty, and the country's continued functioning in spite of them only serves to demonstrate a point acknowledged by both Khomeini's devoted disciples and his most committed enemies: he is the linchpin of the whole system. Khomeini is the one who makes it go. Thus, again the question is raised: without him, what will happen to Iran? Indeed, without Khomeini, what is the future of Islamic fundamentalism?

This question takes on added importance when one considers his Shi'a Islamic commitments. Again, it is difficult to overestimate the importance of the Shi'a element in Khomeini's Islamic fundamentalism. Clearly, it has served him well in engendering fanatical commitments among believers accustomed to the Mahdist tradition of Shi'ite thinking, along with the emphasis upon suffering and dying for God under the more direct orders of the Imams—in this case, Khomeini. But it has worked against him as well. Despite, for example, his efforts to stress the internationalist flair of Islam—appealing, for instance to the oppressed throughout the world, including workers in the Soviet Union and blacks and Native Americans in the United States(!)—Khomeini has been seriously compromised by his inability to deal in an impartial manner with even his fellow Muslims. For instance, the Iranian government has supported the Shi'a majority in Iraq, which is ruled by a Sunni minority, as well as the Shi'a minority that rules a predominantly Sunni population in Syria. And Khomeini often seems to prefer dealing with Shi'a traditionalists rather than Sunni fundamentalists![66] Moreover, Iran's well-deserved reputation for being a fearsome and oppressive place to live belies Khomeini's oft-repeated claims about the bliss of living under divine Islamic justice—Shi'a fundamentalist style, of course. All these considerations highlight the rather special character of Khomeini's Islamic fundamentalism, something that remains crucial for a non-Muslim Western observer to understand.

The course of the Islamic revolution is continuously generating new developments that affect Middle Eastern politics and the world at large as this is being written, and to make statements about its long-term impact is clearly to conjecture. Nonetheless, an overview of events thus far permits at least some speculation. First, the political nature of Islam has been established by Khomeini beyond a shadow of a doubt, and will remain relevant in world politics for the foreseeable future. Second, the political institutions of the Islamic Republic of Iran will likely undergo considerable change when Khomeini is no longer around to keep things together. The direction of that change is more difficult to predict; although the *ulama* will undoubtedly continue to exercise an important and perhaps a predominant influence in government affairs, there also will probably be more movement in the direction of relying upon professional administrators, career bureaucrats, and technical experts. Ironically, the war with Iraq has probably retarded this process. The revolutionary fervor to remold domestic institutions never had a chance to burn out; it has been kept alive by the *jihad* mentality that Khomeini has invested in the Iran-Iraq war. Only when this conflict ends will both countries be in a position to assess on more sober terms the meaning of the revolution that has affected them so deeply.

Third, and perhaps most important, Khomeini's role as a practitioner of Islamic fundamentalism and founder of the Islamic Republic of Iran may not rest on his insistence upon the rule by the *fuqaha,* under the guidance of the *faqih,* or even living according to the precepts of the Shari'a. Khomeini actually developed his Shi'a version of Islamic fundamentalism out of a sense of desperation, because he felt that Islamic civilization as a whole was threatened with extinction. But historically, rule by a *faqih* lasted scarcely more than a generation after the death of Muhammad. Further, if Muslims found it impossible to live strictly by the Shari'a a thousand years ago, when the threat of modernity was not present to make matters even more difficult, they are not likely to live strictly according to it today, regardless of the best efforts of Khomeini or any future *faqih* of Iran. Thus, the most important characteristic of Khomeini's fundamentalism may not rest upon the Shari'a or even the institutions that he formed to labor so hard to implement it. Probably his most significant and lasting contribution to the modern world has been his determination to reassert stridently the identity and independence of Islamic civilization. In the final analysis, all of his more specific views about the structure of Islamic government are derived from this one, central commitment.

Thus, Khomeini has electrified radical Muslims everywhere, even as he has exasperated the Western powers and the Soviet Union, and threatened the traditionalist rulers of Muslim countries. He has been the object of unbridled hate as well as slavish veneration—both of which will undoubtedly secure his place as one of the most significant practitioners of Islamic fundamentalism in the long history of *Dar al-Islam* and, indeed, in world politics as well.

ENDNOTES

[1] Quoted in Shaul Bakhash, *The Reign of the Ayatollahs: Iran and the Islamic Revolution* (New York: Basic Books, Inc., 1984), p. 84.

[2] Quoted in Robin Wright, *Sacred Rage: The Wrath of Militant Islam* (New York: Simon & Schuster, 1986), p. 31.

[3] Ibid., in picture group following page 68.

[4] Quoted in Bakhash, *Reign of Ayatollahs*, p. 32.

[5] *Ayatollah* means "sign of God," and is the title for officials of the highest religious rank in Iran.

[6] "The First Day of God's Government," in Imam Khomeini, *Islam and Revolution: Writings and Declarations*, trans. and annotated by Hamid Algar (London: KPI Limited, 1985), pp. 266–67.

[7] For accounts of Islam and Muslim practices, see, for instance, Alfred Guillaume, *Islam* (New York: Penguin Books, 1956); Ceasar E. Farah, *Islam: Beliefs and Observances* (Woodbury, N.Y.: Barron's Educational Series, Inc., 1970); Glenn E. Perry, *The Middle East: Fourteen Islamic Centuries* (Englewood Cliffs, N.J.: Prentice-Hall, Inc., 1983); and, Roy R. Anderson et al., *Politics and Change in the Middle East: Sources of Conflict and Accommodation* (Englewood Cliffs, N.J.: Prentice-Hall, 1982), chapters 2 and 3.

[8] Treatments of Islam almost always contain glossaries explaining the meaning of Arabic terms pertaining to the faith. A very complete one is contained in Caesar E. Farah, *Islam*. Shorter, more easily usable glossaries covering the most basic terms are found, for instance, in Anderson *Politics and Change;* William Spencer, *Global Studies—The Middle East* (Guilford, Conn.: The Dushkin Publishing Group, Inc., 1986); Daniel Pipes, *In the Path of God: Islam and Political Power* (New York: Basic Books, Inc., 1983); and Edward Mortimer, *Faith and Power: The Politics of Islam* (New York: Random House, 1982). The reader should expect some variation in spelling, however, even in frequently used words, such as Shi'a, which is rendered variously as Shia, Shi'i, Shi'ite, or Shiite, depending upon the text and how the word is used in the sentence.

[9] One exception to this pertains to the Shi'a Muslims, discussed later, who add to the *Shahada*, "and Ali is the vice-regent of God." See Henry Bucher, Jr., *Middle East* (Guilford, Conn.: The Dushkin Publishing Group, Inc., 1984), p. 45.

[10] For accounts of Shi'a Islam, see Hamid Enayat, *Modern Islamic Thought* (Austin, Tex.: University of Texas Press, 1982), pp. 18–51; Mahmood Shehabi, "Shi'a," in Kenneth W. Morgan, ed., *Islam—The Straight Path* (New York: The Ronald Press Co., 1958); Bucher, *Middle East*, pp. 41–57; and Mortimer, *Faith and Power*, pp. 31–55. Bucher's review also includes some extremely helpful charts on Sunni and Shi'a Islam and the Five Pillars of Islam, on pp. 44–45.

[11] The account by Mahmood Shehabi, "Shi'a," in Morgan, *Islam*, is particularly instructive here, as it is written from a Shi'a perspective.

[12] Mortimer, *Faith and Power*, p. 45.

[13] It must be noted, however, that Edward Mortimer points out that this explanation "has now been fairly conclusively demolished by Iranian scholars." Nonetheless, he goes on

to say that "it is hard to accept as pure coincidence the fact that the only Shi'ite state is also the only Muslim state in which the *ulama* of modern times played an active opposition role." *Faith and Power,* p. 300.

[14]Shehabi, "Shi'a," in Morgan, *Islam,* p. 202. Interestingly, this essay was written in 1958, before Khomeini had attained much recognition or prominence.

[15]Enayat, *Modern Islamic Thought,* p. 24. The emphasis is in the original.

[16]These paragraphs are based upon Daniel Pipes's excellent discussion, in *In the Path of God,* pp. 48–69. See also Mortimer, *Faith and Power,* pp. 31–55; and the review of Islamic history during the Golden Age in Perry, *Middle East,* pp. 60–94.

[17]Pipes, *In the Path of God,* p. 57.

[18]Ibid., p. 129.

[19]This definition is taken from *Islamic Government,* in Imam Khomeini, *Islam and Revolution: Writings and Declarations,* trans. and annotated by Hamid Algar (London: KPI Limited, 1985), p. 150, note 1.

[20]Daniel Pipes's discussion of Muslim responses to Western European domination, in *In the Path of God,* pp. 114–142, is excellent. See also the brief survey in Cheryl Benard and Zalmay Khalilzad, *"The Government of God"—Iran's Islamic Republic* (New York: Columbia University Press, 1984), pp. 29–48.

[21]These are Pipes's terms. Benard and Khalilzad apply the labels "Islamic Modernists" and "Secularist Westernizers," respectively, to the same concepts.

[22]To my knowledge, there are no English-version biographies of Khomeini, although there are several in preparation. The following information is taken from Bakhash, *Reign of the Ayatollahs,* pp. 19–52. There are several good reviews of the events leading up to his assumption of power, which I also consulted, and the literature on this subject is growing rapidly. See, for instance, Mortimer, *Faith and Power,* pp. 296–376; Kambiz Afrachteh, "Iran," in Mohammed Ayoob, ed., *The Politics of Islamic Reassertion* (New York: St. Martin's Press, 1981), pp. 90–119; Azar Tabari, "The Role of the Clergy in Modern Iranian Politics," and Willem M. Floor, "The Revolutionary Character of the Ulama: Wishful Thinking or Reality," both in Nikki R. Keddie, ed., *Religion and Politics in Iran* (New Haven: Yale University Press, 1983), pp. 47–97. A survey of Iran prior to the revolution is contained in Fred Halliday, *Iran: Dictatorship and Development* (New York: Penguin Books, 1979). America's involvement in Iranian politics is well covered by Barry Rubin, *Paved with Good Intentions: The American Experience and Iran* (New York: Penguin Books, 1981).

[23]"A Warning to the Nation," Imam Khomeini, *Islam and Revolution,* trans. and annotated by Hamid Algar, p. 170. The section is taken from *Kash Al-Asrar.* See also Azar Tabari, "The Role of the Clergy in Modern Iranian Politics," in Keddie, *Religion and Politics,* pp. 60–64, which contains extensive excerpts from Khomeini's book.

[24]Quoted in Bakhash, *Reign of the Ayatollahs,* p. 29.

[25]Bakhash, *Reign of the Ayatollahs,* contains a brief account, pp. 3–18. See also Ervand Abrahamian, "Structural Causes of the Iranian Revolution," and Jerome D. Green, "Countermobilization in the Iranian Revolution," both in Jack A. Goldstone, ed., *Revolutions: Theoretical, Comparative, and Historical Studies* (New York: Harcourt Brace Jovanovich, 1986), pp. 118–38. Also, of course, Barry Rubin's *Paved with Good Intentions,* especially pp. 190–336, is a most readable and fascinating account.

[26]Quoted by Bakhash, *Reign of the Ayatollahs,* p. 32.

[27]Khomeini, *Islamic Government,* in Algar, *Islam and Revolution,* p. 29.

[28]Ibid., p. 38.

[29]Ibid., p. 39.

[30]Ibid.

[31]Ibid., p. 43.

[32]Ibid., p. 46.

[33]Ibid., p. 34.

[34]Ibid., p. 48.

[35]Unfortunately, specific references are scattered throughout the text, and much of *Islamic Government* is repetitive and not terribly well organized. But see, for example, his comments on pp. 40, 47, 56–57, and 59–101 *passim*.

[36]Ibid., p. 60.

[37]Ibid., p. 27.

[38]Ibid., p. 63.

[39]See especially the excellent treatment by Gregory Rose, "Velayat-e Faqih and the Recovery of Islamic Identity in the Thought of Ayatollah Khomeini," in Keddie, *Religion and Politics*, pp. 166–88.

[40]This summarized account is taken from Bakhash, *Reign of the Ayatollahs*, pp. 52–166; Benard and Khalilzad, *"Government of God,"* pp. 103–145; see also Hossein Bashiriyeh, *The State and Revolution in Iran* (New York: St. Martin's Press, 1984), which takes events up to 1982.

[41]Quoted in Bakhash, *Reign of the Ayatollahs*, p. 69.

[42]Ibid., p. 60.

[43]Quoted in Benard and Khalilzad, *"Government of God,"* p. 108.

[44]Khomeini, *Islamic Government*, in Algar, *Islam and Revolution*, p. 149.

[45]Benard and Khalilzad, *"Government of God,"* p. 124.

[46]Bakhash, *Reign of the Ayatollahs*, pp. 110–12.

[47]Quoted in Ibid., p. 229.

[48]Benard and Khalilzad, *"Government of God,"* p. 135.

[49]Quoted in Bakhash, *Reign of the Ayatollahs*, p. 83.

[50]Quoted in Bashiriyeh, *State and Revolution*, p. 167.

[51]Bakhash, *Reign of the Ayatollahs*, p. 84.

[52]Bashiriyeh, *State and Revolution*, p. 175.

[53]Bakhash, *Reign of the Ayatollahs*, p. 67.

[54]Mortimer, *Faith and Power*, p. 352.

[55]For reviews on this matter, see Ibid., p. 352–53; Bakhash, *Reign of the Ayatollahs*, pp. 226–27; Benard and Khalilzad, *"Government of God,"* pp. 116–17; and Bashiriyeh, *State and Revolution*, p. 175.

[56]Bakhash, *Reign of the Ayatollahs*, p. 216.

[57]Quoted in Ibid., p. 233. This statement is taken from preamble of the Iranian constitution.

[58]Quoted in Benard and Khalilzad, *"Government of God,"* p. 148.

[59]Quoted in Wright, *Sacred Rage*, p. 42.

[60]See, for instance, the recent account by Milton Viorst, "Iraq at War," *Foreign Affairs*, 65, no. 2 (Winter 1986–1987), pp. 349–365; Alvin Z. Rubinstein, "Perspectives on the Iran-Iraq War," *Orbis*, 29, no. 3 (Fall 1985), pp. 597–609; and "Forum: The Gulf War, Year Five," *Orbis*, 28, no. 3 (Fall 1984), pp. 437–465.

[61]Wright, *Sacred Rage*, pp. 32–37.

[62]The information in this paragraph comes from Bakhash, *Reign of the Ayatollahs*, pp. 233–35.

[63]Wright, *Sacred Rage*, p. 43, and see her discussion of Lebanon, pp. 69–111.

[64]Alvin H. Bernstein, "Iran's Low-Intensity War Against the United States," *Orbis*, 30, no. 1 (Spring 1986), p. 152.

[65]This is cited in Ibid. The information in this paragraph is taken from his account. Robin Wright, of course, provides a book-length treatment of Shi'a extremism in *Sacred Rage*.

[66]Benard and Khalilzad, "Government of God," p. 186.

IDEOLOGY
and
LEADERSHIP

INDEX